A History of the
Hal Roach Studios

Richard Lewis Ward

Southern Illinois University Press / Carbondale

Library of Congress Cataloging-in-Publication Data

Ward, Richard Lewis, 1953–
A history of the Hal Roach Studios / Richard Lewis Ward.
p. cm.
Includes bibliographical references and index.
1. Hal Roach Studios—History. I. Title.
PN1999.H28W37 2005
384'.8'0979494—dc22   2004021368
ISBN 0-8093-2637-X (cloth : alk. paper)
ISBN-13: 978-0-8093-2727-0 (pbk. : alk. paper)
ISBN-10: 0-8093-2727-9 (pbk. : alk. paper)

Printed on recycled paper. ♻

The paper used in this publication meets the minimum requirements of
American National Standard for Information Sciences—Permanence of Paper for Printed Library Materials, ANSI Z39.48-1992. ⊚

*For Jane
and
for Stan Laurel and Oliver Hardy*

Who could have imagined that watching your films on television as a child in Chattanooga, Tennessee, in the 1950s would begin a lifetime of inquiry that would lead to this book? Boys, here's another nice mess you've gotten me into.

Contents

═══════ Illustrations

Acknowledgments

I thank, first and foremost, my wife, Jane Egan Ward; my parents, Mary Catherine Ward and the late Judge McInnis L. Ward; and my sister, Dr. Mary Catherine Olmsted, for their continued support, love, and encouragement over the years. Also, many thanks to my friend Bill Lindholm, who has forgotten more about film restoration and the films of Hal Roach than I will ever know.

This project would not have been possible without the cooperation of the Department of Special Collections at the University of Southern California's Doheny Library, which houses the Hal Roach Studios records; the Wisconsin Center for Film and Theatre Research of the State Historical Society, home of United Artists' corporate records; and the Margaret Herrick Library of the Academy of Motion Picture Arts and Sciences, which holds the files of the Production Code Administration. Special thanks in this connection goes to Ned Comstock of USC, for his professionalism (new boxes of material were always waiting for me at the beginning of every day), kindness, and patience with my repeated requests of "Are you sure this can't be photocopied?" My deepest appreciation goes as well to Marc Wanamaker, whose Bison Archives supplied most of the photographs in this book.

I also express my gratitude to those who watched over my initial development and exploration of this area of research: Horace Newcomb, Charles Ramirez-Berg, Bill Stott, and, most especially, Tom Schatz and Janet Staiger.

Tom and Janet's high standards and encyclopedic knowledge of American film history are truly amazing and inspirational, and they have my eternal gratitude for the careful and serious guidance they have given to me in this work.

Thanks also to my students and colleagues at Eastern Connecticut State University during the early 1990s who were very supportive as this work began, and to my current students and colleagues at the University of South Alabama who encouraged me as the present incarnation slowly took shape.

Finally, I am very grateful for the Sons of the Desert, the international Laurel and Hardy appreciation society. Year after year, this group endeavors to introduce new generations to the wonderful work of the Hal Roach Studios. May they do so forevermore.

A History of the Hal Roach Studios

1

Introduction

From very early in its development, the American motion picture industry functioned as an oligopoly. A handful of powerful companies controlled virtually every aspect of the business, leaving little room for new competition from outside the established cartel. The independent companies that did find some success despite their outsider status usually did so by specializing in a market niche either underserved or completely ignored by the major producing studios. Hence Republic Pictures and Monogram found financial reward as producers of low-budget westerns and serials, and Walt Disney Productions (long before it ascended to major studio status) succeeded as an independent producer of short and feature-length cartoons.

This book examines the history of another niche player, albeit one that was in business for such a long time that its niche was continually being redefined as the industry around it changed. The Hal Roach Studios functioned from 1914 until 1960 as a producer of short comedies (running thirty minutes or less), independent features and featurettes, and ultimately, weekly television series. Its forty-six-year survival makes it a unique subject for study, a study that yields insight into not only the production and marketing strategies of a film organization on the periphery of the theatrical film industry but also the interconnected nature of the studio system during the classic era from the early 1920s through the late 1940s and into the early television era.

The Hal Roach Studios never rose to prominence as a major player within the studio system, yet its product was occasionally more popular in its time and is sometimes better remembered today than contemporary productions from the major studios. Roach launched the careers of Harold Lloyd (considered, along with Charlie Chaplin and Buster Keaton, one of the greatest comedians of the silent era), Our Gang, and Laurel and Hardy. Mack Sennett, Roach's chief rival in the production of silent short comedies, had a legendary eye for spotting talent. It was Sennett who introduced Chaplin to the movies. Yet Sennett rarely retained top talent for very long: only a year in Chaplin's case. Conversely, Roach nurtured talent. Lloyd, Our Gang, and Laurel and Hardy spent the prime of their careers at Roach. Even during periods of decline or misdirection, the Roach studio could turn out genuinely original material, such as the screwball classic *Topper* (1937), the brutally frank *Of Mice and Men* (1940), and the silent-film experiment *One Million B.C.* (1940). In the early days of television, the Hal Roach Studios embraced the new medium to briefly become the most prolific of all telefilm producers. Clearly this filmmaking organization deserves more scholarly attention than it has received to date.

This work is intended as a history of the Hal Roach Studios, not as a biography of Hal Roach, the man. Such a biography is long overdue but is simply not the task at hand. Clearly Roach's life was thoroughly intertwined with the studio that bore his name, and some biographic elements, particularly as they concern matters of decision making and creative control, will arise in brief.[1]

In these glimpses, a sketch of Roach's personality will emerge. He will appear as a man with a rather healthy attitude toward his work: enthusiastic and talented (although more so as a promoter of his studio's product than as a creative filmmaker) but not consumed with moviemaking. Roach did not have to make films to lead a happy life. His successful business permitted him to live large—he was an avid sportsman—but on more than one occasion when the studio was in desperate financial straits, he appeared quite willing to walk away. In other words, Roach was a pragmatist. Filmmaking was his livelihood but not his obsession. This practicality is perhaps underscored by a statement Roach made to the *Los Angeles Times* when the studio facility (which had passed on to other owners) was demolished in 1963. Far from being a sentimental old man weeping about the past, Roach flatly declared, "I have no feeling of regret. Passing of the stu-

dio has no effect upon me. It's just brick and mortar." Then the irrepress-
ible entrepreneur in him spoke up: "The developers are making a mistake.
They could invest a half-million in making comedies and make a million
a year. They won't make that kind of money in markets and apartments."[2]

To properly frame the history of the Hal Roach Studios, it is necessary to
occasionally refocus away from the Roach studio itself to the larger motion picture industry in which Roach functioned, to scrutinize industrial
changes and trends that impelled Roach periodically to shift the types of
films he produced. This effort to place Roach in the context of the industry begins with an overview of the type of film on which Roach's enduring appeal rests: the theatrical short subject.

The Short Subject During the Hollywood Studio Era

Short subjects, the principal Roach product during its first two decades (its
most successful period), were an essential if subsidiary part of the theatrical film program throughout the classic Hollywood studio era. Shorts
were generally made in series built around a star or stars (Roach's Laurel
and Hardy and Our Gang, Mickey Mouse) or sharing a common theme
(Crime Does Not Pay). Each series usually comprised eight to twelve films
per year, and as is the case with television series today, they were renewed
or canceled on an annual basis, with extremely unpopular series canceled
before their full year was up. The motion picture release year, or "season,"
ran on a schedule derived from theatrical seasons and similar to television
seasons, beginning around the first of September and running through the
following summer. From the beginning of the studio system around 1915
until the early 1930s, a theatrical program characteristically would consist of
a cartoon, a short comedy, a newsreel, possibly an additional short in the
form of a travelogue, a drama or, after the advent of sound, a musical, and a
feature-length picture. In 1932 Roach studio executive Henry Ginsberg estimated that on average, shorts constituted 40 percent of a two-hour program.[3]
Nevertheless, even though it consumed little more than half the running
time of a typical theatrical presentation, the feature always received the lion's
share of the box office split, leaving the producers of the multiple shorts
on a given program to divide up among them what was left over.

Because the revenue provided by short comedies was not adequate to
allow Roach or the other short-comedy producers to expand into distribution or theater ownership, they were usually forced to depend on other
organizations to distribute their films to the theaters. Then, as now, industry wisdom held that he who controls distribution controls the industry.

The short-comedy producers faced a buyer's market, in which the distribution firms were able to set the terms. Being able to pick and choose which product they wished to handle, the distributors influenced which film series were made and on what sort of budgets.

Further complicating the situation for short-subject producers were the film-booking practices of the large, vertically integrated film studios that controlled most of the major theater chains during the studio era. These companies adhered to a "run, zone, clearance" system, in which theaters were designated as first-run, second-run, third-run, and so forth. A first-run theater would be permitted to play a new film exclusively in its area, or "zone," before any other theaters could get it. This "run" would be followed by a "clearance," or period of time during which the film would not be exhibited within that zone. After the clearance, the film would play in the designated second-run theater, followed by another clearance, another run, and so on. Characteristically, the admission prices charged by first-run theaters were higher than those charged by second-run houses, second-run theaters charged more than third-run venues, and each subsequent-run theater charged less than the run before it. The problem for short-subject producers was that in many of the first-run movie palaces from the mid-1920s until the early 1930s, a live stage show virtually eliminated the need for short subjects, meaning that the shorts in those markets might receive their first run in reduced-admission second- and subsequent-run theaters.

A second problem that faced short-film specialists like Roach, Mack Sennett, and Educational was the major studio distribution policy of block booking, or selling films in packages rather than individually. This practice assured the studios of being able to sell even their weakest films by tying them to the stronger ones: to obtain a single hit film, a theater might have to agree to run any number of duds. The practice of block booking extended, until the late 1930s, to short films as well as features. To secure a high-quality feature, an exhibitor was often coerced into accepting a package of shorts, regardless of the quality. While this system worked well for short-subject producers who were affiliated with the major distribution companies, it was designed to lock out producers without such affiliations. Moreover, as the major studios expanded their own short-subject production output in the mid-1930s, the traditional independent specialty shops found it increasingly difficult to place their products in any but the most forsaken rural and subsequent-run situations.

The financial return for shorts became even tighter because of the theatrical practice of showing multiple features. This strategy intensified in the early 1930s with the start of the Depression and lasted until the end of the studio system in the 1950s. With two or more features on the theatrical program, precious little money or screen time was left over for short subjects, particularly those of the two-reel or twenty-minute variety that comedians from Charlie Chaplin to Laurel and Hardy had found perfectly suited to their work.[4]

2

The Rolin Film Company, 1914

The year 1914 came at the very center of a period of great change for the young American cinema. The relative order resulting from standardized business practices created through trade agreements among the original film companies was being thrown into disarray by government lawsuits, new competitive strategies, and the introduction of multiple-reel films. The resultant period of flux would last for several years until a new set of industrial practices, those leading directly to the vertical integration of the Hollywood studio era, became established.

The original motion picture producers had attempted to control the industry and to bar new producers from entering the business through the formation of a patent cartel, the Motion Picture Patents Company. As a group, these producers controlled enough viable patents on processes, equipment, and film specifications to make it impossible to legally produce a film without their permission, and this permission was granted only to members of the cartel. From the outset, this company proved to be an unreliable means of controlling renegade production by unlicensed producers, who would shortly embark on their own, more successful, methods of controlling the industry. By the midteens, the producers of the Motion Picture Patents Company were losing antitrust actions brought by the U.S.

government. They had already lost the allegiance and patronage of many leading exhibitors because of the strong-arm tactics of their distributor, General Film. Still worse for General Film, even Motion Picture Patents Company producers were abandoning it and seeking other distribution arrangements for their films. Although General Film had controlled 60 percent of the U.S. film market in 1912, its standardized sales and pricing strategies, which charged exhibitors a uniform price per foot for all films, proved inadequate for the handling of longer, more expensive pictures.

While some of the Motion Picture Patents Company producers would adapt to the changing industry and remain viable into the 1920s, Vitagraph being the notable example, two of the industry's early leaders, Biograph and Edison, would be out of the movie business before 1920. The archrivals of the Trust producers—the independent, nonlicensed producers, led by Adolph Zukor and Carl Laemmle, and new distributors and exhibitors such as William Fox and the Warner brothers—were consolidating their power within the growing industry, a process that would be complete by the mid-1920s. Having gained the upper hand in the economic war with the Trust producers in the marketplace, they were well on their way to forming their own vertically integrated monopolistic empires.[1]

The methods and operating base, as well as the management structure, of the young industry were changing. The individual roving filmmaker who functioned as writer, director, camera operator, and editor was being replaced by a more "scientific and efficient" division of labor, an assembly-line approach based in a film factory, or "studio," which permitted a predetermined number of films to be turned out on a regular and reliable basis.[2] The one-reel film, running between ten and fifteen minutes, depending on the speed of theater projection (something not standardized until the advent of sound), was being supplanted as the industry standard by longer movies. Multiple-reel "features," initially two to three reels in length and ultimately standardized at five to six reels (with "special" features running as many as nine reels or more), were becoming established as the preferred vehicle for drama, while a healthy market existed for short-form comedies, newsreels, and travelogues to serve as "opening acts" for the longer films.

Additionally, as Kristin Thompson has illustrated, film was moving from its primitive period into its classical mode during the early part of the century's second decade. Specific film techniques that involved all aspects of photography, direction, and editing and were intended to enhance verisimilitude and narrative clarity were becoming standard industry practice.[3] Films that did not adhere to these standards stood little chance of receiving theatrical distribution.

Finally, the geographic center of film production was shifting. Having originated in the New York City area, the motion picture industry in 1914 was already a national endeavor. While southern California was rapidly gaining strength as the new film capital, economically viable production centers included Chicago, Jacksonville, and San Francisco, and individual production companies were spotted virtually throughout the Sunbelt. This situation was to be short-lived, however. By 1920 virtually all production was centered in the Los Angeles area, while New York City remained the seat of corporate and financial power for most studios.

Hal Roach and the Founding of Rolin

The excitement and glamour of the movie business, the chance for instant wealth, and the then-pristine environment of the Los Angeles basin proved to be a powerful lure for young hopefuls from all over the United States. As Buster Keaton was to rhapsodize many years later, "We were all young, the air in southern California was like wine. Our business was also young and growing like nothing ever seen before. . . . In Hollywood you could all but feel prosperity in the sun-bleached air."[4]

One of those drawn to the area was twenty-year-old Hal Roach, a native of Elmira, New York, who had spent the previous few years working his way down the West Coast, starting in Alaska, on a personal odyssey to see the world. Arriving in Los Angeles in 1913 as a construction worker, Roach answered an ad for western extras at the 101-Bison Company. Roach's first-hand knowledge of life in the Northwest, combined with possession of several authentic western costumes, made him readily employable as a dress extra, and by 1914 he was part of the pool of bit players used regularly in Universal westerns. Within a short period, Roach found employment as an assistant director, responsible for various stage management functions, such as costuming, prop acquisition, and the hiring of extras. Excited by this experience (and by the potential fortunes to be made) and convinced that he had already absorbed as much knowledge about filmmaking as any studio executive, Roach decided that his future lay in the California film industry rather than in a return to the middle-class business life of Elmira, as originally intended.[5]

He organized his own film-producing firm. The name selected for the new concern, Rolin Film Company, was derived from a combination of the first letters of the last names of Roach and his principal partner, Dan Linthicum, an acquaintance from Roach's acting experience. A third partner, I. H. Nance, appears to have been drafted strictly to satisfy the legally mandated minimum of three corporate officers. Nance resigned his position as vice president at the very first meeting of the board of directors, less than a month after the date of incorporation.[6]

The Rolin articles of incorporation, dated July 23, 1914, outline an ambitious and far-ranging entertainment conglomerate. The stated purpose of the firm was to

> carry on the business of furnishing amusement to the public: to purchase, acquire, lease, own, buy, sell and manage theaters, play-houses, gardens, roof gardens, opera houses, parks, concessions, motion picture houses and other places of amusement . . . to carry on the business of managers, proprietors of theaters, opera houses and other places of amusement; to employ vaudeville performers, actors, singers, musicians . . . to acquire, own, purchase or dispose of plays, copyrights and dramatic and musical productions . . . to conduct public and private amusements, consisting of literary and musical performances, parks and picnic grouns [sic] containing dance pavilions, roller coasters and similar amusements . . . to carry on the business of restaurant keepers and vendors of wine, spirits and tobaccos, mineral waters and provisions . . . to print and publish . . . any play, poem, song or words of this the company may have copyright . . . to buy, sell, lease and generally deal in motion picture films.[7]

Whether any of the aforementioned activities, aside from the very last, were actually intended by the young firm is doubtful: the Rolin Film Company seems to have been established for the sole purpose of becoming a film producer. The other endeavors mentioned in the corporate charter more than likely were included simply to cover any foreseeable eventuality in an industry in which it was common to have various entertainment interests.[8]

At the first meeting of the board of directors, Roach was elected president, Nance became vice president, and Linthicum was named secretary-treasurer. The board made available for sale an additional fifty-seven shares of stock with the idea of increasing each board member's stake to twenty shares. No more stock was to be sold without the express approval of the board: a tactic designed to keep company ownership and control in the hands of the founders or their approved successors. Roach announced that he had money in hand for his shares. Linthicum indicated that he would have to pay for his new shares later, and Nance introduced to the board a young automobile dealership executive, Dwight Whiting, who would assume Nance's stock interests and his place on the board.[9]

By mid-September of 1914, the Rolin company had produced four one-reel comedies. Few details are known about these films, other than that they were all directed by Roach and were highly improvisational in nature.[10] The cast and crews for these films were acquaintances from Roach's stint as a movie extra and assistant director, and included Harold Lloyd. Lloyd's aim at this point in his career was simply to become a screen actor. He had no particular interest in comedy and, unlike most other players in film comedy of that era, he did not come to film from a vaudeville or music hall comic career. It was to the great fortune of Roach, Lloyd, and Rolin that Roach seized on Lloyd's athletic ability and pushed him into slapstick comedy. Despite comedy not having been his focus, Lloyd would become one of the screen's most popular comedians by the 1920s and would be the sole reason for the early survival of Rolin.

Rolin, needing a distributor to deliver its films to the nation's theater screens, entered into a contract with Sawyer, Inc., of New York City.[11] Under the terms of the deal, Rolin would receive 50 percent of the net profits from film rentals.

Sawyer, Inc., however, turned out to be a bad choice. The firm's history is a case study of the transient nature of some participants in the film industry during this period. A distributor primarily of multiple-reel features, Sawyer had been incorporated, with much fanfare in the trade press, in May 1914 by Arthur H. Sawyer, the former general manager of the Kinemacolor Company of America. *The Moving Picture World* was greatly impressed by the elegance of the new company's office suite, particularly the "Pompeiian Projection Room," which was kept at a constant cool temperature by electric fans circulating air over a spraying, multicolored water fountain at the base of the screen. Sawyer's stated goals were summed up by the company's general manager, W. H. Rudolph.

> Our aim is to provide expert service in the matter of marketing features—that is, in getting the pictures which producers make before the public in a way which will make them most profitable to those who own or control them. To the makers of pictures we offer the argument that all they have to do is provide the negatives. After we have accepted the negatives, we take care of the remaining details.[12]

Although establishment of new film distribution systems was still possible after 1914, as Pathé, Vitagraph, and others would demonstrate, Sawyer, the self-proclaimed world's largest film mart, proved not to be up to the competition it faced from the existing major distributors: the standard short film exchanges operated by General Film, Universal, and Mutual and the multiple-reel feature release systems operated by Warners' Features, Paramount, World Film Company, and Fox's Box Office. Without a national sales force or a system of film exchanges, Sawyer relied initially on the efforts of its contracting states'-rights distributors to move its films into the marketplace. Under the states'-rights system, a producer (in this case, Sawyer) divided the country into regions and contracted with local firms for the distribution of films within each region. This practice amounted to the farming out of distribution responsibilities to subcontractors, diminishing Sawyer's share of the box office receipts and virtually eliminating any hope for adequate financial return to the original producer.

In the fall of 1914, Sawyer announced the inauguration of an alternative distribution system, opening several branch offices throughout the United States, and including one-reel comedies in its release schedule. By this point, though, Sawyer lacked the resources necessary to gain a real foothold in the film industry, and in January 1915, less than a year after its formation, it placed its last film into distribution.

Whether Sawyer actually distributed any of the early Rolin product is difficult to establish. An absolute lack of any mention of Rolin product in Sawyer's release schedules tends to indicate that it did not. If any of the early Rolin films did receive theatrical exposure, given the disorganized and deteriorating state of the Sawyer firm, their release was probably not widespread.

By the end of 1914, Rolin was actively seeking a new distributor. A deal with United Film Service, an organization with close ties to the Warner brothers' growing film interests, for new one-reel comedies and two-reel dramas seemed a certainty in March 1915, only to fall apart at the last moment. By this time, the situation at Rolin was becoming grim. The company had nothing but red ink and a stack of unsold films to show for its nine months of production. Linthicum, who had never been able to purchase more than three shares of stock in the company, began to withdraw from active participation. Even Whiting, whose combination of enthusiastic high spirits, business acumen, and financial connections had proven to be a real asset to the company, was beginning to wonder whether continuing to make pictures that could not be sold wasn't a case of throwing good money after bad.[13] Then Rolin began negotiations with the Pathé Company.

A Distributor for Rolin: Pathé

Before it became apparent that the war with the independent producers was lost, Trust producers began searching for new distribution arrangements to allow their product continued access to theaters, particularly for their multiple-reel films. One of the first Patents Company members to break rank was Pathé Frères, a Paris-based firm that was one of only two non-U.S. film producers to gain membership in the Trust.[14] Pathé management became frustrated early in the arrangement at the relatively small percentage of its prodigious output that was accepted for distribution by General Film. Even more irksome to the Pathé executives was their perception that those Pathé films that were permitted by the Trust to enter the marketplace were not being as vigorously sold as other Trust productions. That Pathé was painfully aware of this problem is suggested by a line that appeared at the bottom of Pathé's *Moving Picture World* advertisement of February 28, 1914: "Insist upon these films at your exchange. If you can't get them, write us and we will help you."[15]

The strained relationship between Pathé and its distributor broke into open war on May 9, 1914, when Pathé published in *Moving Picture World* a letter that accused General Film of breach of contract as a result of the latter's substituting another weekly newsreel for Pathé's in many of its exchanges.[16] The following week, Pathé announced that it was setting up its own series of exchanges.[17] Starting in early 1913, Pathé had been distributing some of its product through Eclectic Films. Now its bond with Eclectic became stronger and was supplemented by the new Pathé exchanges.

During the summer of 1914, Pathé experimented with a pair of innovative marketing tactics. The first was the inauguration of the *Pathé Daily News,* a newsreel that would be issued on a daily, rather than the usual weekly, basis. Additionally, the *Pathé Daily News* was printed on Pathé-manufactured safety stock so that it could be shipped directly from Pathé via U.S. mail to subscribing theaters.[18] Most motion pictures during this period (and until 1950) were distributed on nitrate-based film stock, whose explosive nature prohibited its being mailed, requiring somewhat slower special courier services.

Pathé's other innovation of 1914 was the release of its latest (and most famous) serial, *The Perils of Pauline,* on one hundred forty-seven film prints. Pathé claimed that the previous record mass release was thirty prints, and that this larger figure would permit *Perils* to open nationwide simultaneously. The large quantity of prints was also intended to guarantee a certain amount of pictorial quality control well into the serial's run, something not possible when the total release amounted to twenty-five or thirty prints that were often torn and scratched by the projection equipment before they reached the secondary theaters.[19]

Despite the innovations, Pathé's initial efforts at independence were counterproductive, resulting in fewer theatrical bookings than it had managed to obtain through General Film.[20] At this point, however, fate and global conflict intervened. Having seen his film empire in Europe all but cease operations due to the outbreak of the First World War, Charles Pathé decided to turn his considerable personal energies toward the revitalization of his American subsidiary. Arriving in the United States in October 1914, he announced that

> the present upset in France has seemed to me to afford a splendid opportunity ... to study American conditions, to get acquainted with the American market. . . . To attain the most desirable end I shall devote much time to watching ... in the theaters what kinds of subjects most thoroughly meet with the public approbation and also to completing my own organization here that I may the better meet the requirements of the time. . . . My intention is to become a picture publisher or editor—to publish films as others publish books. I accept negatives where they accept manuscripts.[21]

Pathé's meaning when he expressed a desire to take "a greater interest" in film distribution became quite clear at the beginning of 1915 when Eclectic officially became a Pathé subsidiary, incorporated in the United States and legally separate from the already functioning American branch of Pathé Frères, and was renamed Pathé Exchange, Inc.[22]

One film form that had definitely received public approbation was the short comedy, particularly of the Keystone slapstick variety. Charles O. Bauman and Adam Kessel had founded Keystone in 1912, placing Mack Sennett, a former associate of influential filmmaker D. W. Griffith, in charge of production. During its first two years of existence, Keystone had established itself as the nation's leading supplier of one- and two-reel comedies, and in 1914, the year that Rolin was founded, Sennett introduced Charlie Chaplin to movie audiences. While Chaplin left Keystone after only one year, his rapid rise to fame and the enormous popularity of Keystone comic Roscoe "Fatty" Arbuckle during the same period, seemed to confirm Mack Sennett's infallibility at judging the public's comedic tastes. The success of Keystone also inspired the advent of a number of short-comedy specialty production companies, including Joker (a Carl Laemmle subsidiary), L-KO (founded by former Sennett employee Henry Lehrman), Komic, Nestor, Christie, and others.

In the midst of this frenzy of new studio formation, Rolin submitted nine one-reel comedies and three two-reel dramas for "publication" through the ambitious and greatly expanded Pathé organization of March 1915. Initially, despite its open-door policy, Pathé seemed uninterested in handling the Rolin product. Its screening committee of six judges completely dismissed the dramas and complained that the comedies were crude and vulgar, full

of censorable material.[23] Further, they criticized the inferior technical quality of the films, citing the presence of onlookers photographed in the background of some scenes, the generally mediocre photography, and poor
direction by Roach. The judges summarized their feelings about all of the
comedies by saying the films were imitations and not very good ones.[24]
Despite this judgment, one comedy was accepted by Pathé for distribution:
Just Nuts, featuring Lloyd as a character named Willie Work. While this film
contained most of the amateurish traits found in the others—including
Lloyd's blatant imitation of Chaplin's Tramp persona—the Pathé judges
thought that both the film and Lloyd had real comic merit. They encouraged Rolin to produce more films along the same lines while improving
on the specific defects that had drawn criticism.

During the summer of 1915, Rolin continued to produce films on speculation, only some of which were accepted by Pathé. Finally, in October
1915, Pathé committed to a long-term distribution contract with Rolin for
a series of one-reel comedies that would feature Lloyd as a new Chaplin
knock-off named Lonesome Luke. As part of the contractual agreement,
all Rolin films would still be judged on their individual merits by Pathé's
screening committee, which would reject any films deemed substandard.
This stipulation remained a major point of contention between Rolin and
Pathé for several years, particularly since Pathé was not obligated to pay
for any films its committee rejected.[25]

The bulk of the early Rolin product that was not accepted by Pathé was
turned over to Motion Picture Specialties Corporation with Rolin's instructions to sell the pictures under any terms possible. Under this arrangement,
two of the dramas and at least one of the comedies received limited exposure under the auspices of a variety of production-distribution firms. The
comedy, *Why the Boarders Left,* turned up on the screen in the fall of 1915
as a MINA (*Made IN America*) production for General Film release, a surprise to Roach and his associates, who received no notice of, screen credit
for, or money from the film's release.[26] By this time, though, unauthorized
releases of what Whiting himself had termed the "old junk" were but a
minor irritation for the Rolin management.[27] The company was embarking on what was to be a successful if occasionally acrimonious association
with a major distributor, cranking out a new Lonesome Luke "Phunphilm"
one-reeler every week for release through Pathé Exchange.

3

Lonesome Luke and the Glasses Character, 1915-19

With his company barely having survived its first year, Roach concentrated on two areas between 1915 and 1920: improvement of the quality of the Lloyd series and initiation of additional series. He was successful enough in his first goal to carry the company through a notable lack of success in the other.

During the latter half of the century's second decade, power was being consolidated within the motion picture industry in at least two different ways. By decade's end, the Los Angeles area was firmly established as the center of movie production in the United States. As talent and, perhaps more important, industrial support services such as processing laboratories and equipment and film stock suppliers became concentrated in southern California, other potential production centers like Jacksonville and Chicago saw their studios close. Even New York City, with its powerful base of Broadway talent, became largely inconsequential as a film production center, with production dwindling primarily to cheap short subjects and an occasional feature.

The other area of power consolidation was within the corporate structure of the industry itself. Starting about 1915 and firmly set by the mid-1920s, the companies that dominated the motion picture industry were vertically integrated, controlling production, distribution, and usually, exhibition. Although the production centers were on the West Coast, the seat of corporate power was in New York City, where central offices held the ultimate authority over the distribution process and the theater chain operations, as well as the budgets and production programs of their Hollywood operations.

One of the leaders in this corporate strategy was Adolph Zukor. Merging his Famous Players production company with a distributor named Paramount in 1916, Zukor formed the industry's largest producer-distributor combination. Paramount almost immediately extended its control to exhibition by buying and leasing first-run movie theaters in major metropolitan areas and by acquiring whole theater chains in some regions. By 1920 this strategy had made Paramount the most powerful company in the film industry. Other companies, with First National as one of the earliest, began to follow the Paramount model of vertical integration. The film producer-distributors that did not vertically integrate to the point of theater ownership, such as Pathé and Universal, would find themselves at a serious competitive disadvantage by the end of the 1920s. Small, independent producers like Hal Roach who did not even control their own distribution would have little power in this system.

Within the realm of comedy filmmaking in the years leading up to 1920, product standards were changing as well. Even though Douglas Fairbanks was starring in a successful series of feature-length comedies at Triangle, the comedy field remained largely the province of short-film producers, with feature length reserved generally for dramas. However, stars began to emerge within the short-comedy form and demonstrated box-office drawing power beyond that of the routine short comedy from a given producer.

After leaving Keystone, Charlie Chaplin embarked on a successful series of two-reel comedies, first at Essanay (1915), then for Mutual (1916–17), and finally for his own company (1918 onward). Upon leaving Mack Sennett in 1917, Fatty Arbuckle was launched in his own series of two-reelers by Joseph Schenck for Paramount release. It was this series of films that introduced Buster Keaton, in support of Arbuckle, to film audiences. These series, which featured the two most popular comedians of their day, instantly established themselves as more prestigious than the generic production-line shorts of Sennett and his rivals, which emphasized fast-paced action and rapid-fire gags over plot and characterization. As Peter Kramer has noted, the style of Chaplin, Arbuckle, and others, including Lloyd, who would join the ranks of the star comedians, integrated "the persona, the comic and acrobatic performances of the star comedians into seriously presented dramatic story patterns."[1]

The star comedians worked with their own personal creative staffs and frequently shot their films in studios reserved for their exclusive use. More time and larger budgets were allocated to the star comedies than to those produced by the production-line studios.

The qualitative gap between the films of the star comedians and those of the production-line studios would widen over the next decade, particularly after 1920, when the star comics began appearing in feature-length films, a move made possible in part by the star comics' reliance on conventional dramatic plotting to carry their films. As Henry Jenkins has argued, by the mid-1920s even the production-line studios had shifted to a more character-oriented style of comedy, "breaking with a disreputable past and progressing toward a higher standard of screen entertainment."[2] As will be suggested in the next chapter, Roach's ability to conform to this emerging standard considerably enhanced his studio's reputation during the 1920s.

By 1920, those studios that specialized in production-line comedies would dwindle to four primary producers: Mack Sennett Comedies, formed in 1917 when Sennett left Keystone (which folded shortly thereafter), and, far below Sennett in prestige, Christie, Educational, and Rolin. Sennett's advantage over his rivals was an established track record and a seasoned staff of writers and comics, most of whom he had carried over from Keystone. The Mack Sennett name was well known among theater operators or "exhibitors," if not with the public itself. As Janet Staiger has noted, film companies used brand names "to spread the value of each film to all the films, hoping to entice repeated consumption of the manufacturer's offerings. If the manufacturer could succeed in this, the firm would gain the advantage of an apparent monopoly."[3] A Sennett film was perceived as a known quantity and hence was more readily bookable than a Rolin product. While Rolin and the others scrambled desperately for theatrical distribution, Sennett was able to affiliate with the best distributors in the business, aligning with Paramount briefly after leaving Keystone, then going to Paramount's chief rival, First National. Sennett's reputation permitted him to present most of his films before 1920 as two-reelers, while the competition was still stuck largely with the less profitable single-reel efforts, which were frequently regarded as little more than filler material. For the remainder of the second decade of the twentieth century, Sennett, Educational, Christie, and Rolin would follow the basic Keystone style of fast-paced slapstick, violent knockabout comedy that often bordered on surrealism, hoping that an occasional comedian would rise above the material and emerge as a possible rival to Chaplin and Arbuckle.

Having overcome the substantial hurdle of finding theatrical distribution for its films, Rolin was able to embark on a standardized production schedule during its first half-decade, generally secure in the knowledge that most of the films it produced would reach theater screens and bring in financial returns. However, despite several attempts to diversify with additional series, the only films that found success in the marketplace were those that featured Lloyd. In addition to the economic disadvantages of having the entire studio overhead supported by the proceeds from a single series of short comedies, the situation gave the star of that series an enormous amount of power. If he chose to walk out, Harold Lloyd might close down the studio. Once, when Lloyd left briefly after a dispute with Roach over working hours, Rolin was able to cover the star's absence by substituting another actor in Lloyd's costume and makeup, but this solution was only a short-term one. Rolin, during this period, needed Lloyd to survive, and both Lloyd and Roach knew it. This situation would seriously limit Roach's managerial authority over the Lloyd series: control would continue to slide away from Roach as Lloyd's popularity grew.

A second influence on Roach's decision making grew from the need to produce films whose form and content met the tastes of the American public, particularly as perceived by Rolin's distributor and its executive staff, most of whom had been brought over from France. Pathé was in a position to accept or reject films on an individual basis. It could prevent Roach from entering entire spheres of filmmaking; it would not accept features or dramas from Roach until the 1920s, and it exercised absolute control over which Rolin comedies reached theater screens. Despite continual confrontation over the issue, Roach knew that for the films to reach the marketplace, he had to produce comedies that pleased the members of Pathé's screening committee. Roach's one alternative, finding another distributor for his films, failed despite repeated attempts. This failure was due, in large measure, to the inconsistent quality of his product during the period.

Standardizing Its Product

The Rolin mode of operation during the first few years of activity could best be characterized as one of frantic desperation. Films were turned out as quickly as possible, with Roach and his staff learning the craft of filmmaking by trial and error. Payrolls were not always met on time: the company was chronically short of general operating funds, necessitating frequent requests for advances from Pathé and occasional excursions into Dwight Whiting's personal resources.

Establishing standardized procedures for the production of slapstick pictures required a certain amount of experimentation as well. One avenue of exploration was to discover set and prop materials that would appear solid but at the same time would not contribute to the premature demise of the cast as they engaged in roughhouse antics. "We take great pleasure in advising you that we have found this to be the best processed board for our use on the market," Whiting wrote to the manufacturers of Upson Processed Board. "It is necessary to throw Mr. Harold Lloyd, who plays the leads, against walls and through doors, and we have found that using Upson Board instead of canvas for our interior scenes we do away with practically all shaking of the walls of the interior sets."[4]

Rolin had a rather transient nature and meager physical plant needs during its early years. The summer of 1915 found it leasing studio facilities from Norbig Film Manufacturing Company at 1745–51 Alessandro Street in Edendale, the same Los Angeles suburb that hosted Sennett's Keystone comedy studios. For a single rent payment of $150 per month, Rolin received office space, five dressing rooms, use of a carpenter shop and a filming stage, projection facilities, a cutting room, a dark room, and all utilities. Norbig also ran its own film-developing lab that, despite occasional problems with water spots on the finished product, Rolin used for the processing of its negatives and the printing of its positive editorial work prints. After these positive prints were edited, they were shipped to Pathé in New York along with the unedited negative. Upon approval of a film by the screening committee, Pathé cut the negative to match Rolin's edited copy and produced the theatrical release prints in its New York laboratories. The Rolin staff never knew exactly how the finished film looked until it played in the local Los Angeles theaters. As awkward as this practice might seem, it was not uncommon for the period.

In March 1916, Rolin moved its operations to Pacific Laboratories on Santa Monica Boulevard in Los Angeles. The rental price at this new facility for accommodations similar to those at Norbig was $125 per month. Starting in late 1916, Rolin also leased a vacant lot on Olive Street for ten dollars per month. This exterior location was used until early 1918, when the Los Angeles Fire Department ordered cessation of film production on the site. By 1917 studio operations were on the move again, relocating to the Bradbury mansion at 406 Court Street in Los Angeles. This would remain the studio's home until the move into permanent facilities in Culver City in 1920.[5]

During its formative years, Rolin relied heavily on Keystone as a model for its own operation. A series of letters between Whiting and Dorothy Twist, an aspiring scenario writer, reveals the extent to which Rolin's product was patterned after that of its more successful rival. Writing to Twist on June 10, 1915, Whiting asks,

> Would you like to try your hand at comedy of the Keystone order, making about 100 scenes per reel, all short, snappy, full of comic situations, writing same about a character named "LONESOME LUKE?" This is for a new series we are putting on.[6]

After purchasing Twist's first submission for twenty dollars, then rejecting her second as substandard, Whiting recommended a specific Keystone model for her future efforts.

> You have perhaps noticed in seeing some of the Keystone stuff, that there are two separate threads of comedy all through the story. That is—there are two separate and distinct pictures run together, of different people, who simply come together at the end with a big splash. You probably have noticed how hard it is to end up a scenario, also how weak all those we sent you were, and how weak your own was. That is the reason for putting in extra factions.
>
> For instance in your golf story, we introduced an eccentric German gentleman with an eccentric wife, both good comedians, who have nothing at all to do with Luke and the rest of the story, but the idea is this. Suppose on seeing the picture, some of Luke's stuff falls flat. In other words, it does not get over or is slow. You can then cut in the other faction and get a laugh from them. When it begins to get stale, flash back to Luke and his story. It thus gives you a chance to cut the picture where not interesting, and put in good stuff. Of course, it is essential for the whole thing to wind up together in a rough house finish, so that there is a logical end to the picture.[7]

Twist apparently took Whiting's instructions to heart; she sold another three scenarios to Rolin during the next few months. Her career as a writer for Lonesome Luke came to an abrupt close in late October 1915, when Hal Roach received permission from Pathé to make comedies without a pre-approved scenario. From this point on, Rolin comedies would rely on little more in the way of a written shooting script than a loose string of scribbled gag ideas with most of the plot improvised on the set.[8]

Despite some concessions from Pathé on the use of scenarios, Roach and Whiting were not pleased with the financial terms of the Pathé contract. The initial euphoria over simply obtaining a distributor for their films passed rapidly with the sobering realization of the low profit margins they were receiving. Thus the company, from a very early point in the relationship with Pathé, actively solicited distribution contracts with other major companies. Although obligated to Pathé for the Luke series, Rolin was under no restrictions regarding the production of other series for other distributors. Answering an inquiry from a British distributor (who, it turned out, was interested only in acquiring the Luke pictures for U.K. distribution), Whiting quoted the following rates for producing "a special brand of comedies along any lines you would suggest."

> We are fully equipped and are capable of turning out the highest quality of 1, 2, 3, 4, or 5 reel comedies, which we can make for you on a so much cash per foot negative contract. We can make comedies from 60 cents a foot to $10.00 a foot, and we have found that about the best average price is $2.50 per negative foot. This enables us to put in new effects, hire the best people, and we believe that we could put you out something that would put you in a position above all competitors.[9]

One wonders what type of film would result from ten dollars per foot, if $2.50 would buy the best of everything. And all this from a company that was still mired in substandard imitation of the Keystone roughhouse comedy style.

In late 1915 and early 1916, Rolin pitched the idea for a new comedy series to Metro, Paramount, Fox, and virtually every other major distributor. Only Paramount expressed any interest in Rolin's proposal, and that never came to the point of contractual commitment.[10] Rolin was stuck with Pathé for the foreseeable future.

Rolin was also stuck producing a single series, the Lonesome Luke comedies starring Lloyd (see appendix 2, synopsis 1). Not only was the fiscal operation of an entire production company extremely difficult on the profits from a series of one-reelers (the profit on the most successful Luke one-reelers averaging around $460[11]), but there was also great danger in placing the entire studio's future on the shoulders of a single starring actor. Slapstick comedians were, by the very nature of their craft, constantly flirting with serious injury. Rolin was one misplaced banana peel away from ruin. And Lloyd's rapidly increasing popularity made him potentially attractive to larger studios with more money to offer. Thus it was more than a simple desire to expand that led Rolin to initiate a second series.

The first effort along these lines was in April 1916, when Hal Roach attempted to hire Arnold Novello, an Italian circus clown who was working in American burlesque under the stage name "Toto." Despite Pathé's enthusiasm for Toto as a prospective film performer, the comic's short-term stage commitments were too heavy to permit him to accept Rolin's film offer.[12] Rolin's next stab relied more on imitation than on innovation. If Lonesome Luke was successful despite being a rather obvious if unstated imitation of Chaplin's Tramp, why not imitate the second most successful screen comedian, Fatty Arbuckle? Roach decided to build a series around Dee Lampton, an eighteen-year-old actor who was five feet tall and weighed 285 pounds. Lampton had previous film experience, most notably as Chaplin's pie-toting loge companion in *A Night at the Show* (1915), and had been playing supporting roles at Rolin since late 1915. The Lampton series, dubbed Skinny comedies with obvious irony, commenced production in August 1916 under the directorial guidance of Harry Russell, a veteran of the Keystone studio. Both Roach and the Pathé organization agreed that the seven shorts produced in the series were extremely poor. When the films finally reached theater screens in early 1917, five had been cut to seven minutes, half of the normal running time of a single-reel comedy. Four of these "split-reel" comedies were released in pairs to form full reels, and the fifth was teamed with an old half-reel short that featured French comedy star Max Linder. Rolin accepted a flat payment of five hundred dollars for each of the Skinny comedies without argument, despite the fact that the films had cost one thousand dollars apiece to produce.[13] After the failure of his solo series, Dee Lampton returned to the Rolin stock company, where he remained until his death in 1919 at the age of twenty-one, the result of a ruptured appendix (see appendix 2, synopsis 2).

The Skinny fiasco was but a temporary setback for Rolin. In the fall of 1916, citing favorable public reaction to the series, Pathé ordered an increase in the length of the Lonesome Luke comedies from one to two reels. This change would elevate the films from the filler status Rolin shared with most of its rivals to a distinctive position alongside the films of Chaplin, Arbuckle, and Sennett. By the early 1920s, two reels would become fairly routine for short comedy, but in 1916 the extra length was still a mark of achievement.

The greater budgets, prestige, and anticipated profits promised by this shift to longer pictures were welcome news indeed and fired the ambitions of the tiny company. "We are moving heaven and earth to give exhibitors the best single reel comedies in the world," Whiting wrote to one California exhibitor. "We are soon going to make some two reel Lukes to buck Chaplin."[14] In spring 1917, however, just when the first of the two-reel "Lukes" were reaching the screen, new developments sent Rolin into a program of expansion and change: Toto Novello was now available and willing to act in two-reel comedies. Furthermore, Lloyd would return to one-reelers, retiring Lonesome Luke in favor of a new screen persona: a timid-looking, bespectacled youth.

Hal Roach's intent was to have the new Toto series handled by a production "unit," or staff, separate from that which worked on the Lloyd films. In a 1918 letter, Warren Doane wrote that the ideal production schedule, only occasionally realized at Rolin, called for each one-reel production unit to have three directors who would rotate, spending a week each on preproduction planning, production, and postproduction. This timetable would produce a new one-reel comedy weekly. In actual practice, however, Rolin frequently had only one or two directors per unit. Roach, Alf Goulding, Gilbert Pratt, and Fred Newmeyer constituted the Rolin directing staff during the period, with J. Farrell MacDonald serving briefly as a director as well. Although surviving Rolin one-reelers do not include director credits (following the lead of Keystone), period accounts suggest that all of these people were involved with the Luke series at one time or another.

Under Roach's plan for a separate Toto unit, Roach would remain the supervising producer for both Toto and Luke but would direct only the Toto series, with assistance from Fred Newmeyer. This arrangement would leave Goulding, Pratt, and initially, MacDonald as the directors of Luke. With Roach concentrating on the Toto series, Lloyd assumed a substantial amount of supervisory control over his own series.[15]

Roach took an extended absence from Rolin in February 1917 to direct the Toto pilot film in a rented studio in New York City, a venue demanded by Pathé executives who wanted to personally observe its production. With Roach on the East Coast, Whiting found himself facing a problem not at all unique to filmmaking: namely, getting the workers to work while the boss is away. While Roach complained in correspondence to Whiting about working with "strangers" and under artificial lights,[16] Whiting reported back to Roach that

> I am instituting a new proposition at the studio because I am having a great deal of trouble in getting people started in the morning, and seeing that they do not take too much time off at lunch. The system consists of a big triangle which will be rung at nine o'clock for a signal for everybody to be on the stage if they are not already

there. At twelve the triangle will be rung again which will be the signal for everybody to go to lunch. At 12:30 the triangle will be rung again which will be the signal for them to be back on the stage, and at 3:30 it will be rung again, which will be quitting time, as that is when the light goes now. A little later it will be four o'clock.

With you away, things are inclined to be a little slack and the hams need all the pep that can be injected into them. They are getting pretty good stuff, but it is coming in pretty slow.[17]

The following week, Whiting happily informed Roach that "the new system of the bell is working out fine."[18]

Despite early enthusiasm about Toto as a film performer, the Pathé screening committee was consistently disappointed in the resulting films once regular series production was under way on the West Coast. Responding to a report from Whiting (who was in New York for a change) that Pathé wanted to reedit one of the Toto pictures and "improve" it with joke subtitles, Roach angrily wired,

> TELL BERST [the managing director of Pathé Exchange, Inc.] I REFUSE TO MAKE PICTURES FOR PATHÉ TO BE EDITED IN NEW YORK. HAS BEEN PROVEN BY PAST EXPERIENCE THAT PATHÉ CANNOT EDIT COMEDY. . . . IF THEY WILL NOT ACCEPT PICTURES AS THEY LEAVE HERE THEY NEED NOT ACCEPT THEM AT ALL AS FAR AS I AM CONCERNED.[19]

In a separate telegram on the same day, Roach informed Whiting that he was going to show the Toto film under discussion to Jesse Lasky and Adolph Zukor of Paramount for their possible distribution. Both this and a similar overture to William Fox failed. The next day, Whiting relayed even more bad news. Pathé was accepting Roach's challenge and rejecting the Toto film completely, saying that

> the [street] car stuff was the only good part and that the rest was worthless. Tell Doran [the cameraman] to stop panning as Berst said Pathé discourages same and nearly every scene in Toto Three had panning needlessly up and down or sideways in new stuff.[20]

Recommending that the entire story be built around the streetcar scenes that Pathé had liked, Whiting concluded, "I think we should finish retakes Toto Three before Saturday next and fire whole Toto company then, as otherwise we will get in so deep that we can't get out."[21]

Responding to Whiting's suggestion about lengthening the streetcar footage, Roach urged,

Wish you could explain to Pathé while the street car stuff is good that to make two thousand feet on street car would surely drag and get monotonous. I think we left the street car at the psychological time and it would be hopeless to make one thousand feet more of street car.[22]

Whiting dutifully relayed this information to J. A. Berst and his committee, then reported to Roach the cornucopia of comic suggestions for stretching the streetcar material, including having "somebody get on with limburger. People think woman with baby inside car guilty of odor. Everybody [at Pathé] thought very funny so if made they have to like same."[23] The nature of Pathé's low-comedy suggestions for improving this film were in marked contrast to their overall complaints regarding the series, finding Toto to be too "contortionistic and burlesque," too close to his classical circus roots for the illusion of reality created by the movies. Unlike the Limburger gag, these complaints were entirely in keeping with the movement in comedy filmmaking toward a more refined and sophisticated style.

Sensing that the Toto films would never progress to an acceptable quality or style, Roach and Pathé agreed to cut the series to a single reel (see appendix 2, synopsis 3). By summer 1918, Novello began to experience health problems, and on February 16, 1919, the last Toto short, appropriately named *Toto's Troubles,* was released. Novello remained in the United States and performed in vaudeville, never returning to the movies. He died in 1938 at the age of fifty.[24]

Roach made two more efforts before 1920 to launch additional series, both of which failed. In the fall of 1917, Roach featured Snub Pollard, Lloyd's ever-dependable and durable supporting player, in a short of his own. This pilot film was a great disappointment, and only in a reconciliatory moment after the storm over Toto did Pathé agree to accept it for release in early 1918 under fire-sale terms similar to those of the unfortunate Skinny comedies.

With the Toto series in its death throes in the summer of 1918, an English comic named Stan Laurel came to work at the studio. Laurel had been Chaplin's understudy in the music hall show that had brought them both to America. Like Chaplin, Laurel decided that his future lay in the New World, but he had not achieved the success that had come so easily to his former colleague. While he had found regular and reliable work as the star of his own vaudeville act, Laurel's real desire, to become a film comic, had met with disappointing results. In a handful of films made prior to 1918, Laurel had managed to produce a few laughs but no long-term studio contracts. Thus it took little from Roach to persuade Laurel to sign a contract for a series of one-reelers (see appendix 2, synopsis 4). In its publicity surrounding the first Laurel release, the Pathé press department referred to Laurel as the British Charlie Chaplin, evidently unaware of Chaplin's own origins and that there really was a Chaplin-Laurel connection that could have been exploited. Pathé further misidentified Laurel's initial Rolin effort as his film debut, although this error could have been less a matter of poor research than of a desire that the earlier Laurel comedies be forgotten. In any case, after only five comedies were produced, all of which received lukewarm reviews, Pathé politely announced that Laurel was concluding his working vacation in America and would be returning to England shortly.[25] Famed director George Stevens, who served as Laurel and Hardy's cameraman in the late 1920s, accurately described the problems with Stan Laurel's comic persona of the years shortly before and after 1920.

> Some time before beginning at Roach, I had seen Stan work, and I thought he was one of the unfunniest comedians around. He wore his hair in a high pompadour and usually played a congenital dude or slicker. He laughed and smiled too much as a comedian. He needed and wanted laughs so much that he made a habit of laughing at himself as a player, which is extremely poor comic technique. How he changed! In those very early days he was obviously searching for a workable form or formula.[26]

The Glasses Character

The change in the screen persona of Harold Lloyd from Lonesome Luke to "the glasses character," which he would play for the rest of his career, marked Lloyd's first step toward the more refined style of character and narrative-driven comedy that would dominate the 1920s and would propel him to the front ranks of comedy stardom. The new character came about reportedly because Lloyd was tired of imitating Chaplin and wanted to establish a screen personality all his own, something he thought he could achieve with the glasses character despite his admission that he appropriated the idea from a fighting parson character in a feature film. It is clear that Lloyd exerted some creative control over his films even at this early stage of his career. Correspondence in the Rolin files mentions that Lloyd scouted locations, and one telegram from Roach to Whiting, sent while the former was on a business trip to New York, suggests that it would be all right to proceed with the production of a certain picture in Roach's absence "if Lloyd thinks it is good enough."[27] Nevertheless, another telegram from Roach to Whiting sent during the same New York trip indicates that the change in

Lloyd's persona actually may have resulted from negotiations with Pathé regarding the new Toto series. Preparing to board a train to return to the West Coast, Roach wired his partner, "Toto pictures length two reels. . . . Luke pictures one reel every ten days. . . . Do not start picture with Luke till I arrive. Am changing make up and style of one reel pictures so they will not conflict with two reel Luke releases."[28] Although production of the two-reel Lukes was discontinued, enough of the shorts had already been made to meet the series' release schedule through the end of 1917.

Whatever degree of collaboration between Lloyd and Roach was responsible for the change in persona, the full characterization took several years to develop. Lloyd suggested that his model was a film character who appeared meek and timid but who, when pushed to the limit, could fight like a tiger to defend himself or his love interest. While this characterization may be fairly true of the mature glasses character, it does not accurately describe the offerings of the early years. The character may look meek, with his owl-rimmed glasses and flowing Windsor tie, but the discrepancy between the character's appearance and his demeanor is usually made clear within the first few moments of a film. The early glasses character is, in many ways, just Lonesome Luke without Chaplinesque makeup. He is brash to the point of being obnoxious: as late as 1919 in *His Royal Slyness,* one of the first glasses two-reelers, the Lloyd character is introduced by a subtitle that reads "if lightning ever strikes his nerve, goodbye lightning." This character is hyperactively out to achieve his goals in life (one gets the impression that wooing the love interest in these films is simply one more goal to be accomplished for its own sake), and he has no reservations about kicking or stepping on anyone who gets in his way.

Despite this odd behavior the character, even at this early phase, was being described in all-American, boy-next-door terms by both the studio and the critics. Lloyd, the person, was exhibited as a model of the virtues of clean living from the very beginning. A press release sent to *Motion Picture News* in January 1916 claimed that Lloyd was so clean-cut, "he becomes physically ill when he has to smoke a cigarette for Lonesome Luke."[29] If so, Lloyd's first five years of film work must have been wretchedly painful for him, so often does his character sport a cigarette carelessly dangling from his lips. And as late as 1919, in *His Royal Slyness,* Lloyd briefly addresses a crowd with a cigarette in the corner of his mouth. The effect is to suggest the character's supreme indifference to those around him and to the world in general. In short, the early Lloyd character is not just an ambitious youth in wholesome pursuit of the American Dream; he is often an unprincipled and unsympathetic individual for whom winning is everything.

Although the comedies were formatted along rather predictable lines, with Lloyd playing "The Boy" to Bebe Daniels's "Girl" and Pollard providing a comic foil, they were hailed as a comic innovation. In a film review quoted by Pathé in a *Moving Picture World* ad of August 24, 1918, Tamar Lane, film critic for the *Boston Evening Record,* praised Lloyd as

> one of the screen's finest comedians, and one whom we think will some day take his place along side Chaplin and Arbuckle as a whole-sale producer of laughs. . . . He is original in his work and imitates no one either in make up or in acting. He is unique as a slapstick comedian for the reason that he wears absolutely no trick make-up or character clothes.[30]

Mr. Lane had apparently never seen a picture of Lloyd out of character; without his glasses and pancake makeup he was virtually unrecognizable. This underscores the degree to which the heavy movie makeup of the early silent era was accepted as "normal" rather than stylized to the particular needs of the film medium. Similar kudos came from a *Moving Picture World* columnist, who in early 1919 hailed the Lloyd films as "an entirely new comedy spirit, an evolution from the broad, coarse and oftentimes messy slapstick pioneer work."[31] Commenting on the success of the Lloyd series, Hal Roach declared,

> It isn't so surprising that Lloyd is going over so big in his new work. I firmly believe the vogue of screen comedians who depend largely upon grotesque make-up or physical infirmities to get them over is going out. I believe that more legitimate methods will be demanded by the public even in slapstick.[32]

Roach's philosophy regarding the need for more legitimate methods may have been the result of painful experience with the Skinny and Toto series but would be applied with an uneven hand in the productions that followed, which often were populated with midgets, obese and cross-eyed persons, and a variety of ethnic "types." Nevertheless, this important early public statement suggests that Roach had finally ascertained film comedy was taking a more cultured and refined direction, emphasizing situation and character over mindless physical violence. This style would become the trademark of his studio and would distinguish his work from that of his rivals by the mid-1920s.

By the fall of 1918, Lloyd's popularity was so great that Pathé was inspired to run trade ads inviting a comparison between Lloyd and Chaplin and even going so far as to suggest superiority of Lloyd's films over those of Chaplin. The Pathé press department must have been using Lloyd's brash and nervy screen persona as a role model. Lloyd, whatever his popularity, was still appearing in cheap one-reelers, while Chaplin had recently signed a widely publicized million-dollar contract with First National. However, Chaplin's increasingly slow working pace, which resulted in only two three-reel comedies and one split-reel sales pitch for war bonds during all of 1918, was creating a comedy void into which the eager young man with glasses was more than willing to jump (see appendix 2, synopsis 5).

This jump was made a bit easier in the spring of 1919, when Rolin and Pathé agreed to begin producing the Lloyd comedies in two-reel length, the first of which would appear in movie theaters in the fall, with the start of the 1919–20 movie season. Typical of the Rolin-Pathé relationship, the green light on a two-reel series was the culmination of tense negotiations between the producer and his distributor, beginning with Roach demanding release from his contractual obligations to Pathé after a series of rejections by the screening committee. That Roach remained in the Pathé fold, happier and with better terms than before, was due in large part to the efforts of new Pathé manager Paul Brunet, a man considerably more skilled in diplomacy than his predecessor, the autocratic J. A. Berst.

Upon completion of the second two-reeler, Bebe Daniels, Lloyd's leading lady since the earliest days of Lonesome Luke, left the studio to take a contract with the Lasky Company as a leading player in the features of Cecil B. DeMille. Lasky and DeMille had first seen Daniels at a local cafe in May 1917 and had tried to hire her on the spot, offering her twice what she was getting from Rolin. Despite an immediate protest from Rolin, citing that such talent raids were barred under the guidelines set by the Producers' Association, it is obvious that neither DeMille nor Daniels forgot the matter. Daniels was replaced in the Lloyd series by Mildred Davis. Davis and Lloyd clicked as a team, and production of the two-reelers continued almost without a pause.[33]

Harold Lloyd's popularity continued to climb during the summer of 1919. One Iowa exhibitor staged a Harold Lloyd week and reported that at week's end, his patrons still had not seen enough of the comic. A theater manager in Montana echoed this sentiment when he wrote to *Moving Picture World* that "every last man, woman and child hereabouts has just gone nutty over him."[34] Theaters across the country eagerly anticipated the new two-reel Lloyd series. Lloyd and Roach had finally achieved a happy synchronization with the tastes of film audiences.

Exit Whiting

As Rolin struggled to define its house style, emphasizing character, situation, and deliberate plot pacing over the high-speed slapstick Sennett formula, its management changed in a major way. Early in 1918 Rolin once again suffered cash-flow problems due to its heavy investment in the Toto series, which was just beginning to be accepted (and paid for) by Pathé. In a letter to freelance writer H. M. Walker, Rolin assistant manager Warren Doane apologized for being unable to send Walker the full amount due for his services, assuring that "this delay will only be temporary. Should worst come to worst, Mr. Whiting will come to bat again and liquidate all that is against the Company."[35] As in the past, Whiting's private financial reserves could always be relied on to keep the company afloat in case of an emergency. The following month, February 1918, Whiting answered a letter from a job seeker:

> [P]icture conditions here on the Coast are a trifle slow; Universal has shut down three companies, and all the rest of the studios have recently laid off large amounts of people. In the spring I look for better opportunities.[36]

He closed by suggesting that the applicant recontact him in a few months.

However, less than two months later, Whiting himself was out of the film business. He resigned his position in Rolin during a special meeting of the board of directors on April 4, 1918, and sold his stock in the company to Roach.[37] The exact reason for Whiting's departure from the company that he had bailed out on more than one occasion has always been vague, Hal Roach simply saying, many years later, that Pathé management had insisted on the change and had financed Roach's purchase of Whiting's interest.[38] No documentation, aside from this statement, exists on the matter, and it is difficult to understand why Pathé would have dictated an administrative change within Rolin and why, if it did, Roach would have obliged, considering his combative stance on the subject of Pathé meddling with his productions. Despite Roach clearly being the senior partner in his collaboration with Whiting, the latter's exit left Roach with no partner, junior or otherwise, whose opinions would have to be considered when the company's future course was being charted.[39]

Roach replaced Whiting by installing his father, C. H. Roach, as the secretary-treasurer of Rolin. Earl Wisdom, a former business associate of Whiting who had served as Rolin's vice president and attorney, tendered his resignation at the same time as Whiting but indicated he was in no hurry for it go into effect. Taking him at his word, the board of directors did not replace him until January 26, 1920, when it elected Warren Doane as the new vice president. Doane had been Whiting's assistant in the automobile business and had joined Rolin with his boss but decided to remain with the firm after Whiting left.

With Whiting gone, Roach withdrew from the regular directing pool to concentrate on company management and to act as a strong central producer for what he envisioned as an expanding production slate. Although he would return to direction periodically throughout his career, the day-to-day directorial chores would be handled by a staff of five: Goulding, Pratt, and Newmeyer, joined by Albert Glassmire and Charles Avery, a recent acquisition from Triangle Keystone.[40] Reorganization of the studio brought Rolin's management structure more closely in line with that of the Keystone-Sennett model, in which the studio head supervised all production in a general sense without becoming intimately involved with the details of individual pictures. However, this structure was rather fluid and subject to permutations during the 1920s and 1930s.

As the second decade of the twentieth century drew to a close, Rolin had only a single series in production. Although the pitfalls of relying on a single series were very real, Roach had discovered that both financial danger and immense frustration also lay in production of failed pilot films and short-lived series (ironically foreshadowing the studio's demise in the television era of the 1950s). What made a conservative approach even more appealing, beyond the fact that Whiting was no longer around to provide a financial safety net, was that the Lloyd comedies were extremely popular. Then, on August 24, 1919, midway through production of the fifth Lloyd two-reeler, what started out as a routine publicity photo session for Harold Lloyd threatened to send his future, and that of Rolin, up in smoke.

4

Pathécomedies, 1919–27

As the 1920s began, Paramount Pictures continued its dominance in the motion picture industry, a position enhanced by the purchase of several large theater chains during the first half of the 1920s. Two companies, First National and Loew's, Inc., attempted to emulate Paramount's model of vertical integration, combining the functions of producer, distributor, and exhibitor under one corporate roof. Unlike Paramount, however, both were primarily theater operators that had moved into production and distribution as a direct competitive reaction to Paramount. First National, formed by a group of first-run exhibitors who had tired of Paramount's film booking practices, achieved financial success early on, placing major film stars like Mary Pickford and Charlie Chaplin under exclusive contract. However, the company had lost its initial momentum by mid-decade and was absorbed by Warner Brothers in 1929. The other theater chain to enter the production-distribution arena had a bit more staying power. Loew's, Inc., was primarily a vaudeville-movie theater chain when it purchased Metro Pictures, a producer-distributor, in 1920. Loew's shot to an industry position second only to Paramount in 1924, when it purchased Goldwyn Pictures and merged that studio with Metro to form Metro-Goldwyn-Mayer. Loew's-MGM would surpass Paramount to become the industry leader in the early 1930s when Paramount's heavily mortgaged theater chains dragged it into receivership and reorganization.

Although Paramount and Loew's wielded considerable power over the film industry in the 1920s, there was still room for entry into the market by less powerful studios. Fox and Warner Brothers, vertically integrated companies with origins in the film industry dating back to the previous decade, would find their pioneering efforts at talking pictures boosting them to a position near the top of the industry by the end of the 1920s. RKO was a new producer-distributor-exhibitor formed in 1928 from a combination of the financial strength (and talking-picture process) of the Radio Corporation of America with the Keith-Albee-Orpheum vaudeville theater circuit and the Film Booking Office, a low-budget producer-distributor. Together, Paramount, Loew's-MGM, Fox, Warner Brothers, and RKO formed the big five, those fully integrated companies that dominated the Hollywood studio system in the 1930s and 1940s.

Generally less profitable or prestigious than the big five, but usually holding a viable industrial position during the studio era, were the little three, companies that were not fully vertically integrated. Universal and Columbia were full-fledged film factories specializing in routine program pictures that were aimed at rural and subsequent-run markets. For most of the 1920s through the 1940s, both companies were producer-distributors that owned no movie theaters. The last member of the little three was United Artists, a distribution company for independent producers (filmmakers not working for one of the major producer-distributors) formed in 1919 by Chaplin, Pickford, Douglas Fairbanks, and D. W. Griffith. By the 1930s, United Artists served as the distribution outlet for the prestige productions of Samuel Goldwyn and David O. Selznick. After the coming of sound and the formation of RKO, the Hollywood industrial structure remained fairly stable until 1948, when the film industry was forced to spin off its theaters after signing a consent decree in the *U.S. v. Paramount Pictures* antitrust suit. The eight major companies dominated the industry during the 1930s and 1940s in such a way as to virtually eliminate any possible competition from outsiders. After 1928, entry into the American motion picture industry by a new company became extremely difficult. Those companies formed in the 1930s and 1940s that did survive for any length of time usually did so either by merging with an established company (Twentieth Century with Fox, International with Universal) or by going after the low-budget, marginal markets that were of little interest to the majors (Republic, Monogram).

One company decidedly in decline during the still-fluid industry environment of the 1920s was Roach's distributor, Pathé Exchange, Inc. Believing that the French film industry would never recover its former prominence after the First World War, Charles Pathé began to divest himself of his various film interests after 1918. His American branch was particularly harmed by this process: Pathé Exchange suffered from poor management throughout the 1920s. Additionally, Pathé did not own any U.S. theaters. As Paramount, Loew's, and others began to dominate the choice theatrical venues, Pathé, like Universal, was forced to place most of its feature-length films in rural and subsequent-run theaters. Even when Pathé or one of its producers made an exceptional feature whose profit potential dictated that it be given play in the most prestigious theaters, like Roach's Harold Lloyd and Rex, the Wonder Horse, films to be discussed later, Pathé's generally weak industry position gave it little leverage to set rental terms that would maximize the box office split for it and its producers. Pathé became known primarily as a distributor of short subjects, and it became marginal to the mainstream industry.

The breach between the two tiers of comedy films (star and nonstar production-line pictures) became wider in the early 1920s, when most of the star comedians moved into feature-length films. Chaplin and Arbuckle (whose career was cut short by a scandal in 1921) were joined in the feature form by Arbuckle's former supporting player, Buster Keaton (who began a solo starring career in short comedies in 1920), and by Harold Lloyd. Comedians and producers who remained in short comedies were widely perceived within the industry as minor league, a fact that was confirmed when the onetime industry leader in comedy, Mack Sennett, who had once had his films distributed by Paramount and First National, signed a distribution contract with Pathé in 1923.

Rolin Comedies

It is ironic that Harold Lloyd, who had survived the rigors of heavy slapstick filmmaking with only minor cuts and bruises, finally met serious injury on August 24, 1919, in the relative calm of a Sunday publicity still session at Witzel Photography Studio in Los Angeles. Lloyd had assumed a characteristic devil-may-care pose lighting a cigarette from the fuse of an anarchist-style bomb when the bomb exploded in his hand. Rather than being an empty shell, the bomb was actually of the variety designed by comedy filmmakers to discharge with a large puff of smoke. It had been misplaced in a box that was supposed to contain only nonexplosive models and from there had found its way into the hands of the unfortunate Lloyd. When the smoke cleared, Lloyd was alive but suffered severe facial burns, seriously impaired vision, and the loss of the thumb and forefinger of his right hand.

Roach and Pathé were faced with an immediate dual problem: handling the public relations aspect of the accident and coming up with a replacement for the Lloyd series. Most Lloyd biographers have characterized the permanent damage to his hand as one of Hollywood's best kept secrets, indicating that the very fact of the missing fingers did not become public knowledge until after Lloyd's death—when, presumably, his confidants were released from their solemn obligations and could finally tell all. While it is true that Lloyd tried to suppress information concerning his maimed hand, in fact this information had been a matter of public record on the pages of *Moving Picture World* since 1919. In the September 6 issue, Paul Brunet of Pathé released a telegram that he had received from Hal Roach on August 27.

> Harold Lloyd's condition greatly improved. He will lose a portion of finger and thumb of right hand. His face is in good condition. There will only be slight scars easily covered with makeup. His right eye, which we feared to be injured, is in good shape and will not be deformed in any way. This is far better than we expected.[1]

The Pathé press release concludes with

> It is expected and hoped that Lloyd will have regained complete health within two months, but if his recovery should not be complete before the end of the year, Pathé would still have enough of his films to supply exhibitors.[2]

While this announcement displays a rather callous tone, emphasizing the damage to studio "property" rather than concern for Lloyd as a person, at least both Roach and Pathé were open about Lloyd's injuries. On October 4, the *Moving Picture World* printed an update on Lloyd's condition, including a September 16 telegram from Pathé's Los Angeles representative, a Mr. Carmichael.

> Saw Lloyd today. He looks fine. His face not injured in any way. Eye doing nicely. Will not be affected. Worst feature loss of part of thumb and index finger which can be easily camouflaged. He expects to be able to work in a few weeks. Personally feel his future will not be affected in any way.[3]

Despite the somewhat excessive optimism in trying to reassure the readers of *Moving Picture World* that a popular box office draw was only temporarily out of action (it would be a matter of months rather than weeks before Lloyd was fit to return to work), none could deny that Lloyd and Rolin had been lucky. The explosion at Witzel's could have just as easily killed Lloyd or, at the very least, left him with career-ending injuries. Instead, it was a relatively minor setback to a career that was on the verge of skyrocketing.

Most of Lloyd's biographers, including Schickel, Dardis, and Reilly, have stressed that the injury was something of an embarrassment to the perfectionist Lloyd, who went to great lengths to keep it from his public after the resumption of his career. His staff was reportedly sworn to secrecy on the matter, and a casual glance through supposedly candid and informal photographs of the star out of character reveals him either to be wearing gloves or situated with his right hand conveniently buried in his pocket. The big mystery that remains is how public memory of such an initially highly publicized injury to a popular star ever could have faded to the point that the charade of denying the injury, which Lloyd does in his 1928 autobiography, was as effective as it was.

Still, the accident did clearly demand a new course of action at Rolin, despite its considerable backlog of unreleased Lloyd films (eight one-reelers and four two-reelers). The studio could not sit idle while its star began what could be a very long convalescence. With no plans in the works for a second series, Roach and his staff opted for the only solution within their grasp. Two days after Lloyd's accident, when it seemed possible that the damage to his eyes might prevent him from ever acting again, production started on the first of a series of one-reelers starring Lloyd's second banana.[4]

Australian comic Harold Fraiser had come to the United States as a member of the vaudeville troupe Pollard's Lilliputians. When the act broke up, Fraiser continued to use the stage name "Snub Pollard" and ultimately found his way to Hollywood and film work.[5] A member of Lloyd's stock company practically from the beginning of the Lonesome Luke series, Pollard had retained his Keystone-inspired makeup of whiteface, oversized moustache and eyebrows, and ill-fitting clothing even after Lloyd had abandoned his slapstick clown persona for the more "normal" glasses character. Despite both Roach's expressed desire to move away from the type of comedy that relied on grotesque makeup and the fact that an earlier pilot film for a Pollard series had fared badly, Snub happened to be the only comic on the lot at the moment who could even remotely be considered as a series lead. Started as an emergency stopgap, the new Pollard films actually became one of Roach's most reliable series during the next several years.

The new Rolin Comedies, as the Pollard series was named, debuted with *Start Something,* released on October 26, 1919. Unlike the earlier solo Snub Pollard effort, *Start Something* was well received by both exhibitors and audiences, with *Motion Picture News* noting that

[i]t was only a question of time before Pollard would shine by himself. He is too capable a fun-maker to unload his comicalities for the
benefit of anyone but himself. . . . He has a style of his own. . . . He
has his own keen sense of humor. . . . They can imitate his make-up
but not his style.[6]

Pathé happily reported to Roach that "so far we have not lost an account
in replacing the one-reel Lloyds for Pollards."[7] In fact, the only exhibitor
complaints about the series occurred when, just a few months into production, Roach attempted to "normalize" Pollard's appearance by taking
away his moustache. Snub's reliance on his trademark prop for humor was
instantly apparent, and the moustache was quickly restored.[8]

While Roach was fundamentally correct in his belief that screen comedy was moving away from the excesses of slapstick makeup, his experience in trying to "reform" Pollard demonstrated that the audience was not
willing to embrace this trend in all situations.

A vital element in the success of the new Rolin Comedies was the presence of Ernie "Sunshine Sammy" Morrison, a gifted African American child
actor who had joined Rolin as a member of the Lloyd stock company shortly
before the accident. Roach recognized that the child's naturally engaging
personality came across quite well on film, an observation confirmed by
Pathé sales executive Fred C. Quimby. One month into the production of
the Pollard films but prior to the series debut, Roach signed Morrison to
a two-year contract with the intention of featuring him in his own starring series. This idea was vetoed by Pathé's U.S. chief Paul Brunet, not on
the basis of racism but rather because of Brunet's conviction that "kid pictures" were box office poison, a conviction that would be debunked a few
years later to the great profit of both Pathé and Roach. This decision left
Roach with no alternative for the present but to continue using Morrison
in supporting roles in the Pollard films, with Pathé featuring him almost
as prominently as the star in trade paper ads, suggesting a costarring partnership (see appendix 2, synopsis 6).[9]

While Pollard and Morrison were busily cranking out the weekly one-reelers that were now Rolin's staple product, the Lloyd phenomenon was just
shifting into high gear. The star's growing popularity, undoubtedly given
a bit of a boost by public sympathy and admiration at the resilience, quite
in character, with which he rebounded from his brush with death, set the
stage for a spectacular opening for his first glasses two-reeler, *Bumping into
Broadway*, on November 2, 1919. Pathé mounted an elaborate ad campaign

that promoted the new series of "Special Two Reel $100,000 Comedies," which were to be released once every four weeks. While the films actually wound up being released on average a bit less frequently than promised, they were instant successes. *Bumping into Broadway* (see appendix 2, synopsis 7) broke house records in many places, and the film's title, along with Lloyd's name, received billing equal to or greater than those of the feature film at numerous theaters, including the Strand and Rialto in New York City.[10] All of the subsequent Lloyd shorts were released to the type of fanfare and exhibitor excitement usually reserved for special features. Thus, after five years of marginal success, Rolin ended 1919 with two significant gains: Lloyd was now a first-rank comedy star, and the new series of Rolin one-reelers was a popular production-line replacement for the one-reel Lloyds.

A New Facility and a New Name

Roach was quick to capitalize on Rolin's newfound success and embarked on an expansion of both his product line and his physical plant. The product-line expansion included unrealized explorations into dramatic feature production. While none of these projects proceeded beyond initial negotiations, they indicate that Roach understood the need to expand beyond short-comedy production if his studio were to attain a position of prominence in the industry. Additionally, Roach and Pathé continued their attempt to place the name *Hal Roach* on a par with that of *Mack Sennett* as a quality trademark.

In early September 1919, Roach was negotiating the production of a western serial, *The Winking Idol,* to star Art Accord; he was also investigating the practicality of purchasing the studio's leased facilities in the Simone Bradbury building. Neither project survived negotiations. By November Roach had purchased a tract of land for studio development south of Los Angeles in developer Harry Culver's Culver City.[11] As construction commenced, Roach tried to provide some relief for his hard-pressed production staff, which had been faithfully producing a new Pollard one-reeler every week since August with only Sundays off. During a trip to New York in November, Roach wired the studio to "tell Alf [Goulding, director] as soon as I can start another company we will make the Pollard pictures every other week. Tell him not to slight the quality of the pictures in trying to get them out too fast."[12] Exactly how Goulding was to accomplish this feat of quality control on his schedule was not suggested.

The new studio in Culver City was still under construction when production units first began using it in February 1920. After moving in on the facility's official completion date of April 20, the Rolin staff discovered that they had landed in a spot that was lacking some of the modern amenities to which they had become accustomed in Los Angeles. For a company trying to be taken seriously as a viable industry participant, the problems encountered were embarrassing at the very least. Worse, they placed new obstructions in the path toward quality production.

The first problem concerned the telephone service. There wasn't any. Culver City and the Southern Telephone and Telegraph Company were at loggerheads over the city's refusal to allow its citizens to be charged long-distance fees for calls into Los Angeles. The telephone company had responded by placing a freeze on all new Culver City service. By September and despite a formal complaint to the proper governmental regulatory commission, the best Roach had been able to do was to secure a single telephone on a party line shared with other Culver City residents.[13] Electric service to Culver City also left much to be desired. In August 1920, Warren Doane complained to Southern California Edison of Santa Monica that

> the voltage at our stage is so low and irregular that at times we are unable to use the lights at all. Approximately a dozen lights is about the limit we are able to pull at any one time. . . . The lack of service which has prevailed since we moved to Culver City has been an extremely serious handicap.[14]

The solution to this problem was revealed in a promotional blurb from December, which boasted that "the studio has its own electrical plant and is modern and complete in all departments."[15] The Culver City building inspector apparently took issue with the last part of that statement. In December 1921, with the studio less than two years old, he condemned two of the studio's stages as unsafe and unfit for use. The two buildings were razed and replaced some time later with new stages that were up to code.[16]

One other bit of corporate business received attention shortly after the move to Culver City. The name *Rolin,* which commemorated the short-lived Roach-Linthicum partnership, had no place in either the new scheme of expansion or the new facility. The necessary paperwork to legally change the studio's name was filed in the summer of 1920, and on August 16, Rolin Film Company was officially renamed Hal E. Roach Studios.[17]

The new studio name marked the beginning of a publicity policy to more aggressively promote Hal Roach as the author of his studio's films. The Pathé trade announcement for the 1920–21 movie season hailed the "master comedy producer" in the following item, sandwiched between plugs for the Lloyd and Pollard series:

HAL E. ROACH, PATHÉ COMEDIES PRODUCER

For six years Mr. Hal E. Roach has been producing comedies for Pathé. He found and developed Harold Lloyd; he found and developed "Snub" Pollard. He has never made a comedy for any other distributor than Pathé.

Mr. Roach today is the greatest comedy director and producer in the business. The quality of his product is preeminent. He personally directs [*sic*] the sensationally successful Harold Lloyd comedies; he supervises the production of the Rolin one reel comedies.

Pathé is proud to announce the continuation of the harmonious and advantageous relations with Mr. Roach.[18]

While this ad clearly was designed to bolster the often less than harmonious relations between Pathé and Roach, it also perhaps suggests a growing realization on the part of Pathé that it might have a salable commodity in the Roach name. Just as Mack Sennett's name had frequently received star billing over his featured players, so might Roach's name ease the burden of selling exhibitors on the idea of new and unproven comedy series. Thus product differentiation might focus on a reliable Roach trademark. On its path toward building up the Roach image, Pathé showed little concern for the egos of Roach's directing staff. Contrary to the advertising claim, Roach directed few of his studio's productions during this period.

The new fall 1920 movie season heralded by Pathé's announcement finally made good on Roach's promise of the previous November to Alf Goulding to introduce a second series of one-reelers that could alternate with the Pollard comedies, ending nearly a year of weekly releases for that unit. Relief of a sort had been provided by a short series of single-reel comedies produced in spring 1920 featuring comedienne Beatrice La Plante. Yet another Keystone knockoff, this time "inspired" by the films of Mabel Normand, the results of the La Plante series were not encouraging enough to warrant extension of her contract beyond the initial five films. However, since those five films were cycled into the Rolin Comedies weekly release schedule at the rate of one per month from May to September, the La Plante series had at least permitted the Pollard unit to reduce its output to three films every four weeks. The new series mentioned in the Pathé ad that was to alternate weekly with the Pollard comedies was dubbed the Vanity Fair Maids (later, Vanity Fair Girls) comedies. Pathé proclaimed the series a bold innovation, unique in that it featured "not one star but six."[19] The six unknown actresses starring in the series would be selected by Roach, and with particular irony considering the Bebe Daniels incident, the finished films would be screened by Cecil B. DeMille prior to release so that DeMille could select his future stars from the Vanity Fair company. DeMille, for his part, would publicly endorse the Vanity Fair comedies as an excellent starting ground for aspiring actresses.[20] The series itself was little more than a pale variation on the old Sennett Bathing Beauty formula, with the actual lead not one of the six starlets but rather a comic named Eddie Boland. Boland played a timid character whose embarrassed efforts to deal with his costars formed the focal point of the comedies (see appendix 2, synopsis 8). By April 1921 the series was officially redesignated Eddie Boland Comedies, and in the fall it was canceled completely, a victim of poor theatrical bookings and the star's health problems. Boland would continue as a supporting player at other studios, most notably as the Obliging Gentleman in F. W. Murnau's masterpiece *Sunrise* (1927), until his death in 1935.[21]

An interesting project discussed during the summer of 1920 but never realized was a film to star popular vaudeville headliner Al Jolson. This picture would have been the first feature-length film for both Roach and Jolson. Despite extensive contractual negotiations, Jolson was unable to arrange his stage schedule to accommodate production, and the film was never made. Too bad, Roach told Pathé, because "I am sure he would be a good bet for one or two pictures."[22] Seven years later, Jolson's exuberant performance in Warner Brothers' part-talking picture *The Jazz Singer* would help to usher in the sound era and would establish Jolson as one of the first stars of the new sound-film medium.

The chief architect of the aborted Jolson deal was not Roach himself but rather Pathé sales executive Fred Quimby. Quimby, who eventually would become the executive in charge of MGM's "Tom and Jerry" and Tex Avery animated cartoons, had taken a strong personal interest in seeing the Rolin comedies succeed. Though Quimby had urged Roach to sign Sunshine Sammy Morrison to a long-term contract only to have "kid pictures" nixed by Paul Brunet, Roach considered Quimby to be a valuable ally and gladly would have taken him into the firm had it not been for Quimby's insistence on a partnership stake in the studio. Roach and Quimby remained close throughout the 1920s; their relationship was to bring great success to both of them when Roach moved to his next distributor.

The All-American Youth

Whatever disappointment Roach may have felt in his inability to lure Al Jolson onto the lot, and in a similar failure the following summer when a proposed feature to star vaudeville headliner Will Rogers never made it to the cameras, his most successful production unit was coming ever closer to finally making him a producer of feature-length pictures, a step toward greater profitability and industry prestige. However, as Lloyd's popularity increased, so did his autonomy from the Roach operation and his share of the box office take.

Lloyd had returned to work at the end of 1919, and his popularity continued to grow with the release of each two-reel special. The heightened public expectations also meant greater pressure on the Lloyd unit to maintain its quality standards—something that, as Chaplin had discovered a few years earlier, could produce a fair measure of anxiety. Writing to Quimby on August 6, 1920, Roach confided,

> We were very disappointed with our preview on picture No. 8, *Get Out and Get Under* and have made it over twice. We have only about a third of picture No. 9 completed, so it will be very hard for us to know what we are going to do with No. 10 for a couple of weeks or so.[23]

Adding to the pressure was the fact that number ten was supposed to be the first in a highly publicized series of six comedy specials to be funded by Associated Exhibitors with physical print distribution to be handled by Pathé.[24] Despite the creative difficulties facing the Lloyd unit, the five films actually produced for Associated, which represented Lloyd's entire output for the calendar year 1921, were the most ambitious and best-received Lloyd comedies to date. Of the first four films, only one was a conventional two-reeler and the remaining three were released in three reels; the relatively unusual extra length gave the shorts a distinctive status and was a positive step toward feature filmmaking. All were extremely successful, capable of attracting large audiences on their own merits regardless of the features with which they were shown. In fact, the three-reel *Among Those Present* was actually run as the featured attraction at New York City's prestigious Capitol Theater.[25]

Explaining the reasoning of the Capitol's chief executive, S. J. Rothafel, Arthur S. Kane of Associated Exhibitors confirmed the importance of Roach's shift toward refined comedy. Rothafel, Kane said,

> knew that even a comedian must be of a more or less realistic type to drive the humor of the situation home. In fact, the more realistic the type of the comedian, the more convincing and sincere is his acting bound to be, and the public, seeing itself confronted with familiar situations in the screen, is bound to appreciate such a picture.[26]

The crowning triumph for the year was the Christmas release of the final film for Associated: Lloyd's (and Roach's) first feature-length picture. *A Sailor-Made Man* went into production as a three-reeler, but Lloyd and his crew shot so much usable footage in this tale of a wealthy fop whose character is strengthened by a hitch in the navy that he and Roach decided to release the film in four reels—a minimal feature running between forty minutes and an hour, depending on projection speed. The decision to release the film in feature length proved wise. A Pathé ad of April 8, 1922, announced that *A Sailor-Made Man* had broken box office records in thirty cities and had broken another type of record by running "fifty continuous days as the feature attraction at the Symphony Theatre of Los Angeles."[27]

As Harold Lloyd rose to first-rank comedy stardom, Hollywood was rocked by several scandals involving drugs, sex, and murder. One of these scandals terminated the career of Paramount's starring comedian, Fatty Arbuckle; another ruined Mabel Normand, Mack Sennett's former leading comedienne, who had recently begun making feature comedies for Samuel Goldwyn. Lloyd's popularity actually benefited from the scandals, as he and his associates cultivated his public image as a wholesome, all-American youth. "Candid" footage of Lloyd at play outside the studio was prepared to accompany a nationwide lecture tour by Robert Sherwood intended to reverse Hollywood's tarnished image.[28] *Health and Life* magazine requested and received "Harold Lloyd's Maxims for Good Health," actually ghostwritten by the studio publicity department. "Lloyd's" recommendations for a long and happy life were

Plenty of sleep and little to eat.
Worry only brings gray hairs—and shortened life.
Lots of play keeps one young and gay.
Twenty minutes calisthenics a day keeps the doctor away.
Smile, and you have the surest cure for all ailments.
Alcohol preserves the bootlegger—but not the stomach.[29]

At the end of 1921, Roach made yet another distribution overture to Paramount for handling of the Lloyd features. Such an arrangement would have given Paramount a percentage of the box office proceeds from one of the fastest-rising comedians in the film industry while giving Roach and Lloyd access to some of the choicest theatrical venues in the United States. The proposition generated much interest on both sides but ultimately no results: the Lloyd films, along with the rest of the Roach product, remained with Pathé.[30] Lloyd was now the undisputed star of the entire Pathé organization, a status he had held at Roach for quite some time. With this position came power, and Lloyd was quick to exploit it. Long gone were the days when Hal Roach could dock Lloyd's salary if he showed up late for work. In November 1921, Lloyd negotiated a new contract with Roach that gave him 80 percent of the net profits on his films, versus 20 percent for Roach.[31] Lloyd's unit, a creative staff of twelve including writers, directors, and camera operators assigned exclusively to his films, became increasingly autonomous from the Roach studio organization during the production of the four features made during 1922 and 1923: *Grandma's Boy, Doctor Jack, Safety Last,* and *Why Worry?*

As Lloyd's control over his work grew, Roach's diminished. In early 1922 Roach had to wire his impatient distributor that he was uncertain about the length of the next Lloyd film because "Harold Lloyd [is] confined to bed with influenza, therefore picture has not been previewed and cannot determine length until previewed."[32] That summer, Lloyd dictated that trade paper reviewers and critics were to see *Grandma's Boy* with full audiences only; there would be no exclusive press showings. Later in 1922, Roach was forced to wire a vacationing Lloyd to obtain permission to "strike the *Safety Last* sets so we can get new sets started."[33] Rather than being an employee working for Hal Roach, Lloyd was virtually an independent producer using Hal Roach Studios as his production facility. This shift in control, however, was not accompanied by a change in the style or content of Lloyd's films; he continued to work largely with the same creative team that had helped mold both his screen persona and the Roach house style, emphasizing character and situation over the fast-paced, often unmotivated and clownish slapstick of Mack Sennett.

With a string of successful pictures behind him, a creative staff that had mastered the knack of producing films tailored to his talents, and a popular image perfectly in tune with public tastes of the early 1920s, Harold Lloyd decided that he was ready to follow the path taken by Chaplin several years earlier and set up an independent production company. On July 7, 1923, *Moving Picture World* announced that Lloyd and Roach would terminate their relations in a friendly way. The paper reported that the split was seen as mutually beneficial, allowing Roach more time to concentrate on his other projects and permitting Lloyd greater freedom in the production of his films.[34] Lloyd reiterated the harmonious nature of the split in his 1928 autobiography and even suggested in a 1966 interview appended to a 1971 reprint of the autobiography that the split was actually Roach's idea.[35] As part of the separation, Roach contractually released twelve studio employees who had worked exclusively with Lloyd, including directors Sam Taylor and Fred Newmeyer, assistant director Robert Golden, writers

Tim Whelan and Ted Wilde, and cameraman Walter Lundin, so that they could join the comedian's independent company, which would, for the time being, continue to distribute with Pathé.[36] Within a few years, Lloyd switched distribution from Pathé to the company that would, with only two exceptions, release his films for the remainder of his career: Paramount.

In 1932 Lloyd bought Pathé's remaining interests in all of his films from *Bumping Into Broadway* (1919) to *The Freshman* (1925). Roach retained his rights to a fraction of the producer's share of any new revenues the films might generate in future distribution, including foreign and substandard, ranging from a fifty-fifty split on the first ten films to a one-fifth interest in the last three made at his studio.[37]

After Lloyd's departure, Roach made the first of what would be several attempts through the years to find a new All-American Boy to star in Roach features, hiring a young comic actor named Glenn Tryon. Breaking the usual pattern of introducing new comics in one- or two-reel shorts, Roach debuted Tryon with a pair of comedy features in the latter half of 1924, *The Battling Orioles* and *The White Sheep* (see appendix 2, synopsis 9). By the time these films were ready for distribution, Pathé also had lost Lloyd, as the star-producer had signed a new distribution contract with Paramount. Hence Pathé was as eager for Tryon to succeed as was Roach. Roach's New York representative, W. B. Frank, reported back to the studio in early October 1924 that he "ran into Pearson in front of the building today, talking with four gentlemen. He hailed me in their presence, and said, 'Frank, we have lost Lloyd now, and I want you fellows to hurry up with Tryon and Stone.'"[38] Unfortunately it became almost instantly apparent that neither Tryon nor Arthur Stone, a new two-reel headliner, was destined to be the next Lloyd. The Tryon features were released to mixed reviews and generally negative exhibitor response, with one exhibitor in South Carolina writing of *Battling Orioles,*

> A few more like this one and our batting average would be the size of a hat and we would be on the bench. Stay off, please. Tone, rotten . . . pleased nobody.[39]

By mid-November, Frank reported that in Pathé's judgment "unless a much better grade of Stone pictures is made in the forthcoming releases he will be too dead to revive. . . . Tryon has possibilities" but only in shorts, not as a feature star.[40] Within a few weeks, Roach had decided to terminate Stone's contract. Tryon was to remain at Roach until 1927, appearing in a series of shorts that were only intermittently successful. Among the most memorable accomplishments of this series were the frequent casting of Fay Wray as Tryon's leading lady[41] and the fact that the last film of the series, *Forty-five Minutes from Hollywood,* was the first Hal Roach comedy to include both Stan Laurel and Oliver Hardy in its cast (although the two do not appear together in the same scene).[42]

New Series

With Dwight Whiting's departure in 1918, Hal Roach found himself increasingly absorbed with the business affairs of his studio, permitting him less time to become actively involved in the production of individual films. After 1920, he directed his company's films only occasionally, although he frequently took story credit. In 1921 he hired Charles Parrott as supervising director, placing him in overall creative control of the studio's entire production output with the exception of the Lloyd pictures. Parrott had entered film from vaudeville sometime between 1910 and 1920. His early film work had included a stint at Keystone where he played supporting roles in a number of Chaplin's comedies. By the late teens, he had turned to directing and, in this capacity, piloted several comedies at Kay-Bee starring his brother, James. In April 1921 Charles joined the Hal Roach Studios as a director for the Pollard series, and within five months he was the new supervising director of the studio, in addition to being an officer of Hal E. Roach Film Laboratories, Inc. James had actually signed with Roach a short time before his older brother, appearing in the Hal Roach Comedies one-reeler series under the name of Paul Parrott.

The one-reel series during this period became a rotating forum in which to try out new comedians. With Pollard and the Roach name as reliable foundations, the series could be sold successfully to theaters regardless of the strengths of individual films. During the 1921–22 season, the Hal Roach Comedies featured Pollard, Gaylord Lloyd (Harold's brother, whose screen career was to be remarkably short), Paul Parrott, and Sunshine Sammy Morrison. The income from these films was supplemented by profits from the reissue of the early Harold Lloyd one-reel comedies. These reissues were sold as a separate series from the Hal Roach Comedies and, owing to Lloyd's great popularity at the time, met with fair success, although some theater managers complained that the two- to four-year-old comedies seemed rather antiquated by 1921 standards.

With Charles Parrott one year into his tenure, the Hal Roach Studios geared up for a major product expansion in the 1922–23 movie season. Just before fall 1922, the studio's fortunes had rested principally on three areas of production. The first was the highly prestigious and profitable Harold Lloyd feature production unit, soon to leave. The second was a limited return to dramatic production for the first time since the earliest Rolin days. These dramas will be discussed later. The staple product, however, was the third area, the one-reel Hal Roach Comedies series.

While both Roach and Pathé boasted that the Hal Roach Comedies were shown in eight thousand theaters, more theaters than any other series of short comedies,[43] just so much income could be derived from one-reelers. They simply lacked the prestige and higher rental rates commanded by two-reel comedies.

It was with these facts in mind plus an eye toward diversification that Roach announced the inauguration of two new two-reel series for the 1922–23 season. The first series would feature Pollard, whose continuing popularity as the standard bearer for the Roach one-reelers seemed to justify his promotion to the two-reel form.[44]

The second series was to be a group of "children and animals" comedies written by Tom McNamara, creator of the *Us Boys* newspaper comic strip, and directed by Robert F. McGowan.[45] The series was initially called Hal Roach's Rascals, but the title of the first film, *Our Gang*, eventually became the official series designation. Many years later, the original series title was partially restored when the films were released to television as The Little Rascals.

Roach, McGowan, and McNamara painstakingly cast the series with children who represented seemingly natural group dynamics, including a leader and his sidekick, a tag-along younger child, a bully, and a female. Once the series was off and running, primary production responsibility fell to McGowan. McNamara left toward the end of the first season, and the extent of Roach's continuing creative contribution to the series is an open question. Roach claimed responsibility for all of Our Gang's storylines, stating that McGowan would come up to his office upon completion of each short and ask "Well, Boss, what do we do next?"[46] While it is true that Roach took story credit on the copyright registrations for virtually all of the Our Gang shorts produced for Pathé, this credit may well have had more to do with Roach's contractual arrangements with his distributor than with his actual creative input. Roach's story credit disappeared when his studio switched distribution to MGM, and at that moment McGowan began to take writing *and* producing credit on the copyright registrations for the series.

In point of fact, the value of Roach's creative contributions to his studio's films has always been rather ambiguous. At times he could be extremely precise in articulating directing or editing instructions to his subordinates. For example, while on a business trip to New York in the mid-1930s, he wired fairly detailed cutting instructions to his staff for the feature film *General Spanky* (1936).[47] On the other hand, consider this observation by George Marshall, a prolific if somewhat undistinguished director of Hollywood features who spent several years at Roach in the early 1930s. According to Marshall, Roach

> would suggest the vaguest outline of a story, say "Know what I mean?" and then walk away, leaving us to try and figure out what in the hell he *did* mean. So we just went ahead and did our own stories.[48]

The Our Gang series, initially built around Sunshine Sammy, was an immediate success and became Roach's longest-running two-reel series. When Roach finally closed production on the series in 1938, two years after the general phasing out of all his other short film series, MGM bought the stock company and series title and continued production for another six years. The last Our Gang comedy was produced by MGM in 1944, twenty-two years after the first entry in the series, making it one of the longest short comedy series in film history.

The positive response to Our Gang prompted a flood of requests from manufacturers and retail chains for commercial tie-ins, many of which were granted by the studio. This was not the first time the Roach company had been involved in such activities. In 1916 Roach had entered into an agreement with the Kellogg Switchboard and Supply Company of Chicago in which the studio would feature Kellogg telephones and switchboards prominently in Lonesome Luke films in return for Kellogg publishing publicity stills featuring Harold Lloyd and Bebe Daniels, posed with Kellogg equipment, in its *Telephone Facts* periodical, which was distributed to one hundred thousand readers.[49]

Although Roach hit a winning formula with Our Gang, the same cannot be said for the expanded Pollard shorts. The problems involved in stretching Pollard's comic persona to cover two reels proved insurmountable, and by the following year he was back to the grind of supplying one-reelers for the Hal Roach Comedies.

Because of the promotions of Sunshine Sammy and Pollard out of the one-reel series and the failure of Gaylord Lloyd to be carried over from the previous season, James "Paul" Parrott was left to shoulder much of the burden of the weekly release schedule for the Hal Roach Comedies during the 1922–23 season. Relief for the Parrott unit came in spring 1923, when a new series featuring Stan Laurel was released on alternating weeks with the Parrott comedies. Shortly thereafter, a new one-reel series made its debut. Released on a one-per-month schedule independent of the Hal

Roach Comedies series, the Dippy Doo Dads featured an all-animal cast headed up by trained monkeys wearing human-style clothing and cavorting on miniature sets. Most of the plots were burlesques of standard melodrama (e.g., farm monkey goes to big city to make good; despite setbacks at the hands of city sharpers, he triumphs in the end). Though considered clever by the reviewers of *Moving Picture World*, the Dippy Doo Dads lasted only one year.

During this period, Roach renewed his efforts to position his studio as a purveyor of refined comedy. Although Roach had rarely drawn complaints previously for censorable content in his films, all Roach films for 1922–23 were produced under a new studio morality code. Attempting to capitalize on the Hollywood scandals in much the same manner as Lloyd was doing, Roach convened a highly publicized meeting of his entire staff on May 24, 1922. The primary purpose of this meeting was to discuss plans for the upcoming season, but during his address, Roach made the following grand statement of policy, clearly intended for press publication:

> If you can't make comedies clean, don't make them at all. . . . I would rather that a thousand persons be disappointed by a comedy that is poor because of a lack of laughs than to have one person offended by a questionable bit of business. I want the world to know that when a Roach comedy is advertised, women and children will be protected against anything that even borders on the questionable. The confidence of the general public is worth more to me than the following of the handful of those who crave the risqué.[50]

At the end of the following season, however, Roach's efforts to establish his studio as the premiere producer of short comedies received a setback from the studio's own distributor. In March 1923 Pathé signed a distribution pact with Roach's chief rival, Sennett.[51] Roach later complained that this was a bad business move on Pathé's part, giving the distributor a supply of far more two-reel comedies than it could possibly sell successfully.[52] Even though Sennett's stock within the industry had slipped considerably, leading him to Pathé's door, Roach feared that exhibitors still might opt for the more famous Sennett name when they selected from Pathé's offerings for the upcoming season. The picture grosses would bear this out during the 1924–25 season. Sennett's three shorts series, Ben Turpin, Harry Langdon, and the Mack Sennett Comedies, averaged per-picture bookings of sixty thousand, forty-five thousand, and fifty thousand dollars, respectively. Roach was grossing $22,641 for each Tryon and Stone short and $17,905 for each Spat Family picture (a series that will be discussed later).[53] Average bookings for Roach's most popular series, the Our Gang Comedies, totaled around fifty thousand dollars.[54]

Despite concerns over the amount of short product that the Pathé sales force was going to have to handle, the 1923–24 movie season, Charles Parrott's last as supervising director, saw even greater expansion in the Roach Studio's release schedule. Pollard was back in one-reelers, but Our Gang was going strong and was joined by three new two-reel series: Stan Laurel, Will Rogers, and the Spat Family. Both the Laurel and the Rogers series lasted but a single season, each gathering only fair reviews from the trade press and strongly negative ratings from some exhibitors. The Laurel series met much the same fate as Pollard's two-reelers; exhibitors thought they were paying more for a padded product that was actually inferior to the cheaper single-reel series that had preceded it.

The failure of Will Rogers to make an impact in silent pictures, despite the fame and popularity he had already obtained on the stage, may be attributed to Rogers's heavily verbal, not visual, style of humor. The Roach films show him shifting uncomfortably between forced slapstick (getting soaked by a lawn sprinkler and eating a lace coaster in *Our Congressman*) and more characteristic Rogers' wit delivered via wordy and too-frequent title cards.

The Spat Family comedies survived into a second season by default. These comedies were not considered particularly good by anyone, including the Roach staff; their failure was simply less spectacular than that of the Laurel or Rogers series. One interesting aspect of the Spat Family was that it was set up as something of a situation comedy. Rather than a single starring comedian engaging in totally unrelated exploits from one picture to the next, the Spat Family centered on the continuing dysfunctional relationship of the fussy J. Tewksberry Spat, his combative wife, and her loutish, know-it-all live-in brother. In a typical entry, *Heavy Seas* (1923), the Spats win a yacht and sink it on its maiden voyage. Mr. Spat announces the inevitable moment with a characteristically stilted "Consternation! We are submerging!" Perhaps learning what *not* to do from these films, Frank Butler, who played Spat, became a successful screenwriter in the 1930s and 1940s.

Meanwhile, the Hal Roach Comedy one-reelers of 1923–24 briefly once again became the sole domain of Pollard following the demise of Paul Parrott's series. At this point, the Parrott brothers decided to switch to opposite sides of the camera. Paul Parrott reassumed his given name, and as James Parrott he would become one of Roach's most prolific writer-directors, piloting numerous Laurel and Hardy shorts of the early 1930s. As for Charles Parrott, his two and one-half years as Roach's supervising director had been a rather discouraging procession of failed series. The only hit series to emerge from his entire tenure had been Our Gang. Parrott resigned his post in late 1923 to star in a new one-reel series to alternate with Pollard. For this new series, he adopted the stage name Charley Chase and initially played a go-getting character named Jimmy Jump. Shortly after the debut of the Chase series, Pollard left Roach, ending a relationship that stretched back virtually to the beginning of the Rolin studio. As for Chase, his comedies proved to be so popular that after only one year he was promoted to star in a two-reel series that would run until 1936. Chase's departure from the one-reel Hal Roach Comedies series in 1925 marked the last time that the series would rely on a single starring comedian. By that point the profits split by Roach and Pathé on each one-reel comedy was between one and two thousand dollars, compared with ten thousand on a Chase two-reeler.[55] The continued production of the one-reel series became such a low priority to the studio that Roach chose to use it as a showcase for supporting players from the Roach stock company who were between other assignments, giving them an opportunity to play leading roles. During its final days in 1926, the one-reel series consisted almost entirely of the belated distribution of films produced during the first half of the 1920s and shelved as too poor for release. The studio had moved beyond the low-profit, low-prestige, one-reel form by 1926, concentrating instead on "quality" series of two-reelers.[56]

The production of these quality two-reelers seemed an increasingly difficult task to the Roach staff by the middle of 1924, a situation exacerbated by the absence of a strong supervising director. Faced with the almost complete failure of the previous season's new product and piqued at a perceived preferential treatment on the part of the Pathé sales force for Sennett's comedies, Roach and his employees reevaluated their goals during the summer of 1924.

One of the problems for the Roach team was to determine the right balance between refined and roughhouse comedy. In this connection, the rivalry between Sennett and Roach took a new turn in September 1924, when Elmer Pearson of Pathé suggested in a *Film Daily* interview that Pathé preferred Sennett's roughhouse and "vulgar" style of comedy to Roach's more subdued variety, seemingly undercutting Roach's promotional efforts concerning the value of refined comedy. After speaking personally to Pearson, Roach employee W. B. Frank sent a vaguely contradictory report to the studio on September 20.

Mr. Pearson's thought was that it was better for us to continue to make clean, uncensorable comedies, but not to be too exacting in the matter. . . . [I]f we could make the Spat comedies with a little more risqué atmosphere it might be the thing that would put them over, namely, have another girl in the troupe, of vampire type, as the sweetheart of the husband. A lot of funny sequences could be built up around a foursome of this kind, and it might be just the thing that the present day audiences would take to because we seem to be living in a jazz era. . . .

Now then . . . Mr. Pearson's idea [in the *Film Daily* article] was that Sennett had always made comedies more or less of a hodgepodge nature, and that the exhibitors and motion picture fans as a whole did not expect anything of very much importance from the Sennett lot other than of the risqué, censorable type of comedy, and that Sennett was able to get away with it because of this fact.[57]

Frank concluded that the feeling in the industry was that the public would not stand for this type of film from anyone other than Sennett, and that exhibitors "expect something more dignified, high-tone and up-to-date from us than they do from Sennett."[58] The problem facing Roach in the short term, however, was that, high-tone or not, with the exception of Our Gang, his two-reel comedies were not finding great favor with the film audiences of 1924. Roach began to consider an alteration of his house style, looking both to the exhibitors and the Sennett model for guidance.

Trying to achieve the taste balance that Pathé seemed to desire, as well as understanding the need for a strong executive producer, Roach hired away Sennett's supervising director, F. Richard Jones, to serve in the same capacity at the Roach lot.[59] Despite Sennett's understandable annoyance at this raid from his chief competitor, Roach's perusal of Sennett's talent did not stop here. During this turbulent period, Roach also made overtures to up-and-coming Sennett comedian Harry Langdon, whose popularity would briefly approach Chaplin's a few years later.[60] Roach also contemplated a new formula sitcom series with faded Sennett alumnus Ford Sterling as a harried store manager.[61] Ultimately, Roach decided not to imitate Sennett and hired neither of these comics in the mid-1920s. He similarly refrained from employing another ex-Sennett star, Ben Turpin, when he went freelance in the late 1920s.

A large measure of Roach's determination to stay with his standing house style came, surprisingly, from his new supervising director. Rather than moving the Roach studio toward Sennett's brand of humor, Jones actually polished the refined style of comedy already in place at Roach, banishing crude slapstick unless it could be justified by the plotline of a film. This would lead, in part, to the concept of "short films with feature polish" to be discussed later.

The other factor in influencing Roach to stick with his established style was the response to a poll he circulated among theater managers nationwide in January 1925. Breaking down the Roach studio output by series, the questionnaire commented that the Our Gang comedies were quite popular and that Pathé wanted a Gang feature. Exhibitor input on this idea was solicited, as well as any ideas on whether the same cast should be kept or replaced as they grew older. Both questions drew split responses, although most exhibitors thought that the series worked best in two-reel form, and some who liked the idea of an Our Gang feature believed that it should not exceed four reels. Most exhibitors felt that new Gang members needed to be rotated in and older ones phased out, although some thought that the public "knows and loves each member now" and would not stand for any changes. Partially as a result of the poll, the gang members were gradually replaced and a silent Our Gang feature was not made.

General questions of quality about the Tryon, Chase, and Spat series revealed that most theater managers were unaware of the former two, although those who had seen Chase and Tryon liked them. The Spat comedies drew an almost universally negative response, with managers stating that the series was a good idea with a bad cast, that too much of the comedy was low, and that the quality of the films, never good to begin with, had steadily declined during the series' run. The questionnaire also asked about the public image of the Hal Roach Studios, the value of the Hal Roach name, the value of leading ladies in comedies dominated by a male lead, audience feelings about slapstick, and the importance of trying to make short comedies appear as polished and handsomely mounted as the features with which they played. The consensus among managers was that audiences did not object to slapstick and that leading ladies were not particularly important. Responses to the other questions were mixed. On one hand, an exhibitor wrote, "Audiences would walk one mile for an 'Our Gang' comedy when they might not even walk one hundred yards to see a comedy simply advertised as coming from the studios of Hal E. Roach. Your name has become an institution to the exhibitor" but was of little value on a theater marquee. On the other hand, another manager wrote, "I think it will only be a matter of a short time, if you continue your policy of producing standard comedies that you are now doing, that you will be to the comedy field what Griffith and DeMille and others are to the feature field." With regard to the importance of a polished feel, while some exhibitors thought that a cheaper look would actually enhance the comedy, most expressed the desire to see Roach continue to produce shorts with a feature polish. "You seem to have the lead," wrote one manager. "Why not keep it?"[62]

The King of Wild Horses

Roach never intended to produce only comedy films, either short or feature-length. The initial Rolin offerings had included several dramatic two-reelers. That Roach was able to interest Pathé in only his early comedies started a chain of events that led him to preside over a comedy studio. He never lost interest in dramatic productions, however, and eagerly seized the opportunity to produce dramas when the situation permitted.

Roach desired to produce drama for two reasons. First, the type of drama that interested him most was the outdoor adventure, something akin to the rugged lifestyle he encountered during the West Coast odyssey of his youth. Roach never lost his yen for the great outdoors, and right up until his death at age one hundred, he reportedly relished a good hunting or fishing expedition in the rough.[63]

Second, and more pragmatic from a business standpoint, much was to be said for product diversification. Roach was never satisfied with his status as a minor producer, and given the still fluid situation of the American motion picture industry in the early 1920s, he actually had good reason to hope for the attainment of major status. This climb could be accomplished only through a production schedule that included feature-length dramas.

Roach embarked on his career as a dramatic producer through the device of the serial, combining what his studio knew (the production of two-reel pictures) with the less familiar area of long-form drama (with the storyline being spread characteristically over ten to fifteen chapters). The Roach studio began its dramatic production schedule with a pair of Ruth Roland serials, *White Eagle* and *The Timber Queen,* filmed in 1921 and 1922 and released in 1922. The exact business arrangement behind these productions is unclear. It appears as though Pathé, distributor of Roland's previous popular serials, "placed" her at Roach, possibly to appease Roach's desire to expand into drama and thus keep Roach and the Lloyd comedies under the Pathé banner. The Roland serials were promoted in the trades as being produced at the Hal Roach Studios by "Ruth Roland Serials, Inc. under the supervision of Hal E. Roach."[64] Both serials were well received, but after their completion, Ruth Roland Serials, Inc., moved on to another production facility. Roach produced one final serial, the ten-episode *Her Dan-*

gerous Path, starring Edna Murphy, before abandoning the dramatic serial form for the next logical step: the production of feature-length dramas.

The first of these features was a 1923 seven-reel picture based on a popular Jack London adventure, *Call of the Wild.* According to trade and exhibitor reviews, the film was quite successful. This warm reception led to another action-adventure feature in 1924, *King of Wild Horses,* starring Rex, the Wonder Horse (see appendix 2, synopsis 10). This film was voted by exhibitors to be one of the ten best pictures of the year and led to three sequels, released annually. The first one, *Black Cyclone* (1925), was another ten-best list entry. The third and fourth Rex features, *The Devil Horse* (1926) and *No Man's Law* (1927), were only slightly less popular, and the demise of the series was probably due more to a change in Roach's distribution than to diminishing box office returns.

On *No Man's Law,* a tale of two desperadoes (one played by Oliver Hardy wearing an eye patch) who terrorize a prospector and his daughter, Roach ran into a bit of trouble with local censorship boards. The Michigan state censor threatened to ban the film in its entirety as "seven reels of brutality without point or redeeming feature." Objections were also voiced by censor boards in Ohio and Pennsylvania, and the film was passed by the New York state censor and the National Board of Review only after the studio made "a few cuts around the scenes where the nude girl is swimming."[65] Despite these problems, studio manager Warren Doane instructed his staff not to make any changes in the negative but rather to alter prints on a local basis as needed.[66] Presumably, most areas of the United States received the full, unexpurgated *No Man's Law.*

The production of action-adventure pictures introduced the Roach company to the problems and perils of filming in remote locations, far from the safety and reliability of the back lot and local southern California surroundings that were home to the short comedy units. During the shooting of the serial *Timber Queen,* director Fred Jackman, who was to helm most of the studio's dramatic outings over the next several years, answered studio concerns over production delays and rising costs by wiring on February 8, 1922, from the shooting location in Truckee, California: "WORKING DOG TEAMS VERY TEDIOUS STOP DOING ALL I CAN TO SPEED UP WORK UNDER ADVERSE CONDITIONS."[67] Two days later, Hal Roach's brother Jack, who was acting as a location production manager, wired even more bad news: "SNOWED THREE FEET HERE LAST NIGHT STOP BLIZZARD ALL DAY STOP NO CHANCE TO WORK STOP HOPE FOR BETTER WEATHER TOMORROW."[68] However, the next day saw a continuation of "THE WORST BLIZZARD IN MANY YEARS."[69] Ultimately, of course, the weather did break and permit completion of the film, but the episode was to be a harbinger of things to come on future location outings. During the production of *Devil Horse,* a crew member drowned in the Gardner River in Montana, and the film's star, legendary actor-stuntman Yakima Canutt, was laid up for two weeks from burns he received when a flare exploded.[70] Upon his release from the hospital, Canutt was welcomed back to work by being bitten in the face by Rex, the Wonder Horse. Perhaps the most bizarre accident to befall a Roach location company occurred during the summer of 1926, when virtually an entire cast and crew in Mopa, Nevada, were poisoned "by drinking lemon water from galvanized canteen[s]."[71] Although no one ultimately died during this episode, several Roach employees became so seriously ill that the doctors did not consider them out of danger for several days.

Two other dramatic features produced by the Hal Roach Studios during the 1920s were to have great impact on the future of the organization: a pair of westerns, *The Valley of Hell* and *The Desert's Toll,* both made in 1926. The importance of these films was not that they led to more feature production. On the contrary, Roach publicly announced before completion of the second that there would be no more in this series, as production of these films took too much of his time and attention away from the production of the "high-class comedy subjects" which were, after all, "his greatest ambition."[72] The significance of these films, rather, was that they were the first Hal Roach productions made for release through MGM, the company that would handle distribution of Roach's entire output from 1927 until 1938. While the alignment with MGM in the fall of 1927 was to guarantee the Roach Studios' stability through the Depression, it did temporarily limit one phase of studio operation. Aside from the initial two westerns, MGM was interested only in Roach's short subjects, not features.

The All-Star Series: Short Subjects with Feature Polish

By the mid-1920s, Roach and Pathé saw clearly eye-to-eye on at least one point: short films were not getting their due in the grand scheme of things. Roach's frustration at being considered a minor player because of his status as a producer of shorts was matched by Pathé's anxiety at becoming principally a distributor of shorts in a market in which the feature picture commanded the lion's share of the box office take.

As part of a Pathé publicity push at the start of the 1925–26 season to prove that "short subjects merit more recognition,"[73] Hal Roach announced a new series of two-reel Hal Roach Comedies that would costar "well-known fun makers."[74] These players were a mixture of recognizable comic-relief character actors such as Lucien Littlefield, comedy stars like Al St.

John and Clyde Cook whose popularity had either waned or had never fully developed, and familiar faces from the Roach stock company.

Within less than a year, this concept had evolved into the All-Star comedies. The idea behind this series was simple. If Roach could not return to the feature-length comedy market, a feat he had been unable to successfully accomplish since the departure of Lloyd, he would make comedy shorts that starred well-known feature-length players and were mounted with glossy feature-style production values that would compete head-on with features. The polished production values were largely accomplished by setting the stories among the social elite, with formally dressed characters cavorting about in mansions and four-star hotels. Quality and big names would undoubtedly win out over mere footage.[75]

Sadly, the circumstances of these stars were somewhat less than advertised. Many, like Theda Bara and Mildred Harris, were at the end of their careers, desperate for any kind of film work. Others, particularly Lionel Barrymore and Harry Myers, were at lulls or turning points in their professional lives. In no case was Roach actually able to convince a star with a truly viable feature career that appearing in short comedies would be a smart move. He failed similarly in an attempt to lure D. W. Griffith to the studio to make two-reel dramas.[76] Additionally, in many instances, the star, including Bara and Barrymore, was signed for only a single short. In this regard, Roach got far more mileage out of months of publicity during which he repeatedly recited his starring roster than he did out of the actual films.

An unforeseen situation occurred on the Bara film, *Madame Mystery*. The director, working in typical Roach fashion with story and gag suggestions but without a concrete shooting script and perhaps overwhelmed at working with someone who had been a feature-length film star, shot so much footage that the "director's cut" of the film was a five-reel featurette. Although Doane and some of the other Roach staffers thought that after years of trying to break into the feature market, the studio should release the film in this long form, Roach held firm in his conviction that doing so would defeat the credibility of the All-Star concept. The film, in Roach's opinion, had to be released as a two-reeler and that is the version U.S. audiences saw, although some evidence indicates that the five-reel *Madame Mystery* may have been released in some foreign markets (see appendix 2, synopsis 11).[77]

One project somewhat related to the All-Star comedies was the return of Mabel Normand to the screen in a series of Hal Roach Comedies. Normand had been one of the leading comediennes of the teens and early 1920s

until she was involved, in rapid succession, in a pair of the scandals that
rocked Hollywood in the early 1920s, including implication in the still-un-
solved murder of director William Desmond Taylor. Normand had not made
a film in several years when she accepted an offer from Roach to appear in
not simply a single All-Star picture but an entire series of Mabel Normand
Comedies for the 1926–27 season. Instrumental in coaxing the star out of her
unplanned and troubled retirement was the promise of personal supervision
of her films by F. Richard Jones, with whom she had worked successfully
during her last days at Sennett. Normand's arrangement with Roach called
for her to make eight two-reel comedies during the 1926–27 season with
an option for an additional two if desired. Furthermore, Normand would
stay with the studio beyond the first year, either moving into features or
staying in shorts, depending on audience and trade acceptance.

Thus the planned Roach release schedule for 1926–27 was to consist of
four series: Chase, Our Gang, Normand, and All-Star.[78] A threatened renewal of the controversy surrounding Normand, fueled by an opportunis-
tic, headline-seeking Los Angeles district attorney, actually produced a wave
of sympathy and support for the actress, reflected in fan letters received
by the studio and a "best wishes" ad taken out by Mary Pickford.[79] As had
happened with *Madame Mystery,* an enthusiastic director produced a five-
reel featurette for Normand's first film, *Raggedy Rose,* which only the se-
verest of editing could whittle down to a three-reel short (see appendix 2,
synopsis 12). Even at this length, half again as long as the usual comedy
short, the film was well received, and Normand's return to the screen was
hailed as a cause for celebration in the film industry. Yet, after only one
more three-reeler and a pair of two-reelers, the series came to an inexpli-
cable end. Normand never made another film, and she died of tuberculo-
sis in 1930 at the age of thirty-five.

By the beginning of the 1927–28 season, Roach abandoned most of his
original aspirations for the All-Star comedies, and the series reverted largely
to being a vehicle for the supporting players of the Roach stock company.
The difference this time, though, was that the company now included Stan
Laurel and Oliver Hardy. Even though both of these players had well over
a decade of film experience behind them, neither had attained anything
approaching star status. Hardy seemed destined never to be anything more
than a reliable comic heavy, while Laurel entered the All-Star series as yet
one more also-ran comic who had failed to make a substantial impression
on the moviegoing public. In fact, after Laurel's two previous unsuccessful starring series for Roach, Pathé expressed reservations at the comic's
return for a third try in 1926.

Thrown together in the potluck All-Star series, however, Laurel and Hardy achieved a team chemistry that was totally unanticipated. The "feature polish" expectations of the All-Star comedies required an even greater refinement of the already-subdued Roach house style, and Laurel and Hardy, first under the guidance of Jones and later Leo McCarey, softened their standard screen personae to fit the needs of the series. Dropping the time-honored comic-lead-versus-towering-heavy formula, Laurel and Hardy's screen characters became grown men of childlike innocence and intellect who, despite Hardy's occasional selfish bullying and Laurel's chronic ineptitude, were dedicated buddies who knew that surviving life's trials and tribulations (and "the boys" faced an incredible array of them) was possible only as a joint undertaking, a theme that would resonate even stronger as the nation entered the Great Depression. In their new screen incarnations, the duo rapidly became the stars of the All-Stars, and in the 1928–29 season they were officially launched in their own starring series.

As the idea of shorts with feature polish faded and their popularity grew, Laurel and Hardy embraced the brand of violent physical humor that Roach had recently eschewed, resulting in a sort of give-and-take between the team and the house style. Laurel and Hardy brought a bit more low slapstick, but in keeping with the Roach style it was never unmotivated and was deliberately paced. Small incidents between adversaries (Laurel and Hardy and someone with whom they are trying to conduct important business; buying a glass of soda, for example) lead to larger incidents and, ultimately, all-out war. A sharp word leads to a tweak on the nose, which finally begets the total demolition of all of the antagonists' worldly possessions. Dubbed "reciprocal violence," the conflict is carried out as a ritualistic ceremony. The person who is being violated is not permitted to defend himself; he must stoically accept whatever indignity is being meted out, secure in the knowledge that it will be his turn next.

The End of the Roach-Pathé Relationship

The fall of 1925 brought the news that Paramount, the most powerful company in the film industry and the owner and operator of the nation's largest chain of movie theaters, was going to commence distribution of two-reel comedies in addition to their usual feature release schedule beginning with the 1926–27 movie season. Frank wrote to Doane that word in the industry had it that Paramount would try to lure distribution of Sennett's product away from Pathé, and he noted with some irony, considering Roach's attitude when Pathé signed Sennett initially, that Roach, in his opinion, would actually be better off if Sennett stayed with Pathé.

If Sennett and Christie [another two-reel comedy producer] went
with Paramount, Pathé would have a very difficult time selling all of
the Paramount houses our product next year unless we can outshine
all the rest of them as far as quality is concerned and force our way
in on the merits of the pictures. If Sennett remains with Pathé, we
will not have very much to worry about from the Paramount producing companies' product at least the first year because of the inferior quality of comedies they would no doubt make.[80]

Elmer Pearson of Pathé added to this argument by saying that with Roach
and Sennett under the same distributor, that distributor would be the undisputed leader in the field of short comedy and hence would have an easier
time selling the films of both producers. Roach and his staff evidently saw
some merit to this logic; however, in their version Roach and Sennett would
both be better off releasing through Paramount. Roach's future with Pathé
was summed up by Doane, who wrote Frank,

I am convinced that their ideas are costing us hundreds of thousands
of dollars through lack of distribution, and if they persist in this
course which is so ruinous to their producers there is only one thing
for us to do, which is to get better distribution.[81]

Better distribution, however, was not, in Doane's mind, restricted solely to
a deal with Paramount. In late January 1926, Doane wired F. Richard Jones,
who was on a business trip with Roach in New York City, that he was

EXTREMELY WORRIED OVER THE FACT THAT WE ARE EVIDENTLY STRAINING EV-
ERYTHING TO PERSUADE PARAMOUNT INTO THE IDEA OF SELLING SHORTS AND
APPARENTLY NEGLECTING WIDE OPEN OPPORTUNITY OF DEALING WITH METRO
WHO WILL PROBABLY GO AHEAD EITHER WITH OR WITHOUT US STOP PLEASE GO
INTO THIS CAREFULLY WITH MR ROACH AND MR FRANK AS IT IS EASY FOR EN-
THUSIASM TO LEAD A PERSON ASTRAY STOP PARAMOUNT HAVING PREVIOUSLY
TURNED PROPOSITION DOWN DEFINITELY WILL PROBABLY NEED LOTS OF COAX-
ING TO NOW ACCEPT AND MEANWHILE UNLESS WE ARE CAREFUL METRO WILL
GO AHEAD WITHOUT US AND WE WOULD HAVE TO FALL BACK INTO PATHÉ'S LAP
STILL WORSE OFF THAN WE ARE NOW.[82]

Doane's advice was evidently taken to heart, because on March 16, 1926,
Hal Roach Studios signed an exclusive distribution contract with Metro-
Goldwyn-Mayer Distributing Corporation.[83] It was virtually inevitable that
Loew's-MGM, in its quest to challenge Paramount for industry supremacy,
would match its rival move for move. If Paramount was going to start dis-
tributing short comedies, then Metro would do the same. Paramount wanted

Sennett, so MGM had to settle for the runner-up, Roach. Rarely has finishing in second place paid off so handsomely. MGM became the most powerful and profitable studio of the Depression, and Roach and his studio shared in Metro's good fortune.

Despite what appeared to be obvious benefits of an affiliation with the industry leader, Sennett was unable to come to satisfactory terms with Paramount and remained with Pathé for a few more years. With Sennett and Roach thus unavailable, Paramount signed a contract to distribute the short comedies of the Christie Studio. The corporate fates of Sennett, Christie, and the fourth short comedy specialist, Educational, will be covered in the next chapter.

Before its prosperous association with MGM could commence, Hal Roach Studios had to extricate itself from its obligations to its old distributor. Roach was operating under a five-year Pathé contract that was to be in effect from September 1, 1925, until September 1, 1930.[84] Pathé was extremely unhappy about the prospect of losing Roach and threatened to make him finish out the contract. Faced with this situation, and eager to begin making pictures for MGM as soon as possible, Roach negotiated with Metro to commence production of a series of eight western features in late spring 1926.[85] Under this plan, Roach would continue to produce his comedy series for Pathé while doing the westerns for Metro. For reasons unclear at this time but most likely having to do with a weakening of resolve on the part of Pathé, the western series was terminated after only two pictures, the previously mentioned *Valley of Hell* and *Desert's Toll*. By late 1926, Pathé had indeed relented, agreeing to permit Roach to shift distribution to MGM beginning in the 1927–28 movie season. In exchange for releasing him from his contract, Roach agreed to produce a few extra comedies at the end of the 1926–27 season for release by Pathé during the first half of the 1927–28 season.

The Roach-Pathé relationship did not end without one final twist. Pathé executives informed Roach in early 1927 that their deal would not permit Roach to begin producing films for MGM until September 1, and that all films produced prior to that date would be the distribution property of Pathé. Roach and MGM contended that the agreement called for MGM to begin releasing Roach films on September 1, and that obviously these first releases would have to be produced prior to that date. Not surprisingly, given Pathé's deteriorating state in 1927, MGM and Roach won their point, and Pathé was obliged to be content with a final group of twelve Hal Roach two-reel comedies for release against the new Roach-MGM product for 1927–28.[86]

5

Roach-MGM Short Features, 1927–33

The move by the major studios into the distribution of short subjects during the mid-1920s, led by Paramount and Loew's-MGM, was simply one more step in their quest to dominate the film industry. *Moving Picture World* noted the shift in the attitude of the majors in late 1926.

> The short subject, once the orphan of the motion picture family, has become the favorite son, surrounded by herds of fatted calves. In their efforts to offer exhibitors complete programs, big distributors are putting out the welcome mat and offering the glad hand to the formerly unpopular short subject.[1]

Being able to obtain a "full service," that is, short subjects as well as features, from one distributor meant that exhibitors would be less likely to deal with companies that specialized in the distribution of shorts only. Since a firm that distributed shorts could conceivably move into feature distribution, creating more competition for the major studios, squeezing out such specialty companies before they could offer a full service of their own was a prudent business move.

As the major film companies built more theaters and purchased existing theater chains, the exhibition end of the business rapidly split into two factions: affiliated and nonaffiliated theaters. Affiliated theaters were those that were owned or controlled by the major film companies. They were situated in the key locations of major metropolitan centers and had first pick of the best Hollywood productions. Since they were an integral part of the film industry, those theaters that ran shorts (instead of a live stage show) were inclined to rent their shorts through the major distribution outlets rather than from specialty distributors.

Nonaffiliated theaters operated independently of the major studios and encompassed both large chains and small operators of individual theaters. Since the major companies did not have a direct financial interest in the operation of these theaters, and since, in fact, these theaters frequently operated in direct competition with affiliated theaters, the majors often forced onerous film booking arrangements on the unaffiliated houses. One of the most common of these methods was block booking, that is, selling features in groups rather than individually. Characteristically, an exhibitor would have to agree to take several routine program pictures, low-budget films with little marquee or star value, to obtain a single feature with real box office potential.

The practice of block booking was extended to shorts. To get a supply of features, an exhibitor would have to agree to accept packages of shorts. Under this system, exhibitors frequently found themselves with more major-studio shorts than they could possibly play in a single season, leaving absolutely no room on the programs for independently distributed shorts.

Even though shorts were often block-booked with features, shorts and features were not exhibited as standardized units at either affiliated or nonaffiliated theaters. A feature did not play consistently with the same set of shorts nationwide, nor did it even play consistently with shorts from the same studio. It was not at all uncommon, for example, to find a Roach-MGM short comedy playing with a Paramount cartoon and a Warner Brothers feature at a Fox theater.

While Educational Pictures operated its own distribution network, which will be discussed later, the other three largest short comedy studios, Sennett, Roach, and Christie, were dependent on companies imperiled by the entry of the majors into short-film distribution (Sennett and Roach through Pathé, Christie through Educational). Roach and Christie eagerly jumped at the opportunity to affiliate with MGM and Paramount, respectively, while Sennett elected to bide his time at Pathé. MGM and Paramount, in turn, received access to short-comedy series of name value (e.g., Our Gang) from producers who were specialists in the field of short comedy. These alliances relieved the major studios of having to start their own in-house production units and produce an entire season of short films with no prior experience in the field. However, the signing of outside producers for their supply of shorts appears to have been a temporary transitional tactic to help the majors ease into short-film distribution. Both Paramount and MGM began producing their own shorts at the same time that they began distributing the work of others. Although the Roach-MGM affiliation would last for more than a decade, MGM's in-house production of short subjects steadily increased, and when Roach voluntarily withdrew from short-film production, MGM's unit was producing enough shorts to easily meet the studio's release schedule. Unlike the Roach-MGM bond, Christie's alliance with Paramount, as well as subsequent Sennett-Paramount and Educational-Fox associations, would be short-lived. In each case, the major studio's own short-film unit filled the company's requirement for live-action shorts upon the expiration of its arrangement with the outside shorts subcontractors.

By the end of the 1930s, only the field of animation remained primarily the domain of independent studios. While MGM had established an in-house animation unit in the mid-1930s, the other majors still relied on subcontractors: Fleischer Studios for Paramount, Terrytoons for Twentieth Century–Fox, Leon Schlesinger for Warner Brothers, Walt Disney for RKO, and Walter Lantz for Universal. During the early 1940s, both Paramount and Warner Brothers assumed ownership of their animation suppliers.

Within a few years of the Roach-MGM affiliation, the motion picture industry adopted two new practices that would have a profound impact on short-film producers: talking pictures and double features. The talkies debuted in mainstream cinema, as opposed to the isolated efforts of various inventors throughout film history to that point, in 1926 in the form of a group of Warner Brothers Vitaphone shorts that formed a prologue for the silent-with-recorded-score feature *Don Juan*. By 1929 the American film industry had virtually converted to the production of talking pictures. The introduction of sound caused production costs to soar. Sound recording equipment and services were expensive. The production of short comedies had always yielded minimal financial returns, and now the profit margins were being squeezed even further. The addition of dialogue also demanded tightly prepared shooting scripts, putting an end to the sort of improvisation that had been predominant, especially among short comedy producers like Roach, during the silent era. Further traumatizing short-film producers in the early 1930s was the rise of the double feature. This booking practice caused theatrical program times to balloon, leaving less time for two-reel comedies.

Faced with these industrial changes, Roach determined once again to enter feature production and eventually to discontinue short-subject production completely. However, Loew's-MGM had sought an affiliation with Roach for a supply of shorts, not full-length films. It was uninterested in receiving features from an outside producer, particularly the type of low-budget, or "B," picture that it perceived Roach would produce—a class of films with which MGM denied, as a matter of product differentiation from other studios, any involvement.

The Transition to MGM

As previously noted, MGM's incentive for distributing the Roach short product was the announcement by Paramount that it would become a full-service distributor by expanding its product line to include short comedies. During his affiliation with Loew's-MGM, Roach answered to MGM distribution executives at Loew's New York City headquarters. He had virtually no dealings with Louis Mayer or MGM production executives, even though MGM's Culver City production center was only a short distance from his own studio.

The March 16, 1926, contract between Hal Roach Studios and MGM Distributing Corporation provides an insight into the responsibilities and expectations of the producer-distributor relationship. The contract starts by stating that MGM

> is in the business of distributing and exploiting feature motion picture photoplays and is prepared to expand its organization to include the distribution of so-called short reel pictures, such as comedies, newsreels, etc., and is prepared to add a separate Sales Department for the purpose of handling the product of the Producer, and other so-called short reel pictures, providing it has the exclusive right to distribute throughout the World the product of the Producer.

Hal Roach Studios is described as being "engaged in the production of motion picture comedies, particularly of two reel lengths, and is desirous . . . to have its pictures distributed solely through the facilities of the Distributor." Each of the comedies produced by Roach for MGM was to be "a complete story capable of being distributed as a comedy, and of the same high character and quality as those now being produced by the producer." Roach was to deliver said comedies at the rate of three or four per month, producing "not less than thirty and not more than fifty-two comedies per year," consisting of ten to thirteen from each of the four brands agreed upon.

Other contract stipulations included the following: Twenty production stills were to accompany each completed film, and MGM could make as many release prints of each comedy as it deemed necessary; MGM agreed, in return for the privilege of distributing Roach's films, to do its best to secure distribution and would create a special sales department exclusively for short films. MGM would procure copyright in the United States, Canada, Great Britain, and Australasia in Roach's name and at his expense, and sole rights under copyright would belong to MGM. MGM would retain between 0.5 percent and 1 percent of the gross receipts on each comedy to go to the Motion Picture Producers and Distributors of America. MGM would pay Roach 60 percent of receipts from world distribution for the first eight weeks of each release, but advances on production and negative costs already paid to Roach would be deducted from this amount. After eight weeks, the split between producer and distributor would become fifty-fifty.

MGM was prohibited from making any editorial changes in the comedies without Roach's approval, but such approval was expected to be automatic on changes mandated by the National Board of Review, local censors, "or where necessities of the trade demand the cutting or shortening of said photoplays." MGM would spend up to fifteen hundred dollars in advertising on each film, and would provide Roach films with advertising equal to that given any non-Roach comedies it distributed. Title to all negatives and photoplays would remain with Roach; however, MGM would retain custody of the negatives for two years following release, after which they would be returned to Roach with the understanding that they could be recalled by MGM at any time if needed. MGM alone would determine the length of time each film was distributed. Each release print of every film and all advertising materials for the comedies would state "Hal Roach Presents" preceding the title. MGM "further agrees that in quoting prices in the course of distributing said motion picture photoplays it will not name lesser prices for the same in order to obtain higher prices for other pictures distributed by the Distributor, but that such photoplays shall be priced and designated on an independent and separate basis."

Roach was to deliver to MGM two negatives and one positive copy of each completed picture. This requirement was common at the time, although Pathé had required only a single negative because of the prohibitive cost, for Pathé, of producing two negatives. Both of the negatives were camera originals; hence, two cameras were used on all productions, cranking away side by side. One of the negatives was used for the production of domestic prints, and the other for foreign release prints. An interesting by-product of this process was that one frequently finds variations between the U.S. and foreign versions of films, ranging from slight differences in camera angles to substantially differing shot selection (i.e., material covered in a medium shot in the U.S. version may be represented by a long shot in the foreign edition). This practice would come to an end in the late 1920s with the advent of laboratory processes capable of generating a high-quality duplicate negative for the foreign release printing from a single camera original. Incidentally, MGM predecessor Metro Pictures distributed shorts prior to the merger with Goldwyn. These shorts had included a series with future Roach-MGM Laurel and Hardy star Stan Laurel.

Regarding short comedies accepted for distribution by MGM from sources other than the Hal Roach Studios, "it is understood between the parties hereto that the Distributor shall not distribute comedies provided by any other source than that of the Producer in an amount in excess of fifty percent of the motion picture photoplays produced by the Producer, except in the event that the Producer shall not produce sufficient" films. MGM was permitted by the contract to accept as many outside films as it needed to get up to at least fifty-two comedies per year.[2]

Instrumental in the transition to MGM was Roach's old Pathé ally, Fred Quimby. Quimby was working as short subject sales manager for Fox in September 1926, when he signed a contract to act as Roach's agent in the organization of the new short subject department at MGM. Unbeknownst to Fox, Quimby actually continued to work for Fox and Roach simultaneously during the second half of 1926, a situation that took on something of a cloak-and-dagger flavor at the end of 1926, when Quimby journeyed from New York to Los Angeles by boat via the Panama Canal to keep his destination a secret from his Fox employers. Quimby left both the Fox and the Roach payrolls in February 1927, when he became an employee of Loew's, heading up the new MGM shorts department.[3]

MGM expressed a desire to receive between forty and fifty comedies from Roach during the first year of the agreement. Roach proposed that ten comedies should be produced in each of five series: Our Gang, Charley Chase, All-Star, Max Davidson, and a western series. The Davidson series, featuring a strongly ethnic Jewish comic, had recently become a replacement for Mabel Normand's series. The western series was to be a group of two-reel comedies under the direction of Louis Gasnier, a French-born filmmaker who would later achieve dubious immortality as the director of *Reefer Madness* (1936), and featuring Oliver "Babe" Hardy in the lead.[4] However, by June 1927 the western series was postponed indefinitely and the initial Roach product for MGM was stabilized at ten shorts each from the other four series. As it turned out, Hardy's services were needed in a series other than the westerns anyway (see appendix 2, synopsis 13).

Other details still needed to be ironed out in the new relationship. For starters, MGM wanted a new name for the overall product line. Roach liked "M-G-M Short Features," while Quimby preferred "M-G-M Junior Features." Roach won that argument, although Quimby occasionally managed to sneak his version into trade announcements.[5] In addition, the MGM logo on the ending title cards of many of the early shorts featured a lion *cub* rather than an adult animal. To ensure Metro's feedback on the product, Roach actually requested that MGM set up a screening committee similar to that at Pathé—an ironic turn of events, considering the number of times the Pathé screening committee had been a major bone of contention with Roach.[6]

Roach and his staff had been present during too many theatrical screenings of their comedies in which the laughter had been drowned out and the comedy blunted by overly frantic musical accompaniment played too loudly by either an organist or orchestra. As a final bit of effort to ensure that his comedies would be given proper presentation wherever they ran, Roach decided to have a music cue sheet prepared for each film, with instructions for house musicians to render the score softly, so as not to overwhelm the comedy.[7] Ernst Luz, head of MGM's music department, complained that the first cue sheet submitted to him by Roach, a score for the Davidson short *What Every Iceman Knows,* was far too complicated. With thirty numbers for an eighteen-minute film, an average of forty seconds per song, Luz found the overall effect choppy and said that the better theater organists would simply ignore the cue sheet and do their own material, while those less competent would become thoroughly lost in the rapid changes. In response, Warren Doane admitted that music was not an area in which anyone at Hal Roach Studios had any particular expertise. He suggested that Luz use his own best judgment in reworking the score.[8]

Coincidentally, *What Every Iceman Knows* had trouble on another front, receiving negative ratings from MGM's screening committee. Quimby suggested that this film probably should not be the first Davidson short released by MGM; Doane replied that the second comedy was no better and that both were below the standards set by the Davidson films that had been released through Pathé.[9]

The initial entry in the Davidson series was conveniently unavailable on August 4, 1927, when MGM held a trade press preview of its short subjects lineup at the Embassy Theatre in New York City. Each of the sixty writers in attendance received a program that said,

GREETINGS

More than ordinary interest should attach itself to this showing of Short Features inasmuch as it signalizes in reality the entrance of Metro-Goldwyn-Mayer into the short subject field. This is indeed the birthday of M-G-M Short Features; it is the occasion when for the first time Metro-Goldwyn-Mayer publicly introduces the subjects representatives [sic] of the short feature program of the coming year.

Much has been written regarding M-G-M's announced intention of entering this field; much speculation been invoked as to the variety and quality of the program which would be released. It is with considerable pride that the producers of "The Big Parade" and "Ben-Hur" have requested your presence at this showing so that you may form your own conclusions.

The program which you will see includes the first release of each of the five series of short features to be released during 1927–28 with the exception of one of the four series of comedies being produced by Hal Roach. The print of the first of this fourth series starring Max Davidson has not yet been received from the coast. Each of the subjects shown constitutes the first release of each series and is typical of those to follow.

It is to be regretted that we cannot present at this time the first issue of M-G-M News. The first issue of the NEW Newsreel is scheduled for release during the week of August 15th.

Thank you for your presence on this, the birthday of M-G-M Short Features.

METRO-GOLDWYN-MAYER

The program, which received musical accompaniment from the Cotton Club Orchestra, was presented in the following order and included two one-reel shorts produced by Germany's Ufa studio and an MGM-produced Technicolor short:

1. *Sugar Daddies* (Roach All-Star), featuring Stan Laurel, Oliver Hardy, Edna Marian, and Jimmy Finlayson
2. *An African Adventure* (Ufa), one reel
3. *The Sting of Stings,* Charley Chase
4. *Soaring Wings* (Ufa), one reel
5. *The Flag,* "the story of the birth of the Stars and Stripes," two reels, Technicolor, starring Francis X. Bushman
6. *Yale Vs. Harvard,* Our Gang.[10]

Thus, with a flourish intended to reinforce the notion, planted late in the Pathé era, of the Roach product as short features, the Roach-MGM alliance was officially under way.

Laurel and Hardy

After the high spirits and expectations with which the Roach-MGM association was launched, the fall of 1927 was something of a letdown. Members of the MGM sales force and Loew's theater managers complained that the quality of the Roach shorts was not as high as they had been led to believe, and Roach was unhappy about lower-than-anticipated revenues. The one bright spot on the program—quite possibly, in fact, the salvation of the entire Roach-MGM relationship—was the formation of the comedy team of Laurel and Hardy. As mentioned earlier, the two comics were thrown together in the All-Star series by accident, with Laurel playing the flustered comic hero and Hardy appearing either as a comic heavy or merely as a supporting comic character. The two had appeared in a few of the Pathé All-Star comedies as a full-fledged costarring team, but these films were the exception, and most of them were not released until after the appearance of the first Roach-MGM comedies.

Having worked out the basic ground rules in their last Pathé films, Laurel and Hardy were primed and ready to go virtually from the outset of the Roach-MGM affiliation. After only a single MGM-released All-Star two-reeler, *Sugar Daddies,* which presented the two in a sort of loose amalgamation reminiscent of their Pathé days, Laurel and Hardy were teamed constantly and to good effect under the watchful eye of Roach's new supervising director, Leo McCarey. McCarey had been promoted from director of the Chase comedies to his new position in the spring of 1927 when F. Richard Jones left the studio to become a freelance feature director. This final phase of Jones's career would be extremely brief, encompassing but five features, from Douglas Fairbanks's *The Gaucho* (1927) to Jones's only talkie, *Bulldog Drummond* (1929), before his death in 1930 at the age of thirty-six.

Correspondence from the early days of the Roach-MGM affiliation reflects a growing awareness on the part of the executives of both companies of Laurel and Hardy's potential as a new starring attraction. In 1927, during a disappointing business trip to New York City punctuated by MGM staff complaints about product quality and the corporate uncertainties and court intrigue in the wake of the sudden and unexpected death of Loew's-MGM founder and chairman Marcus Loew, Roach found some comfort in a telegram from Doane, which informed him that "Laurel Hardy picture previewed last night near riot stop one of best laugh pictures for long time stop because picture is very good we feel justified working day or two longer make it still better."[11] One week later, Doane followed with more good news:

LAST LAUREL HARDY PICTURE EXCEPTIONALLY GOOD BY REASON OF GREATLY IMPROVED PERFORMANCE BY PRINCIPALS STOP CURRENT PICTURE HAS GOOD CHANCE TO BEING AS GOOD OR BETTER STOP MCCAREY WALKER MYSELF WISH YOUR OPINION OF A LITTLE LATER ON SUGGESTING TO METRO FURNISHING TO THEM PICTURES WITH THIS COMEDY TEAM IN PLACE OF DAVIDSONS GOING INTO OPENED MARKET FOR TALENT FOR ROACH STAR PICTURES. . . . LEO FEELS WOULD BE ENTIRELY PRACTICAL MAKE VERY GOOD ROACH STAR SERIES WITHOUT LAUREL AND HARDY AND WE ALL FEEL TIME IS HERE TO START INTENSIVE DEVELOPMENT ON LAUREL AND HARDY AT SAME TIME USING ROACH STAR SERIES TO DEVELOP NEW TALENT STOP WE FEEL THIS IDEA WOULD BE EASILY ACCEPTABLE TO METRO AFTER THEY RECEIVE LAST ROACH STAR AND ONE NOW IN PRODUCTION.[12]

Although it took a bit longer than the Roach staff suggested, not occurring until the beginning of the 1928–29 season, Laurel and Hardy did indeed advance into a starring series of their own, replacing the Max Davidson series, and the All-Star series went on as a proving ground for new talent and possible new series.

As the first of the Laurel and Hardy All-Star team efforts reached MGM's New York office, enthusiasm about the new team and about the future of the overall Roach product began to spread throughout the sales organization. After a screening committee showing of the Laurel and Hardy comedy *Hats Off,* Quimby wrote Roach, "I think that this subject is a riot. . . . I think that Hardy and Laurel make a great comedy team, and hope that you keep them working together"[13] (see appendix 2, synopsis 14). In December, Roach informed Quimby that a preview of the latest comedy by "Laurel and Hardy went over with a bang at the Metropolitan Theatre! Looks like we have a big bet in these two comedians."[14] Ending the year on the most enthusiastic note yet, Fred Quimby sent Roach a New Year's Eve report on the screening committee's reception of Laurel and Hardy's latest.

JUST FINISHED SCREENING LEAVE 'EM LAUGHING FOR COMMITTEE STOP TO A MAN IT WAS A CONTINUOUS ROAR I HAD A PAIN IN MY SIDE WHEN I LEFT THE PROJECTION ROOM IT IS A RIOT LAUREL AND HARDY DOING MARVELOUS WORK WE SHOULD GET THOUSAND DOLLARS A DAY FOR THIS ONE REGARDS AND A HAPPY AND PROSPEROUS NEW YEAR.[15]

The Arrival of the Talkers

Through a combination of the better-quality pictures it was producing, quality particularly enhanced by the Laurel and Hardy team films, and a renewed and intensive effort by Fred Quimby and his MGM Short Features sales staff, the Hal Roach Studios was able to conclude the first year of its distribution affiliation "well pleased with the performance of Metro-Goldwyn-Mayer Distributing Corporation." However, a new wrinkle had been added to the film industry's established operating practices. Less than two months into the Roach-MGM relationship, Warner Brothers released *The Jazz Singer.* An early aspect of Warner Brothers' experimentation with sound had been a steady stream of Vitaphone shorts, most featuring vaudeville comics and singers, appearing since late 1926. In 1927, the Fox Film Corporation entered sound with the production of Movietone shorts. As the Board of Directors of Hal Roach Studios put it in their August 31, 1928, report to the stockholders:

> The last few months has witnessed the advent of another element in the production field; that is, the talking or sound pictures. It is, of course, difficult to foretell what the eventual outcome of talking pictures will be or the eventual form they will assume. One thing is certain, however, that is that they are at the present time an element in the amusement field apparently having a definite appeal to the public, and properly handled, it promises to be a great addition to the entertainment value of pictures and a great aid to the producer in building up the interest in the picture intended. The company has placed itself in a position to gain by any and all new methods and devices introduced in the field and is a party to a contract with the Western Electric subsidiaries handling the sound effects prepared and manufactured by the Victor Talking Machine Company in collaboration with the Distributor and this company. Developments in the sound field are carefully watched and its entertainment and box office value will be fully availed of.[16]

This report failed to note that one Our Gang short of the previous season, the April 7, 1928, release *Barnum and Ringling, Inc.,* had received a synchronized sound effect track. The sound tracks for this film and the 1928–29 silent Roach releases with synchronized music and sound effects, as well as for the first group of full talkies produced by Roach, used the sound-on-disk system rather than the sound-on-film system that ultimately became the industry standard. In this method he was following the lead of his distributor: MGM had also opted for a disk system. Like MGM, Roach contracted with the Victor Talking Machine Company of Camden, New Jersey, makers of the ubiquitous Victrola wind-up phonograph, for recording equipment and for the manufacture of the sound track disks that were sent out to the theaters. Within a few years, Victor would merge with the giant Radio Corporation of America.[17]

Commenting on the addition of synchronized music and effect tracks to his late 1920s comedies, Roach outlined his vision for the integration of sound with the art of silent comedy, specifically, the established Hal Roach Studios house style.

> The art of pantomime is as old as amusement itself and there isn't the slightest chance that dialogue ever will entirely displace pantomime on the screen. Dialogue can't possibly take the place of pantomime in causing laughs.
>
> There is no doubt, however, that sound synchronization of the score will be a great help to comedy subjects. I should say that it will increase the amusement possibilities of a comedy from 10 to 20 per cent to have the proper musical accompaniment. . . .
>
> Sound effects in pictures are going to find a definite niche in the market. There is no doubt about that. And they are going to add variety to the program. But they won't necessarily take the place of anything else on the programs. You may say that they take the place of the elaborate presentations, recently so much in vogue. Well, my answer to that is that when presentations came in they didn't take the place of anything.[18]

Roach entered the all-talkie era with the same four short-film series that had constituted his output during the last year of full silent production: Laurel and Hardy, Charley Chase, Our Gang, and the Roach All-Stars. Rejecting a suggestion from Doane that the studio shoot its talkies as silents, preview them that way, and only then add talking sequences[19] and, in the process, contradict somewhat Roach's vision of the integration of sound with pantomime as described to the press, Roach decided to make truly all-talking comedies, with Victor-supervised soundstage construction commencing in early March 1929.[20]

While sound posed no particular problem for the principal players of the Laurel and Hardy, Charley Chase, and All-Star units, most of whom had come to the silent cinema from the stage and possessed both speaking and musical talents, it did create a vexing situation for Robert McGowan, the director of the Our Gang comedies. These films, with their young casts, had been even more reliant than any of the other Roach comedies on the style of silent filmmaking in which the director gave the actors verbal instructions as the cameras rolled. Sound both deprived McGowan of being able to speak while shooting and required that the children actually learn and deliver dialogue, something that had never been necessary before. McGowan and his cast were ultimately able to cope with the changes, although coping sometimes meant piecing a young actor's performance together in the editing process one line at a time. This procedure often resulted in scenes that are full of jump cuts, a glaring technical deficiency in the Our Gang films of the period. (For an example of this problem, see Spanky's rendition of "Tarzan" in the 1933 short *Forgotten Babies.*) McGowan did permit himself one public venting of his frustration over the new demands brought about by the talkies. The unit's seventh talking effort, *Shivering Shakespeare* (1930), supervised by McGowan and directed by his nephew Anthony Mack, deals with the trials and tribulations of a schoolteacher attempting to stage a play in which none of her students can remember his or her lines.

The Hal Roach Studios entered the talkie era with a creative vacuum at the top. Leo McCarey had left the studio at the end of 1928, just as sound production was beginning, to pursue a career as a feature director. Unlike his predecessor, Richard Jones, McCarey would survive long enough to enjoy a long and successful Hollywood directing career. With McCarey gone, Roach and Doane resumed production supervision. This situation was intended to be temporary while Roach searched for a new supervising director. He filled the position in October 1929 with Fred Karno, the British stage impresario whose shows had introduced Chaplin and Laurel to America. Karno's tenure at Roach was extremely brief. Roach discovered instantly that the legendary showman "was just the businessman. He just hired guys that were funny, and he hired other guys to write for them. I finally let him go." Karno's five-year contract was terminated after less than four months, in February 1930.[21]

From this point on, Roach would never again have a designated supervising director. General production responsibilities were handled on new series by Roach and Doane, while production units for the established and long-running series followed the model of Our Gang and acted semiautonomously. Robert McGowan continued to produce and direct Our Gang until 1933. After a four-month hiatus in production, McGowan was replaced by Gus Meins. In 1936 Meins was succeeded by Gordon Douglas, who served as producer-director on the series until 1938, when Roach transferred production of Our Gang to MGM.

With the basic format of the Laurel and Hardy series firmly established by the time of McCarey's departure, creative oversight was assumed by Stan Laurel, who was still working under a contract as a writer-director-actor. Although he received producer screen credit on only two occasions, Laurel exercised a fair amount of creative control over the series until Laurel and Hardy left Roach in 1940.[22]

The Chase series, similarly, was largely the responsibility of its star, who had been Roach's first supervising director in the early 1920s. Chase's control over his series was formalized in 1933, when he began directing his films under his real name, Charles Parrott. In 1934 his contract was revised to redefine his role as actor-supervisor. Chase-Parrott would direct or codirect all of his films from 1933 until the series ended in 1936.[23]

The other series, most of which were short-lived, typically would be assigned to a staff director under the supervision of Roach and his lieutenants. If the films achieved a standard acceptable quality, the director remained in charge. If not, and this was more frequently the case, Roach would revolve other directors through the shorts, trying to find one who could make the series concept work. The only post–Laurel and Hardy series with any durability illustrates this mode of operation. The Thelma Todd–Zasu Pitts series started in 1931 with its entries being directed alternately by Roach and faded Hollywood feature director Marshall Neilan. After the first five shorts, the series was handed to a succession of Roach staff directors, including Gil Pratt, an employee from the Rolin days. At the end of 1932, Gus Meins took over the reins of the Todd-Pitts films. Under Meins the series finally met with Roach's approval. Meins became the series producer-director until late 1934, serving through a change in personnel, as Pitts was replaced by Patsy Kelly. Incredibly, during his last year on this series, Meins also acted as producer-director for Our Gang. Meins was succeeded briefly by James Parrott, then in mid-1935 by former Roach editor William Terhune, who remained in charge until the series ended. The rest of the new series during the first half of the 1930s lasted only one or two seasons and remained the province of rotating staff directors under the general supervision of Roach and Doane or, after Doane's 1931 departure, Henry Ginsberg. Ginsberg, a budget-minded executive whose 1931–36 tenure at Roach was a prerequisite for a loan from the Bank of America, considered the traditionally relaxed creative atmosphere at Roach a waste of time and money and insisted on tighter discipline and stricter adherence to shooting scripts and schedules. The free and easy days so fondly recalled by Roach employees had come to an end.[24]

The concept of unit production at Roach in the late 1920s and early 1930s extended to crew assignments on a routine but nonexclusive basis. Director of photography Art Lloyd worked more consistently after 1930 with Laurel and Hardy than he did with any other unit, but he could be called upon, between Laurel and Hardy assignments, to photograph shorts in other series. Occasionally, when schedules on these other assignments ran long, Laurel and Hardy found themselves working with one of the other Roach staff cinematographers. Similarly, the Our Gang comedies were photographed extensively, but not exclusively, by Francis Corby. This nonexclusive approach applied to editing as well.

Writing credit for the Roach shorts is virtually impossible to establish. Until 1932 the only writing credit to appear on Roach-MGM shorts was "Titles by H. M. Walker" on the silent films and "Dialogue by H. M. Walker" on the talkies. After Walker's departure from the studio in 1932, no one received screen credit for writing the short subjects. Through interviews with Roach employees of the period, Randy Skretvedt has reconstructed the writing procedure used for the Laurel and Hardy films, a method that, presumably, followed similar lines for the other series. Someone—Roach, Laurel, or one of the team's three or four gag writers—would suggest a story idea or situation. Then Laurel and the gag writers would work on the story for approximately one week until they had a script that, according to Skretvedt, consisted of "three to six legal-size pages, single-spaced, with a description of the action and sometimes a few brief dialogue sequences if they were especially funny or important."[25] This "action" script then went to Walker. Walker, a member of Roach's executive staff since before 1920, had written all of the title cards for Roach's silent films. By the coming of sound, however, his contribution to Laurel and Hardy's films consisted of a few pages of dialogue appended to the "action" script. Skretvedt notes that this added dialogue was generally disregarded by Laurel and Hardy, and that the dialogue in the finished films was usually a combination of the "action" script, ad-libbing by Laurel and Hardy, and on-the-set writing by Laurel and his gag men.[26]

The Roach Product of the Early Sound Era

The stampede to full sound production at Hal Roach Studios during the spring of 1929 resulted in a studio record number of two-reel shorts being produced for the 1928–29 season. The normal quota of ten silent shorts per series had already been produced, beyond which additional full talkie shorts were released for each series as follows: Laurel and Hardy, four films; Charley Chase, three films; Our Gang, two films; and All Star, three films. This bonus of talkies resulted in a grand total of fifty-two shorts for the year.

The last Roach silent film, Laurel and Hardy's *Angora Love,* hit theater screens in December 1929. As with its immediate predecessors, it had a truncated commercial life. Before the coming of sound, the studio's shorts had always had an active release life of three years as they worked their way through the national theater circuit. By 1929, sound pictures were driving silents from the theatrical market so rapidly that no short made within the last two years of silent production was able to realize its full release life and earnings potential.[27]

Although the series lineup for the 1929–30 season was identical to that of the previous year, a major change had taken place in the All-Star comedies. During the 1928–29 season, when Laurel and Hardy were moved from the All-Stars to their own starring series, the All-Star comedies had drawn their casts from the Hal Roach supporting stock company. The first three talkies in the series, the last films of the 1928–29 season, continued this practice. However, the 1929–30 season once again saw the series revolving around a single star. After years of negotiations that had never quite reached fruition, Harry Langdon finally arrived at Roach. Langdon had enjoyed a meteoric rise in the late 1920s, briefly enjoying a popularity that placed him in the same company as Chaplin, Lloyd, and Keaton as one of the nation's top film comedians. Then, just as quickly, he fell from public favor. The most commonly cited culprit in his downfall was a misguided temperament that led him to overreach creatively, trying to assume more control over his films than he was actually capable of handling with any degree of success. So, bloodied but apparently not humbled by his tumble, Langdon agreed to come to work for Hal Roach as the star of the All-Star series. Viewed today, the films of this series seem very much in the same league with Langdon's successful shorts for Sennett. Langdon's established screen persona is intact, and he handles dialogue well, with a voice that matches the character. Nevertheless, audiences reacted negatively; perhaps it was just too soon after the spectacular collapse of his popularity in a string of bad films to permit the rehabilitation of his career. Even worse, Langdon apparently still possessed a star-sized ego that alienated his colleagues at Roach, the very people who were trying to help him get back on track. The Langdon All-Star comedies rotated through most of the Roach staff directors in search of the right chemistry, but all in vain. The series was canceled after a single year (see appendix 2, synopsis 15).

While Laurel and Hardy, Charley Chase, and Our Gang would remain strong short-film series through the mid-1930s, the All-Star slot remained problematic for Roach. Langdon was replaced by a two-season series announced as The Younger Set, which finally reached the screen under the series title The Boy Friends. Conceived as an adolescent version of Our Gang, The Boy Friends actually contained in its cast two of the original silent Our Gang members, Mary Kornman and Mickey Daniels. The Boy Friends was not successful, and the fourth short in the series did not even receive a theatrical release—a sure sign of a series in trouble. Perhaps the only really memorable aspect of this series was that several of its shorts were directed by George Stevens who until that point had been one of Roach's primary cameramen—and who, of course, had a brilliant Hollywood directing career ahead of him (see appendix 2, synopsis 16). The Boy Friends was succeeded by The Taxi Boys (see appendix 2, synopsis 17) for a single season during 1932–33; another round of Hal Roach All-Stars for 1933–34, featuring Billy Nelson, Douglas Wakefield, and Don Barclay (see appendix 2, synopsis 18); and finally a series meant to include seven shorts to star humorist Irvin S. Cobb in 1934–35. William K. Everson saw the Cobb films as modeled after those of Will Rogers (who was a friend of both Roach and Cobb), but in many ways they seem to be closer in spirit to the films of W. C. Fields. Cobb was roughly Fields's age and physical shape, and the films had him wandering through a malevolent world of irritating relatives and escaped convicts, spouting homespun witticisms all the way. The Cobb series was so unpopular with exhibitors that it was canceled after only four films, one of which was not even released to theaters. Two one-shot special shorts, one a straightforward filming of an amateur talent contest and the other a no-star story of the battle of the sexes, were produced to complete contractual release obligations, after which the All-Star short series expired.

Roach produced, in addition to the Laurel and Hardy, Charley Chase, Our Gang, and All-Star shorts, a fifth series from 1931 to 1936, the previously mentioned Todd-Pitts-Kelly comedies. During the 1933–34 season, there was actually a sixth Roach series: six musical comedies created to cash in on the popular trend of movie musicals started by 42nd Street. This series lasted only a single season.

At least a few other aspects of Roach's early sound product deserve brief mention. First, as a result of the increased production costs attendant to sound, Roach's annual output declined from ten films to eight films per series. Second, Roach's staff seems to have been rather bold in taking their brand new sound equipment outdoors. While they produced their fair share of studio-bound shorts, there is also a surprising amount of location work, including synchronous sound shots inside the cab of a moving steam locomotive in the second Our Gang talkie, Railroadin'.

Equally sophisticated was the approach to sound in the initial talking entries of the Charley Chase and All-Star series. Chase's *The Big Squawk* (1929) uses dialogue sparingly and only to support the plot. There is none of the incessant talk that marks so many of the earliest sound films. Dialogue supports, but is not allowed to dominate, the type of pantomimic situational comedy at which Chase excelled. Unfortunately, as will be discussed later, the series would soon veer off this proven track.

Hurdy Gurdy (1929), directed personally by Hal Roach, is nothing short of remarkable. The first sound entry of the All-Star series, the cast includes Roach stalwarts Edgar Kennedy (in his frequent characterization as an Irish policeman), Max Davidson, Thelma Todd, and Eddie Dunn. A heat wave sends the residents of a New York City tenement to their fire escapes for whatever breeze is stirring. The tenants are a cross section of melting-pot culture: Irish, Jewish, German, and Italian dialects create a rich aural mix on the sound track. As small talk is exchanged among the residents of different floors, an off-camera hurdy-gurdy supplies an often ironic counterpoint to the action. While the characters swelter, the street organ provides a jaunty rendition of "In the Good Old Summertime." The same song would be used to equally ironic effect in the Laurel and Hardy film *Below Zero* (1930). This time, the boys are street musicians in the middle of a raging snowstorm. The one and only song in their repertoire is—"In the Good Old Summertime." Later in *Hurdy Gurdy,* Officer Kennedy tries to catch a nap between shifts, an impossibility because of the neighborhood chatter, to the accompaniment of "Please Go Away and Let Me Sleep."

Unquestionably one of the major concerns of all U.S. film producers upon the arrival of sound was the potential loss of the highly lucrative foreign market. In the silent era, translation of a film from one language to another was as easy as changing title cards, and it was entirely possible for a German audience to watch an American film, and vice versa, without being aware that they were viewing a foreign film. Beyond the new technical challenges posed for translation from one language to another, sound removed emphasis from the visual and placed it on the verbal, making film much more specific to a particular culture and less international. This situation was particularly acute in film comedy, where witty dialogue and one-liners of the vaudeville aesthetic gradually replaced pantomime as the source of humor. Despite the problems they faced in retaining their overseas market, U.S. filmmakers were not about to let it go without exhausting every possibility.

One of the first methods employed by American feature film producers to hold on to the foreign market was to shoot the same film simultaneously in one or more of the following languages: Spanish, German, Italian, and French. Roach appears to have been the only producer of short subjects to follow this practice, having the dialogue written out phonetically for the principal players and replacing the English-speaking supporting cast with one versed in the appropriate language. A complete list of the Hal Roach films shot in multiple language versions is included in the filmography. These international versions are markedly different from the American versions of the same film. First, since short films were more difficult to place in foreign markets, the feature film having dominated the theatrical bill from an early date, the international versions were usually longer than their English counterparts. This extra running time often was achieved by combining two shorts into a single featurette, joined together by a transitional subtitle; by including material in the foreign-language version that does not appear in the English version; or by employing both methods. An example of the second means of expansion may be found in the Spanish version of the Laurel and Hardy film *Chickens Come Home.* In the thirty-minute English version, a party that Hardy is giving for community leaders is merely a backdrop for his flustered efforts to instruct Laurel, by telephone, in the proper way to keep a blackmailer away. In the Spanish version, which runs fifty minutes, the party consumes a major portion of the film's running time, as Hardy introduces one Spanish-speaking vaudeville act after another as entertainment at his party. Needless to say, these acts have no counterparts in the English version.

Beyond the need for length, another factor sometimes contributed to differences between the English and foreign versions of Roach's early talkies. Following the practice of his distributor, MGM, Roach would preview a short, and if the audience response was less than anticipated, the film would be sent back into production for retakes. This same process evidently was not undertaken, however, on the foreign versions, which, as with Laurel and Hardy's *Night Owls,* provide a tantalizing look at what the original, pre-preview English version was like.

The process of shooting a film simultaneously in several languages was cumbersome, expensive, and not terribly popular with the principal players, who now had to go through the same routines as many as five times what might normally be expected. By the early 1930s, dubbing and superimposed subtitling brought an end to multiple-language production.

Three-Reel Shorts

The Roach short-film output had been standardized since the mid-1920s at two reels, or approximately twenty minutes of screen time per short.

Although some shorts had been permitted to run into a third reel—Mabel Normand's first two shorts being prime examples—this extra length was considered an anomaly, something permissible only when a film previewed considerably better in the longer form than it did at two reels.

During the 1930–31 season, most of the Roach series experimented with the three-reel format. The motivation for this intentional and systematic lengthening may have been yet another attempt at differentiating the Roach product from that of rival comedy producers and to place it on more of an equal footing with features in the audience's perceptions. The first four of the seven Laurel and Hardy releases for the year were in the longer format, as were two of eight Charley Chase films, one of eight Boy Friends films and the first Thelma Todd–Zasu Pitts short. The fifth Laurel and Hardy comedy of the season, *Laughing Gravy,* was shot as a three-reeler but released in two reels after a poor preview in the longer form. Only Our Gang remained exclusively in the two-reel length during this year. By the next season, all series returned full-time to two-reelers except Laurel and Hardy, who had justified their expanded running time by successfully starring in a feature-length picture. During the 1931–32 season, two of the seven Laurel and Hardy shorts were three-reelers. One of these, *The Music Box,* won an Academy Award for best live-action short subject. A third 1931–32 Laurel and Hardy short, *Any Old Port,* was reduced from three reels to two for release, while another, *Beau Hunks,* was actually expanded to twice the normal length, reaching theater screens as a four-reel featurette. After this season, there was to be only one more Hal Roach extended-length short, the 1934 Laurel and Hardy three-reeler *Oliver the Eighth.*

The demise of the three-reeler as a studio standard after less than a season may be attributed to several factors: rising production costs in the face of the Great Depression, which was just beginning to affect the film industry; increased competition for screen time with the rise of double features; and the feeling on the part of some theater owners that the three-reelers were slow and padded compared with the twenty-minute shorts that were the norm.

Laurel and Hardy Features

Although Roach's three-reelers didn't pan out, the early 1930s brought another film-lengthening process that was to have considerably more impact on the future of the Hal Roach Studios: the studio's return to feature-length production. Although only two years into their partnership, Laurel and Hardy were so popular by 1929 that MGM borrowed them from Roach to appear in its all-star extravaganza, *The Hollywood Revue.* MGM used the team again, as comic relief, in its all-talking, all-Technicolor production of the period operetta *The Rogue Song* in 1930, this time also employing the team's most frequent director during the period, James Parrott, to direct their scenes. During the same year, largely as a gesture of good will, Loew's actually brought Hal Roach onto the MGM studio lot to direct one of its own action-adventure features, *Men of the North.*

Despite the admitted star value of Laurel and Hardy—Loew's having begun featuring large portraits of the team with its own MGM stars as well as in the regular Hal Roach product advertisement in the trade papers—Loew's continued to oppose the idea of the Hal Roach Studios producing features for MGM release. Although MGM had handled the feature product of outside producers during the silent days, as with Joseph Schenck's Buster Keaton pictures and the Roach westerns, by 1930 the company had adopted a policy of not distributing any feature-length films that were not produced in-house. Undeterred, Roach launched into production of the first Laurel and Hardy starring feature in 1930. As a precaution, the film was given a short-film production number during the shooting to prevent MGM from discovering that Roach was producing a feature without their consent or approval. Roach presented that film, a one-hour prison feature entitled *Pardon Us,* to the MGM executives as a fait accompli (see appendix 2, synopsis 19). MGM, after viewing the picture and realizing its profit potential, quickly drew up a separate contract, outside and apart from the existing short-film contract, to cover its distribution.[28]

Following the success of *Pardon Us,* Roach was able to negotiate with MGM in advance for distribution arrangements on future Laurel and Hardy features, although this arrangement was strictly on a picture-by-picture basis and permitted no features beyond films starring Laurel and Hardy. This agreement eventually would change: the enormous popularity of the Laurel and Hardy features, particularly in the foreign market (see "Financial Performance of the MGM Features" in appendix 3), and the continuing popularity of the Our Gang short comedies would, within a few years, give Roach the leverage he needed for even non–Laurel and Hardy features to be distributed by MGM on a routine basis.

The extraordinary nature of Roach's accomplishment in persuading MGM to distribute his features is underscored by an examination of MGM's release schedule in the 1930s. Aside from the nineteen features MGM distributed for Roach (eleven of them with Laurel and Hardy), the studio accepted only three other features from outside its walls during the entire decade: the appropriately titled *The Outsider* (1931), a British film produced by Eric Hakim; *Flirting with Fate* (1938), produced by David Loew, the son of Loew's, Inc., founder Marcus Loew; and David O. Selznick's *Gone with the Wind* (1939).[29]

Although Laurel and Hardy in feature-length form had proven successful, MGM Distributing demanded that Roach continue to supply at least a modest schedule of Laurel and Hardy shorts each season. The result of this requirement was rather unusual. While comedians who made the transition from shorts to features rarely returned to shorts unless, like the case of Langdon, a catastrophe befell their careers, Laurel and Hardy remained extremely popular as they alternated between shorts and features from 1931 to 1935.

A second Laurel and Hardy feature, *Pack Up Your Troubles,* appeared in 1932, followed by a third, *The Devil's Brother* in 1933. Based on the nineteenth-century operetta *Fra Diavolo, The Devil's Brother* was a marked departure both for Laurel and Hardy and for the Hal Roach Studios. While the team's previous two features had been rather modestly budgeted films (and looked it, as Loew's had foreseen), *The Devil's Brother* was an "A" picture, an elaborate period costume piece inspired, in part, by the duo's success as comic relief in MGM's *The Rogue Song.* As Roach was to learn, however, making big-budget pictures was not without peril. *The Devil's Brother* cost far more than he had anticipated, and he was forced to turn to MGM for additional financial assistance during production. It would not be the last time.

6

The Demise of the Short Subject, 1933–38

While the short subjects production schedule cranked on, including four to six Laurel and Hardy shorts each year, Roach became increasingly focused on features when planning the future of his company. The reasons for this change were many. First, as already noted, the advent of sound had made filmmaking more expensive while simultaneously making Hollywood's English-language talking films more difficult to sell overseas—a situation exacerbated by the worldwide economic downturn and international strife in the 1930s. In an interview with the *Motion Picture Herald* in mid-1935, Hal Roach said his production costs had increased by at least fifty-two hundred dollars per two-reeler since the silent days.[1] By 1931 this meant an average budget of forty thousand dollars per Laurel and Hardy two-reeler (due largely to the salaries of the stars of Roach's premier series) and twenty-five thousand dollars per picture on all other series.[2]

Additionally, the Depression had begun to affect the "Depression-proof" film industry in 1931. While Roach had posted a profit of $87,085 for the period of July 27, 1930, through August 29, 1931, the studio lost $41,875 between August 30, 1931, and March 12, 1932. As the Depression deepened and the short-subject market was adversely affected by other industrial factors to be explained shortly, Roach would see his losses mount. Although the company turned a profit of $218,155 on the forty-two shorts produced during the 1933–1934 season, it would lose $221,919 on thirty-two shorts produced for 1934–1935 and $34,537 on twenty-four shorts produced in 1935–1936, the year Roach decided to cancel production on all short series except Our Gang.[3] Despite these losses, Roach did not have to go through any sort of bankruptcy or reorganization at that point, unlike several of the major studios. Ironically, Roach would remain solvent in the turbulent 1930s only to face economic catastrophe in the 1940s, a generally prosperous period for the rest of the industry.

In addition to the difficult financial situation, the early 1930s found the Roach studio in a creative slump. The long-running Our Gang and Charley Chase series were at creative midlife crisis points, the Laurel and Hardy partnership was threatened by a growing feud between Laurel and Roach, and the new series were having trouble getting off the ground.

While the Our Gang cast had changed several times since the series inception in 1922, with younger children being brought in to gradually replace those who had outgrown their roles, the series had always been under the guidance of producer-director Robert Francis McGowan. The stress of a decade of riding herd on his juvenile troupe had been aggravated by the addition of dialogue. Twice in the late 1920s, McGowan had taken brief sabbaticals to recover from what one doctor described as "nervous exhaustion."[4] The Our Gang comedies had been directed during these absences by McGowan's nephew, Robert Anthony McGowan, who billed himself as "Anthony Mack" to avoid confusion with his uncle.

At the end of the 1931–32 season, McGowan resigned his position, only to be coaxed back for the following season in a verbal agreement with Roach.[5] This verbal agreement was supposed to cover only the eight shorts produced during 1932–33, but at the end of the year, with no suitable replacement in sight, Roach talked McGowan into staying on for the 1933–34 season. By the beginning of the new production season, though, McGowan was, in Roach's words, "just worn out."[6]

The 1933–34 season had begun with a major change of format for Our Gang. Rather than concentrating on the exploits of a group of children, the first two films of the season, *Bedtime Worries* and *Wild Poses*, centered on Spanky and his parents, played by Emerson Treacy and Gay Seabrook, with the gang itself assuming an incidental status. This change may have been intended to permit the harried McGowan to work more with professional adult actors than with children. If so, the tactic apparently didn't succeed. McGowan left the series after *Wild Poses*, and there was a four-month hiatus in the normally monthly Our Gang releases. When the series resumed in February 1934, it had a new director and several new gang members and had reverted to its original concept, losing Spanky's parents and focusing once more on the children. Although Gus Meins's 1934–36 tenure at the helm of Our Gang was a popular success and introduced Darla, Alfalfa, and several other "definitive" cast members, his work was a bit more formulaic and mechanical than that of his predecessor, lacking the warmth and sincerity of McGowan's efforts.

Meanwhile, the Charley Chase series faced a creative crisis of its own. Concurrent with the arrival of sound (but not necessarily due to sound; Chase had a good speaking and singing voice), the Chase series went somewhat off stride, with the shorts often appearing haphazard and ill-conceived. All too often a story idea is planted but serves only as a springboard for a string of comic bits, and the film ends on a gag without any real resolution of the plot premise (see appendix 2, synopsis 20). Further, Chase was visibly moving into middle age, a transition hastened by a heavy workload and stomach ulcers so serious that they required repeated and dangerous surgery. As a result, he became a bit less credible in the boy-girl plots that had served him so well. Chase's status at the studio was clearly in trouble as early as 1932, when *Variety* reported rumors that he was about to be released from Hal Roach Studios.[7]

Ultimately the Chase series was renewed, and Roach's publicity director informed MGM immediately prior to the 1932–33 season to "eliminate all of the old Chase [publicity] photographs as his present series will reveal the comedian in an entirely new characterization."[8] The metamorphosis wasn't exactly earthshaking. The "new characterization" saw the star donning a pair of wire-framed glasses and, more often than not, eschewing man-about-town plots in favor of films with a married-life, domestic setting. For the 1933–34 season, the studio announced yet another makeover, with Chase playing the fall guy to "a musical quartet of stooges," a group of his war buddies who relied on his financial support.[9] This format, with the Ranch Boys playing the stooges, was introduced with the last film of the 1932–33 season, *Arabian Tights* (originally to be called *A Farewell to Arms* until it was discovered that the title had already been taken),[10] and was continued for the first two films of the 1933–34 season. But the stooges were never really integrated as envisioned, and the Chase series returned to its old ways. With a brief upturn in the Roach studio's financial fortunes, further retooling of the Chase series was deemed unnecessary. Chase's creative control over his work was expanded, to the point that he became the officially credited series director.

As the Laurel and Hardy series was Roach's hottest property, as well as his ticket to feature production, the personnel problems on this series were perhaps the most troubling to the studio. The origin of the Roach-Laurel rift lay in notions of creative freedom and fair compensation. While Roach permitted a certain level of autonomy to his more successful series, he insisted that in the event of creative conflicts between series personnel and himself, his views would prevail. As Laurel and Hardy series supervisor since 1929, Laurel saw the success of the series as confirmation of his own creative instincts and became increasingly resistant to even the slightest input from Roach. The conflict between Roach and Laurel over creative control would intensify during the 1930s.[11]

Perhaps the most serious problem between Roach and Laurel, however, involved money. The first major monetary conflict between the two arose in the summer of 1932 when Laurel and Hardy decided to take a joint vacation to Great Britain: Laurel to visit his father and Hardy to exercise his passion for golf. The duo's trip, which took them to New York City and through Great Britain from London to Edinburgh, became a massive publicity tour, with mobs of fans and newsreel cameramen meeting them at every turn. They returned from their trip profoundly aware of their immense popularity but also thoroughly fatigued from a junket that had been anything but a vacation. They were understandably outraged when the Hal Roach board of directors voted to suspend their contracts (and salaries) from July 10 to September 12, the period of the trip.[12] Laurel reasoned that since the trip had in fact become a publicity tour, they fully deserved to be compensated. Relations between Roach and Laurel became so strained at this point that by mid-November Roach felt compelled to inform MGM of the very real possibility of a breakup of the team of Laurel and Hardy, prompting the following urgent and personal telegram from Felix Feist of MGM to Roach:

AFTER SERIOUS DISCUSSION ON SUBJECT YOUR PHONE CALL WITH MR SCHENCK WE CANNOT SUBSCRIBE TO ANY PLAN THAT WOULD BREAK UP THE TEAM AS IT WOULD INVALIDATE ALL PRESENT CONTRACTS [with exhibitors] AND IT WOULD IN OUR OPINION ALSO MEAN FOREGOING A VERY VITAL PART OF YOUR SETUP SO RECOMMEND YOUR DOING EVERYTHING NECESSARY TO MAINTAIN PRESENT STATUS OF TEAM AND WIRE US THAT SETUP IS TO CONTINUE.[13]

Under these circumstances, Roach had little choice but to placate Laurel and keep his starring team together. This marked the beginning of an unfortunate new phase of the Roach-Laurel relationship, with Laurel characteristically holding out until the eleventh hour at each contract renewal time and Roach resenting his studio's being held hostage by one of his employees.

An interesting prospect grew out of a contract impasse between Laurel and Roach in early 1935. Roach announced to the trade press the termination of the Laurel and Hardy series and its replacement by a series to be called The Hardy Family, a situation comedy featuring Hardy with Patsy Kelly as Mrs. Hardy and Spanky McFarland as their son. This announced series was almost certainly a negotiation ploy to persuade Laurel to sign the contract, since the proposed cast would have gutted Roach's successful Our Gang and Thelma Todd–Patsy Kelly series. And since Roach was much more interested in features at this point, the inception of a new short comedy series to replace his most viable feature property seems an unlikely move. Nevertheless, Joe Rivkin, a Hal Roach publicist in the New York office, wrote his West Coast counterpart on March 16, 1935, that "the new set-up of Hardy-Kelly and Spanky sounds very good to me. Is it definite? You can bet your life that Laurel is a dead pigeon when he leaves Roach."[14] Laurel signed a new contract on April 8, 1935.[15] The Hardy Family was dead, and Laurel and Hardy continued, but so did the Roach-Laurel conflict.

For Roach the Laurel episode must have been reminiscent of the situation he had faced with Lloyd. Like Lloyd, Laurel and Hardy were Roach's only contract stars capable of supporting a feature-length picture. Their loss would mean a return to all-short production during an era that witnessed the demise of the independent short-comedy shop. Hence, Laurel and Hardy were arguably Roach's most valuable commodity, and until he could develop an alternate strategy for the production of features, a task in which he was busily engaged in 1935, Roach was obliged to indulge Laurel's independent streak. Once he developed a full feature production program in the latter half of the 1930s, Roach became ambivalent about the continuation of the Laurel and Hardy features, and the unflattering tone of most of his later comments about Laurel suggest that he never forgave Laurel for usurping his authority.

As noted above, the All-Star series during the early 1930s was little more than a frustrating succession of unpopular one-season experiments. Only the Boy Friends was able to hobble into a second season before cancellation. Roach's attempt to add a sixth series to his roster in the 1933–34 season, the musical series, was dismissed by exhibitors as being devoid of entertainment while glorifying drunken revelry. Depiction of excessive drinking on the screen was still a sensitive subject in this post-Prohibition society, and limitations on the amount of on-screen drinking were included as part of the Production Code of the Motion Picture Producers and Distributors of America (see appendix 2, synopsis 21).

The only successful Roach short series to be introduced in the sound era were the Thelma Todd–Zasu Pitts–Patsy Kelly comedies. Conceived by Roach as a "female Laurel and Hardy" team,[16] the series debuted in 1931 with Todd and Pitts costarring. It underwent a change in personnel in 1933, when Kelly replaced Pitts after a contract impasse with the latter, and lasted until the end of two-reel comedy production at Hal Roach in 1936. The series was quite successful, occasionally running second to Laurel and Hardy and eclipsing Charley Chase and Our Gang in box office take. This achievement may have been due, in part, to the three leads frequently having received prominent supporting roles in features produced at other studios. Pitts, of course, had begun a promising starring career in the late silent era, including a pair of Erich von Stroheim features: *Greed* (1925) and *The Wedding March* (1928). The shorts with Todd at Roach basically provided Pitts with a transitional period, setting her up for starring and character roles in "B" feature comedies for the remainder of the 1930s. Todd and Kelly had both had limited film experience prior to their work at Roach, and both proved popular in sound features, with Todd's non-Roach appearances including the Marx Brothers' *Monkey Business* (1931) and *Horsefeathers* (1932). Kelly's exclusive contract with Roach made her a valuable loan-out property, as she embarked on a highly successful supporting character comic feature career between Roach shorts (see appendix 2, synopsis 22).

The Double-Feature Evil

A fundamental change in the exhibition end of the motion picture industry proved to be the death knell for independent producers of theatrical short subjects. The advent of double features (not to mention triple features and more in some metropolitan theaters) and the concurrent ballooning of overall theatrical program schedules left little time for twenty-minute comedy shorts and forced an even finer slicing of the box office pie, reducing the amount of money available for the rental of shorts.

An anomaly in the history of the rigidly controlled film industry under the studio system, the practice of showing multiple features was actually forced on the industry by independent, nonaffiliated theaters (theaters neither owned nor controlled by the Hollywood studios), who began showing a second feature as a cheap substitute for the elaborate stage shows common at the larger studio-controlled theaters. Seeing two or more features for the price of one proved enormously successful with the bargain-seeking movie audiences of the Great Depression.[17] Needless to say, the film studios took a different view of this heavily discounted selling of their product. However, despite bitter opposition from Hollywood, which dubbed the practice "the double-feature evil," even the affiliated, studio-controlled theaters reluctantly adopted it as a means of survival.

As might be assumed, the big five fully integrated studios attempted throughout the early 1930s to end the double billing practice that they found so abhorrent, although Universal, Columbia, and some smaller studios (e.g., Monogram) that specialized in the production of "B" pictures, perfect for the bottom half of a double bill, actually benefited from the situation. The trade press editorialized against the practice and published opinion polls, conducted under circumstances that were unscientific if not downright suspect, that purported to demonstrate a public aversion to double bills. A ban of double features that was included in the industry's code of practice as part of the National Recovery Act initiative was gradually watered down in negotiations with independent exhibitors, going from an absolute prohibition of multiple bills nationwide to a ban only in markets where a 60 percent or greater majority of exhibitors voted against the practice, after which the entire agreement was junked when the NRA was declared unconstitutional.[18]

The crucial moment in the double feature war came in early 1936, when the U.S. Circuit Court of Appeals in Philadelphia confirmed a lower court ruling that denied distributors the right to include single-feature requirements in their contracts with exhibitors. The court held that the practice would be legal if used by a single distributor but, as an industry-wide practice, single-feature language in all distribution contracts was collusive and monopolistic behavior and constituted restraint of trade. With *U.S. v. Paramount Pictures* just around the corner, this would not be the last time the industry would hear about violation of antitrust laws. But this early salvo in the war that ultimately divorced the producer-distributors from their affiliated theater chains was the end of Hollywood's serious legal opposition to the doubling and tripling of its features in the marketplace. While the industry would continue to conduct audience polls that indicated public opposition to multiple features (but that were contradicted by the successful audience-drawing power of such features) and producers would continue to publicly rail against the double-feature evil, the film community had resigned itself to the situation. By this time, some of the big five, particularly Warner Brothers and Fox, were profitably exploiting the double-feature practice with their own "B" picture production units. With multiple features established as a permanent part of the exhibition landscape, and with little room left in the expanded program schedules for two-reel comedies, Roach decided to end short subject production at his studio.[19]

Sennett, Christie, and Educational

Hal Roach was not the only independent producer of short comedies to wrestle with the new economic realities of the 1930s, but he was the only one to survive the decade. Sennett, Christie, and Educational faced the same set of problems and attempted some of the same strategies as Roach. Their failure illustrates what could well have happened to Roach had his circumstances been somewhat different.

As early as 1931, Earle Hammons of Educational Pictures decried the double feature as "a dangerous substitute for the well-balanced program."[20] At the same time, both Educational and Mack Sennett began attempting to diversify their output by including feature production in their schedules. Educational achieved brief success by merging two poverty-row producers, Tiffany and World Wide, under its management.[21]

Sennett entered the talkie era in a greatly weakened condition, with Andy Clyde and Marjorie Beebe as his major stars. He had left Pathé in 1928, a year after Roach, and had been releasing his product through Educational's exchanges. Sennett was able to claim distinction as the only independent comedy producer of the period to produce and release some of his shorts in color. Although he, like Roach, had produced silent features on an irregular basis (see appendix 2, synopsis 23), Sennett's entry into the feature race of the early 1930s consisted of a single film, *Hypnotized,* starring a pair of Amos and Andy–style white comics in blackface named Moran and Mack.[22] By the time the film went into release through Earle Hammons's World Wide in the autumn of 1932, Sennett had left Educational and joined Paramount.

The Sennett-Paramount combination, an alliance that had been rumored in the mid-1920s, thus sparking the Roach-MGM partnership, resulted in a substantial improvement in the Sennett product. The 1932–33 season saw Sennett produce a series of comedies with up-and-coming crooner Bing Crosby, as well as four now-legendary shorts starring W. C. Fields. However, Paramount experienced severe financial difficulties during the first half of the 1930s and, in the midst of corporate reorganization, declined to renew its distribution pact with Sennett beyond the single year.[23] This breakup proved fatal to the Sennett studio, which was unable to find a new distributor for its product. Mack Sennett, Inc., was automatically declared bankrupt in Los Angeles federal court at the end of 1933; Sennett had failed to even respond to the complaint filed by his creditors.[24] In early 1935, the former Sennett studio plant in North Hollywood was sold to Nat Levine, whose Mascot Pictures had been leasing the facility during the previous year. Within a short time, after a series of mergers, the studio became Republic Pictures, which proceeded to crank out matinee westerns and serials at the old Sennett factory for the next two decades.[25]

The Christie studio began releasing its product through Paramount in 1927, when the latter was unable to come to terms with Sennett. The Christie-Paramount association was short-lived, with Paramount rapidly forming its own short-subject production unit, and by 1930 Christie, like Sennett, was releasing its output through Educational. By 1933, Al Christie had folded his production company into Educational and spent the rest of the 1930s as a short-comedy producer at Educational and Columbia.[26]

Things were moderately better at Educational Pictures. Educational's distribution branch had faced increasingly stiff competition once the majors became involved in short-subject distribution. The studio's response was to sell its distribution and film exchange operations to Fox Films in 1933 and to begin releasing its product through Fox.[27] Buoyed by this major-studio affiliation, Educational announced (as did Roach) that the 1934–35 season would see a 20 percent increase in short subject negative costs in an effort to improve the production values of the films.[28] At Educational, part of that upgrade program included a series of shorts that starred Buster Keaton, the first American films for the legendary comedian since the collapse of his career and his dismissal by MGM in 1933. From March 1934 until March 1937, Keaton starred in sixteen Educational short subjects. However, something else occurred in the 1934–35 season that was to add yet another wrinkle to the already complicated situation for Roach and Educational: Columbia Pictures reorganized its short subject department to favor the production of two-reel comedies. As one of the little three, Columbia had nothing to lose by trying to explore any aspect of the business that the majors generally ignored. (Of the big five, only RKO, the least secure of the lot, produced two-reel comedies on a long-term basis.)

The first season of Columbia shorts featured Harry Langdon and Andy Clyde, both hired away from Educational, and the Three Stooges, who arrived from MGM. The shorts were popular and, perhaps more important, cheap to produce. The studio rushed the pictures through production in as little as three days, compared with the usual two or more weeks per short at Roach. In addition, studio overhead costs could be spread over more productions, including features. The Columbia short comedies appropriated the Sennett roughhouse tradition (and several of Sennett's employees) after the latter's bankruptcy. While the successful entry of Columbia into the two-reel comedy business would play a major role in driving independent producers from the field, the Columbia shorts unit itself was to keep the theatrical two-reel comedy alive for another two decades, with the final Columbia two-reelers going into distribution in the summer of 1959.

Educational finally lost its uphill battle at the end of the 1937–38 season, when Twentieth Century–Fox decided that it would no longer distribute the former's shorts. Citing "little or no market for two-reel shorts because of dual bills," Fox announced that it would commence production of its own one-reel shorts for the 1938–39 season.[29] In September 1938, Earle Hammons assumed presidency of the New Grand National studio, a combination of the Educational assets and those of Grand National, an independent feature producer that had achieved brief notoriety by luring James Cagney away from Warner Brothers.[30] After two mediocre pictures for Grand National, Cagney was back at Warners', and Grand National was facing extreme financial distress. The new setup with Hammons was designed to bail out the feature production program while providing an outlet for shorts to be produced by the former Educational staff. Hammons was unable to raise adequate funds for the venture, however, and in early 1940 the Educational interests filed for voluntary bankruptcy.[31] Nearly a year later, Hammons announced plans to produce a series of features,[32] but, instead, by mid-1942 he was producing a wartime series of short subjects entitled Hands of Victory for distribution as part of Paramount's Headliners series.[33]

The failure of Sennett, Christie, and Educational underscores the dire situation for independent short-comedy producers in the 1930s. Roach survived the early 1930s largely because his three strongest short series, Laurel and Hardy, Our Gang, and Chase, had greater box office appeal than the series of his rivals, which tended to feature faded silent comics (Buster Keaton, Lloyd Hamilton) or newcomers who had not yet reached their potential (Bing Crosby, Shirley Temple). The new performers who demonstrated real talent were typically lured away by the bigger salaries of the major studios before they could develop into box office attractions for the short-comedy studios. Even with a lineup that was superior to those of his rivals, however, Roach could not have remained in business through the decade had he not converted to feature production. The independently produced two-reel comedy was on its way out.

Roach's Conversion from Shorts to Features

In light of the extremely rough going for his competitors, Roach should have been doubly grateful for his strong alliance with the financially secure MGM and his possession of the feature-worthy Laurel and Hardy franchise. After the successful completion of the fifth Laurel and Hardy feature, *Babes in Toyland* (1934), Roach, possibly using the continuation of Laurel and Hardy and Our Gang as leverage, was able to persuade MGM to permit him to produce a non–Laurel and Hardy comedy feature, designated as an All-Star Comedy Feature, in addition to two Laurel and Hardy features and a schedule of thirty-two short films.[34] The feature film, entitled *Vagabond Lady* (1935), borrowed Robert Young from MGM as the lead and was generally considered a lackluster "B" picture.

The 1935–36 season, the second year MGM permitted Roach to make an All Star feature and the season that brought the court decision affirming the right of exhibitors to double and triple features, was to be the last year of full-tilt short-comedy production at the Hal Roach Studios. The studio entered the season with only three short series: Our Gang, Charley Chase, and Todd-Kelly. Laurel and Hardy had made their last starring Roach short during the previous season and were now committed completely to the production of features. The All-Star short series had been retired during the 1934–35 season after the Irvin S. Cobb fiasco.

In February 1936, Roach and MGM agreed that of the remaining three short series, only the Our Gang comedies would continue in production for the 1936–37 season, and that these films would be reduced to a single reel (ten minutes) in length.[35] The Todd-Kelly series was already at an end due to the mysterious death in December 1935 of Thelma Todd. Found in her locked garage behind the wheel of her automobile, the coroner determined cause of death to be due to accidental inhalation of carbon monoxide, although theories and rumors involving suicide and murder began circulating immediately and continue to this day. The last Todd-Kelly short, *The All-American Toothache,* was released in January 1936. To fulfill MGM's distribution obligations for the series, Roach produced three Patsy Kelly shorts, one teaming her with Pert Kelton and the other two featuring Lyda Roberti. As for Kelly, her numerous supporting roles in non-Roach films in the 1930s assured her a place in the new feature scheme at the Hal Roach Studios (see appendix 2, synopsis 24).

A Roach fixture since 1923, the Chase short series was starting to wear thin with audiences, as confirmed by the format tinkering of the early 1930s. Thus it seemed unlikely that Chase, who was beset by illness and an unhappy personal life, would evolve into a feature star. Roach was unwilling to carry Chase on the payroll as a supporting player in the All-Star features, despite his valuable supporting performances in Laurel and Hardy's fourth feature, *Sons of the Desert* (1934), and in the third All-Star feature, *Kelly the Second* (1936). Hence, Chase's days at the Roach studio were numbered. Perhaps out of a sense of obligation to his longtime employee, Roach permitted Chase a final chance to fit into the new production schedule by allowing him to make a pilot feature without MGM's knowledge. The film was basically an expanded version of one of Chase's last silent shorts, *Movie Night* (1929), but this new version, entitled *It Happened One Bank Night*, ran into immediate trouble. First, Bank Night, a giveaway promotional gimmick used by many theaters nationwide to boost patronage, was a registered trademark of Affiliated Enterprises, and the owners threatened to sue the studio for the unauthorized use of their name and idea.[36] Next, the Production Code Administration notified the studio that scenes of tommy gun–toting gangsters would have to be cut, as machine guns in the hands of criminals were no longer permitted onscreen.[37] Finally, Roach's contract with MGM did not specifically permit a feature starring Chase. While MGM was happy to have Chase included in the cast of an All-Star feature, selling MGM on a feature headed by Chase would be difficult. Although Roach was willing to undertake this task—he had done so with Laurel and Hardy's first starring feature and would do the same again on other occasions—the problems associated with this film were simply too great. Recut into a two-reel short and retitled *The Neighborhood House* (1936), this became the last entry in the Charley Chase series for the Hal Roach Studios.

The *Hollywood Reporter* of June 1, 1936, announced that Chase and Roach had made a friendly settlement of the former's contract, ending "one of the longest associations of actor and producer in the picture business."[38] The same publication carried a full-page ad that simply read, "Thank you Hal Roach for a wonderful engagement that lasted over seventeen years. Charley Chase . . . I knew I shouldn't have cleaned up that dressing room."[39] Upon his departure from Roach, Chase returned to his theatrical roots and embarked on a vaudeville tour in the summer of 1936. At his first engagement, the Palace Theatre in Cleveland, Ohio, Chase received a word of encouragement from his longtime professional home: "Hope you open your tour with a bang and end in a blaze of glory. Best Wishes, Hal Roach Studios, Inc."[40] Having said that, the studio forces must have realized the irony in the situation that developed after the release of the third All-Star feature, *Kelly the Second,* in which Patsy Kelly was supported by Chase. Commenting on the film's poor box office drawing power, one Pittsburgh exhibitor found a silver lining in the fact that the film was being backed up, at his theater, by "a very fine stage show headed by CHARLIE [*sic*] CHASE."[41] Perhaps Roach had kept the wrong player on the payroll after all. The 1937–38 movie season found Chase making two-reelers once again, this time at Columbia, after an absence from the screen of one year. This series continued until Chase's death at the age of forty-six in the summer of 1940.

With the Chase and Todd-Kelly series finished, Hal Roach embarked on a features-only policy, with the exception of the abbreviated Our Gang shorts, beginning with the 1936–37 movie season. The Roach-MGM feature distribution contract for that year called for Roach to produce five features along the following lines: two standard Laurel and Hardy pictures; a third Laurel and Hardy film in which they would be supported by Jack Haley (on loan from Fox), Patsy Kelly, and Pert Kelton; one Kelly and Kelton feature; and one Haley comedy. The films were to be furnished to MGM for distribution at the rate of one every ten weeks.[42] The actual release schedules and casts were shifted somewhat before the product reached theater screens, but the season would ultimately prove auspicious for the new studio direction.

It did not start out well, however. Although MGM publicly claimed that it did not handle the lower-budgeted B-class features, Roach's four previous non–Laurel and Hardy features for MGM had been considered "B" pictures. With the new contract, Roach officially entered the ranks of "A" productions. The first of these was *Pick a Star,* the film that was originally announced as a Laurel and Hardy starring feature with Jack Haley and Patsy Kelly in support but that actually turned out to be exactly the opposite, with Laurel and Hardy's participation reduced to a ten-minute guest-starring spot. The resulting film did poorly at the box office (see appendix 2, synopsis 25).[43]

Happily, the disappointments surrounding this first "A" picture would be offset by the third All-Star picture of the season, a film about a pair of mischievous ghosts wreaking havoc on the well-ordered life of a staid, middle-aged banker named Cosmo Topper. *Topper* (1937) was an A-class picture all the way, with a top-rank cast headed by Cary Grant, Constance Bennett, and Roland Young; capable direction by comedy veteran Norman Z. McLeod; and an enthusiastic young producer, Roach newcomer Milton Bren. Considering the influx of new talent onto the lot for *Topper,* it is noteworthy that the film's remarkable special effects were achieved by Roach veteran Roy Seawright, who had been responsible for animating superimposed soap bubbles, bumblebees, and the like on the studio's short comedies since the silent days.

In shifting his studio from shorts to features, Hal Roach was well aware of the need to bring in knowledgeable unit producers to guide the day-to-day progress of individual pictures while he retained ultimate control over the entire studio operation and, if necessary, veto power over his producers. In Bren, Roach had found a capable producer whose ideas about comedy seemed to be in happy synchronization with his own, and *Topper* was the result. A literary property that had appealed to Roach and that had been purchased by the studio before Bren joined the staff, *Topper*, as guided to the screen under Bren's supervision, propelled the Hal Roach Studios into a position that, to many observers, seemed not far removed from the ranks of Samuel Goldwyn and David O. Selznick. As the *Motion Picture Herald* noted in early 1938,

> Not so long ago Mr. Roach seemed firmly cast forever in the category of the two part comedy producer, deep rooted in the traditions of an art of yesterday.
>
> Today he is to be discovered full-fledged and sure handedly engaged in first rank feature production, and production of a type unburdened of reminiscence. This constitutes a performance with few, if any, parallels in the annals of Hollywood. Few have had the elastic capacity.[44]

However, apart from *Topper*, Roach's non–Laurel and Hardy features proved to be inconsistent box office performers. Hence the Roach-MGM distribution agreement for 1937–38 included a rather disturbing clause. Although it increased to six (from the five of the previous season) the number of features MGM would be willing to accept from Roach, two Laurel and Hardy features and four All Star musical comedies, the contract stated that MGM reserved the right to cancel the last two musical comedies if the first of the group was not doing well three months after its release.[45] Although the first two musicals were guaranteed, along with the two Laurel and Hardys and the twelve Our Gang one-reelers, the prospect of losing any ground at this point was not acceptable to Roach. Far from retreating, in fact, Roach was drawing up plans for three feature production units, one for Laurel and Hardy, one to be headed by Bren, and a third under the supervision of former Roach employee-made-good Leo McCarey.[46] Regardless of MGM's dictates and despite McCarey taking a more lucrative offer from RKO, Roach would not be deterred from his shot at the major leagues of production; the goal of being a respected feature producer had been his dream since the days of Rolin. Suddenly, an opportunity seemed certain to make that dream a reality.

United Artists had been formed in 1919 by Charlie Chaplin, Douglas Fairbanks, Mary Pickford, and D. W. Griffith as a distribution outlet for their independently produced films. By the late 1930s, the company was handling the product of David O. Selznick, Samuel Goldwyn, Alexander Korda, and Walter Wanger. And now UA wanted Roach. In the spring of 1938, United Artists' president and leading motion picture financier A. H.

Giannini personally offered Roach a distribution contract that promised a larger percentage of box office gross and the ability to produce more films than MGM was willing to accept.[47] Roach found UA's offer compelling. He voluntarily canceled the last two All-Star musicals under the 1937–38 MGM distribution agreement, rushed the last two Laurel and Hardy films owed to Metro through production, and sold the entire Our Gang production company, actor contracts and all, to MGM. MGM would continue to produce the Our Gang one-reelers until 1944. As for Roach, he was happily embarking on what had every appearance of being the pinnacle of his career as a filmmaker.

Dwight Whiting *(left)*, Dan Linthicum, and Hal Roach prematurely celebrating the Sawyer distribution deal, 1915. (Bison Archives)

Lonesome Luke *(right)*, looking his most Chaplinesque, with Snub Pollard, 1916. (Bison Archives)

Clarine Seymour *(left),* Arnold "Toto" Novello, Hal Roach, Harold Lloyd, and Bebe Daniels outside the Bradbury mansion, 1917. (Bison Archives)

Pathé trade advertisement promoting Harold Lloyd's new character, 1918. The ad obviously refers to Chaplin and his trademark mustache. (Collection of the author)

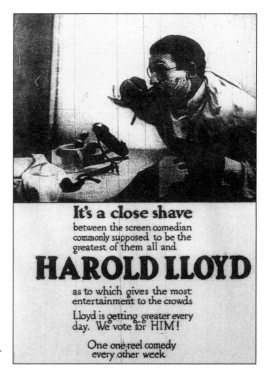

It's a close shave between the screen comedian commonly supposed to be the greatest of them all and

HAROLD LLOYD

as to which gives the most entertainment to the crowds

Lloyd is getting greater every day. We vote for HIM!

One one-reel comedy every other week

Pathé trade advertisement promoting the Snub Pollard–Ernie Morrison series. "These comedies start something with 'Start Something,'" October 26, 1919. (Collection of the author)

The alpha and the omega. The Hal Roach Studios administration building going up in 1920 *(top)* and about to come down in 1963 *(bottom)*. (Bison Archives)

Hal Roach's office, which reflected his love of the rugged West, 1926. (Bison Archives)

Between the Vanity Fair Girls and director Fred Newmeyer, there seems to be little room on the bus for series star Eddie Boland, 1921. (Bison Archives)

The Dippy Doo Dads, 1923. (Bison Archives)

Series star Will Rogers *(left)* sharing Hal Roach's passion for polo, 1924. (Bison Archives)

Glenn Tryon, who was no Harold Lloyd. (Bison Archives)

Theda Bara and director Richard Wallace on the set of *Madame Mystery*, 1926. (Bison Archives)

Our Gang, circa 1923. Pictured *(from left)* are Allen "Farina" Hoskins, Mary Kornman, Mickey Daniels, Joe Cobb, Ernie "Sunshine Sammy" Morrison, and Jackie Condon. (Bison Archives)

Our Gang, circa 1930, preparing to shoot a Spanish-language version of one of their shorts. The gang members *(from left)* are Mary Ann Jackson, Pete the Pup, Bobby "Wheezer" Hutchins, Allen "Farina" Hoskins, Norman "Chubby" Chaney, and Jackie Cooper. (Bison Archives)

Charley Chase outside the studio administration building. (Bison Archives)

Hal Roach (left) conferring with the production chief, Louis B. Mayer, of "that other" Culver City studio, MGM. (Bison Archives)

Hal Roach and Mary Kornman *(center)* on the set of the last Boyfriends short, *Wild Babies.*
The "explorers" *(in headgear)* flanking the group are Charley Hall *(left)* and Charles Rogers,
1932. (Bison Archives)

Irvin S. Cobb *(left)* wondering why audiences aren't laughing, 1934. Hal Roach seems to know.
(Bison Archives)

Oliver Hardy *(left)* in a creative dispute with producer A. Edward Sutherland on the set of *Zenobia*, 1939. (Bison Archives)

D. W. Griffith *(right)* chatting with Adolphe Menjou and Joan Bennett between takes of *The Housekeeper's Daughter*, 1939. (Bison Archives)

Hal Roach *(center)* directing *One Million B.C.*, 1939. Lon Chaney Jr. is to the right. (Bison Archives)

They weren't Laurel and Hardy, but the service comedies of William Tracy and Joe Sawyer were Roach's most popular attraction of the "streamliner" era. (Collection of the author)

Hal Roach Jr. *(right)* visiting the set of his most popular television series, *The Stu Erwin Show.* Stu Erwin is on the left. (Bison Archives)

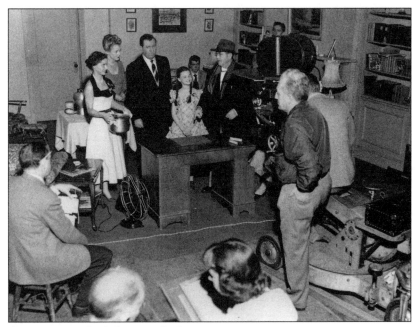

Shooting an episode of *The Stu Erwin Show.* (Bison Archives)

Hal Roach Studios' past meeting
its present in 1954. Stan Laurel
(left) and Oliver Hardy *(right)*
pose with *My Little Margie* stars
Charles Farrell and Gale Storm.
(Bison Archives)

Hal Roach Sr. at one hundred in
1992. (Photo courtesy of Richard W. Bann)

7

From "A" Pictures to Streamliners, 1938-42

In the late 1930s, the administration building at the Hal Roach Studios underwent a major renovation. The mission styling was removed from the roof, and the ivy, which had spread to cover the entire face of the building, was pulled down. The homey, single-level veranda at the entrance made way for a more formal and imposing two-story portico. The result was a more contemporary appearance, with clean lines replacing quaintly graceful curves. In the process of modernization, the building's original charm was completely stripped away. Unfortunately, the same thing was about to happen to the studio's output.

Hal Roach had always had a strong and adventuresome entrepreneurial spirit, as his founding of the Rolin studio on meager capital resources had demonstrated. During the 1920s and 1930s, Roach flirted with diversification by buying a downtown Los Angeles Chevrolet dealership, by becoming a partner in a local jewelry store (Roach and Driver), and on a grander scale, by founding and becoming the first president of the Los Angeles Turf Club, an organization that owned and operated the Santa Anita Racetrack. An interesting footnote to this last operation was the inclusion of Dwight Whiting on the club board of directors more than a decade after his unceremonious departure from Rolin.

Roach's entrepreneurial spirit perhaps blinded his judgment when, in October 1937, he announced that he was forming an American-Italian film production partnership with Vittorio Mussolini, son of the Italian dictator Benito Mussolini. The new company, to be called RAM Pictures (for *Roach and Mussolini*), would "produce motion-picture operas with Italian talent and American technique."[1] Roach found himself an outcast in Hollywood for his affiliation with the Fascist Italian government, a situation that was aggravated when he assured a reporter that while he would not tolerate any attempts to propagandize the RAM productions, the prospect of government interference was moot because "Benito Mussolini is the only square politician I've ever seen."[2] Furthermore, in light of recent policies implemented by the Italian government designed to restrict, if not to completely eliminate, Hollywood productions from Italian cinema screens, Roach's planned partnership was seen by many as breaking ranks with the American film industry and collaborating with the enemy. The death knell for RAM was sounded only one week after the venture hit the trade press. Dr. Renato Senise, an Italian citizen who claimed that the partnership and production scheme had been his idea and that he had been eliminated from the setup despite early contractual assurances that he would be included in the business, filed a breach of contract suit against Roach and MGM.[3] Although this suit ultimately failed, this new embarrassment in Roach's relationship with MGM was the last straw. Only two weeks after the initial grand publicity splash that had announced RAM's birth, a Roach spokesman responded to a reporter's question about the venture with a simple question of his own: "Why bring up a dying duck?" In a settlement that appears to have been mediated by MGM, Roach paid Vittorio Mussolini and his production company, Era, five hundred thousand lire to get out of his contractual obligations and to reimburse Era for its preproduction expenses on what was to have been the first RAM picture, *Rigoletto.*[4]

In a similarly entrepreneurial spirit, Hal Roach's distribution agreement with United Artists in May 1938 held the promise of greater operational freedom than had been possible during his eleven-year association with MGM. No longer would the Roach organization be an oddball independent that had to beg Loew's permission for every feature production and to rely on the long-running and immensely popular Laurel and Hardy and Our Gang series for negotiating leverage. Although UA did request that the Laurel and Hardy series be continued, the Roach Studios would otherwise be permitted at last to shed its slapstick comedy origins and enter the glamorous world of A-picture production on a full-time basis.

Under the terms of the contract, Roach was to deliver to United Artists four to six pictures annually, in black and white or color, with running times of at least one hour. The contract specified that the films were to be of a type "in vogue in first-class theaters in the United States."[5] In addition to these films, Roach would produce up to four pictures per year that starred Laurel and Hardy, bringing to ten the annual total number of Roach features that United Artists was willing to accept, an increase of four over the last distribution contract with MGM and minus the troubling cancellation clause for non–Laurel and Hardy features in the event of poor box office performance.[6]

One significant difference between the MGM and UA distribution agreements involved production financing. While MGM had provided Roach with production advances after 1929, Roach was obligated to arrange his own financing for his UA productions, a situation that would soon place the studio deeply in debt. Roach's share of the domestic U.S. profits from films distributed by United Artists would be 75 percent, as opposed to the 70 percent he was getting from MGM. His Canadian share would be 70 percent, the same as with MGM, but the share on British profits would rise from the 65 percent in the MGM contract to 70 percent. The European and Asian share would actually drop slightly, from 65 percent to 62½ percent, but given the tense international situation of 1938 and with the outbreak of World War II slightly more than a year away, this choice did not turn out to have been a poor one. The United Artists distribution contract was to take effect upon the fulfillment of Roach's current commitment to MGM, to be concluded no later than January 1, 1939, and would run until September 2, 1945.

Ending the long-term relationship with MGM proved relatively easy. In May 1938, Roach still owed MGM one Laurel and Hardy feature (of a promised two) and two All-Star musical comedies (of four) under the 1937–38 distribution agreement. As MGM had never been especially happy with the All-Star films (with the exception of *Topper*), it readily released Roach from his obligation to deliver the remaining All-Stars. MGM did, however, insist on delivery of the final Laurel and Hardy film and further stipulated that Roach was not to place any additional Laurel and Hardy features into distribution for a period of three months after handing this final feature over to MGM.[7] The last Hal Roach–MGM feature, Laurel and Hardy's *Block-Heads,* was released on August 19, 1938.[8]

The final matter of business between Roach and MGM was the disposition of the Our Gang series. Even in the face of declining returns in the short film market, this series had remained profitable in its one-reel form, and MGM had insisted that Roach continue its production after the 1936 termination of all other short film production at the Roach lot. The solution found in the Roach-MGM contract dissolution, again, was a simple one. MGM itself had been engaged in short comedy production since the early 1930s, and by 1938 its one-reel output included the highly popular Robert Benchley and Pete Smith series. With a proven short-subject production unit in place, MGM saw no problem in assuming production responsibilities for Our Gang from Roach. For twenty-five thousand dollars, Roach sold MGM the contracts of the Our Gang cast members along with exclusive rights to the Our Gang name. Roach agreed to refrain from producing any films, in either short or feature form, that were "of the same or competitive nature" as Our Gang or to use any of the Our Gang actors in any film. Furthermore, Roach was forbidden from reissuing any of his old Our Gang pictures or reusing any of the old Our Gang story lines in any new film without first obtaining the express written permission of MGM.[9] These stipulations would prove troublesome after the advent of television.

For its part, MGM released Roach from his obligation to deliver the final two (of twelve) Our Gang shorts for the 1937–38 season. MGM further agreed that if it decided at any point to discontinue the production of Our Gang shorts, it would inform Roach four months in advance and give him the option of resuming production of the series at that time, although if he declined to exercise his option, the exclusive rights to Our Gang would remain with MGM.[10]

With the arrangements for his departure from MGM complete, Roach was ready to pursue a bright and glorious future as one of the elite UA producers—a group that included David O. Selznick, Samuel Goldwyn, Alexander Korda, and Walter Wanger. Yet Hal Roach's anticipated ascension to the industry status of major independent wasn't to be.

In the first place, United Artists was, at that historical moment, in the midst of a serious crisis. In fact, the major reason that Roach had been lured into the UA fold, a more lucrative profit split than he had received from MGM, had only recently been implemented by United Artists in the very hopes of attracting new producers and, hence, new product to prop up UA's failing fortunes.[11] Unfortunately, as Tino Balio noted, many of these new producers were "far below the company's previous standards."[12] UA's most prestigious producers had tired of the company's sloppy business practices and, as summarized by Balio, "the bizarre behavior of the owners [Chaplin, Pickford], which not only demeaned the principles on which the company was based [quality distribution for independent filmmakers] but also prevented it from attracting a steady flow of quality product on a par with

Goldwyn's."[13] Specifically, the original UA founder-producers refused to permit the company's active breadwinning producers from assuming full partnership status in the firm. Within three years after Roach became a United Artists producer, the company crisis reached its apex. Goldwyn left the firm in disgust, convinced that too great a percentage of the profits from his films was ending up in the bank accounts of UA's inactive producer-owners. A deal that would have brought Frank Capra into the company fell through because, in Capra's words, "despite the fact that I have bought at considerable expense three stories which were to be my first three pictures for United Artists . . . it was almost impossible to meet the people who were to be my future partners."[14] Of the other major UA producers of 1941, as recorded in an unusually disparaging historical summary in the 1946 company stock report, "Mr. Korda had completed his commitments and was already looking to new pastures. Mr. Selznick had not commenced to produce and Mr. [Edward] Small, who had numerically given the company most of its product in 1941, had decided to sit down and rest."[15] The product from the remaining producers, the report complained, came in such a sporadic and unreliable flow that, to cite the worst case example, United Artists had no major releases from Labor Day 1943 until New Year's Day 1944.

Several factors were responsible for United Artists' quandary. First, since it owned no theaters, it depended on theaters owned or controlled by the major studios for exhibition, a problem also faced by Columbia, Universal, and a host of minor studios. This dependence often resulted in the films being booked in some of the less desirable venues of the major chains, being shown at slow times of the year, or being scheduled as the bottom half of a double bill, with the top-billed feature receiving the major portion of the box office take. Beyond this problem, however, United Artists encountered difficulties unique in the industry, owing to its corporate structure. As a releasing company for an assortment of independent producers, United Artists management had no control over the quantity, quality, or content of the films it released within any given year. Unlike every other company in the industry, United Artists was contractually obligated to its producers to sell each film individually, rather than in groups or packages.[16] Until block booking was outlawed in the late 1940s with the final settlement of the U.S. government's antitrust suit against the major studios, the practice was vital to the industry's distribution machinery. By tying strong and weak films together in a single sales block, Hollywood could count on some revenue from even the poorest product.

Unable to map out a coordinated program strategy for each year's product, UA simply had to take what its contributors produced, each producer working on his or her own timetable, and do its best to obtain decent bookings for the films in theaters that basically owed their first allegiance to competitors of United Artists. The enormity of trying to coordinate the releases of this unwieldy organization may be best demonstrated by a September 1941 letter from Arthur Kelly, UA vice president, to Mary Pickford, one of the original producer-owners of United Artists:

> Dear Mary:
> Last week, over the telephone, I received instructions from Mr. Raftery that the producers wanted Loew's Criterion as a high-class firstlong [sic] run Theatre and were willing to support the Theatre with GOLD RUSH, all Wanger's pictures, Ed Small's pictures, and Mr. Alexander Korda's JUNGLE BOOK. Further, I was to endeavor to secure back from the Music Hall all the pictures I had booked there and give them to Loew's Criterion. . . .
>
> After working out the preliminaries and dating the first picture, I am informed on Monday by Mr. Raftery that the producers have changed their minds as Mr. Chaplin and Mr. Korda want special terms and Mr. Chaplin wanted United Artists to lease the theatre; further, Mr. Korda stated he did not think Mr. Selznick would tie himself up to any theatre.
>
> The cancellation of these instructions has caused no end of embarrassment for me with the Loew people, to a point where they consider that we, the operators, are a lot of God damn idiots, as we never know what we want.[17]

The Roach-UA Affiliation

Although Roach was embarking on a high stakes and uncharted course (for his studio) with the move to "A" production, his attempt to shift to a unit production system and his heavy reliance on previously published, presold story properties followed two contemporary industry trends and suggest that he was well aware of the changes necessary in studio practices for the new venture to succeed. However, despite a well-reasoned approach to the production of prestige features, Roach simply lacked the financial resources necessary to pull it off. In addition, the industry-wide rush toward the production of quality pictures after the runaway success of *Gone with the Wind* (1939) turned out to be, in Thomas Schatz's words, "a misfired market strategy," resulting in a glut of expensive prestige films during a period of depressed box office returns.[18] As the revenues slowly dribbled in from United Artists and the red ink rose, Roach was forced to radically curtail his plans, having to reassume producing, and often directing, functions on his films. The "A" class freelance and loan-out stars of his early UA efforts (Fredric March, Joan and Constance Bennett) became unaffordable, and Roach was forced to cast his films with unknown newcomers (Victor Mature, Carole Landis, John Hubbard) and somewhat faded "A" leads (Adolphe Menjou, Joan Blondell). The loss of star marquee value did not help the anemic UA sales efforts on Roach's films, and the studio debt deepened.

Even before the United Artists crisis of 1941, dealings with his new distributor must have given Hal Roach a sense of déjà vu. Roach's very first UA release, *There Goes My Heart* (1938; see appendix 2, synopsis 26), brought in disappointing box office returns. Answering a studio inquiry, Roach's New York representative, Tom Walker, explained in a letter that United Artists was having difficulty selling all of its films of the 1938–39 season, a roster that included *Algiers, Drums,* and *The Cowboy and the Lady.*[19]

Despite the chronic and serious disorder within United Artists, problems that led its most gifted producers to either bolt or retire, much of the trouble encountered in selling the Hal Roach features lay with the product itself. During his affiliation with Loew's-MGM, Roach had benefited from having his features, especially the All-Stars, which lacked the Laurel and Hardy marquee value, sold in blocks with stronger MGM product. However, since United Artists did not engage in block booking, each film now had to stand on its own merits, a situation that rarely worked to Roach's best advantage.

In a statement presented at United Artists' twentieth-anniversary sales convention in New York City in June 1938, Roach shared his three secrets for producing a hit motion picture: "(1) a vital story, (2) a director particularly attuned to the complexities of the story, (3) players not chosen because of their sudden vogue or reported popularity, but rather for their outstanding ability to portray the role at hand."[20] While the last "secret" may well be considered the rationalization of a low-budget producer who was unable to afford the services of players who had experienced a "sudden vogue or reported popularity," strongly reminiscent of studio publicity in the All-Star days of the late 1920s, the first two rules may have served Roach well had he only adhered to them. As previously mentioned, a characteristic of Roach's UA feature period was a reliance on previously published material, an increasingly popular trend among studios because of the automatic advance publicity attached to a best-selling novel or a popular play. Seven of Roach's fourteen UA features were based on literary properties and an eighth, *Topper Returns* (1941), was an original story based on the characters from the two Thorne Smith *Topper* novels previously adapted into screen versions by Roach. However, Roach lacked the financial resources to compete with the major studios for the most attractive properties, forcing a selection of second-rate stories that were seldom vital and usually not very original.[21]

As to the directorial assignments, Roach's precarious financial condition prevented his hiring any truly gifted directors, with the single exception of Lewis Milestone on *Of Mice and Men* (1940). A few films were directed by competent craftsmen, such as Norman Z. McLeod (*There Goes My Heart*, 1938; *Topper Takes a Trip*, 1939), Roy Del Ruth (*Topper Returns*, 1941), and Richard Wallace (*Captain Caution*, 1940). However, the bulk of Roach's UA features were directed by Gordon Douglas (three films: *Zenobia*, 1939; *Saps at Sea*, 1940; *The Broadway Limited*, 1941) and Hal Roach (five films: *Captain Fury*, 1939; *The Housekeeper's Daughter*, 1939; *One Million B.C.*, 1940; *Turnabout*, 1940; *Road Show*, 1941). Although Douglas would have a long career as a feature director, his directorial experience prior to 1939 had been limited to short comedies (as the principal director of Our Gang from 1936 to 1938, actually continuing with the series through the first three shorts produced at MGM) and a codirecting position on *General Spanky* (a Civil War–era feature comedy with the Our Gang cast).[22] Hal Roach, on the other hand, had directed occasionally since the studio's earliest days, but he had never really distinguished himself in that arena. The films for which he received directorial credit tended to be among the studio's lesser financial performers, and there were far too many of these during this period. Employees later remembered that he had a tendency to become bored or frustrated with the slow pace of filmmaking, often leaving a production in the hands of an assistant while he attended to the larger matters of studio operation.[23] The intense business pressures on Roach during the UA period doubtless added new distractions.

Compounding the problem of poor product were losses at the production executive level. At the outset of Roach's UA period, Roach had elevated Milton Bren from associate producer to producer. In this capacity, Bren handled three of the five films Roach delivered to UA during the 1938–39 season, with the other two produced by Roach *(Captain Fury)* and free-lancer A. Edward Sutherland *(Zenobia)*. However, in March 1939, Bren left the studio to become a producer at MGM. In January 1940, studio executive Frank Ross departed—during the next two decades he would be employed as a producer at RKO, Warner Brothers, and Twentieth Century–Fox. These vacancies left the studio without any upper-level management who had a sufficient grasp of contemporary film tastes to achieve the prestigious industry position Roach desired for his studio. Although Roach's decision not to hire replacements for Bren and Ross was related to the studio's financial standing, which had already begun to decline by early 1940, it also speaks volumes about his belief in his ability to act as the studio's sole creative producer. This belief may have been unfounded: the deterioration of the company's finances accelerated during 1940, reaching a crisis point by midyear.

Roach's UA Features

Of the fourteen features completed by Roach for United Artists release between 1938 and 1941, ten were comedies (including two starring Laurel and Hardy) and four were dramas (three action-adventure pictures plus *Of Mice and Men*). Of this group, five are worth close examination, since they illustrate different aspects of the difficulties within both the Roach and UA organizations: *Of Mice and Men* (1940), which represented Roach's dramatic apex but which failed at the box office; *One Million B.C.* (1940), which illustrates the failed management-promotional tactic of attempting to "reactivate" legendary producer-director D. W. Griffith; and *Zenobia* (1939), *A Chump at Oxford* (1940), and *Saps at Sea* (1940), which as a group provide a chronicle of the demise of the long-running and consistently popular Laurel and Hardy series.

Of Mice and Men, based on the contemporary best seller by John Steinbeck and produced and directed by Lewis Milestone, was easily the most ambitious drama the studio had ever attempted, a film that might have permitted Roach to distance himself from his slapstick roots and place his studio in the ranks of the other prestigious UA producers. Interestingly enough, shortly after purchasing the screen rights to *Of Mice and Men,* Roach's New York office informed him of the availability of a brand new Steinbeck work, *The Grapes of Wrath.* Roach's representative, Grace Rosenfield, wrote that although the new book had not yet been published, she thought that it was certain to be a best seller and that Steinbeck would likely give Roach the first opportunity to buy film rights. Rosenfield's efforts were rewarded with a terse communication from Roach's secretary which said in part, "as Mr. Roach has informed you, he has no interest in it." The screen rights to *The Grapes of Wrath* were purchased shortly thereafter by Twentieth Century–Fox, which rushed the picture into production.[24]

Production on *Mice* started on August 14, 1939, and wrapped forty-six days later, with two days of pickup shot in November. Considering the rather grim nature of the story, the Production Code Administration found surprisingly little to complain about in the screenplay, cautioning only that the scenes of Curley beating Lennie should not be "too realistically brutal," and that an extreme close-up of Mae after her murder should be eliminated.[25] While Lon Chaney Jr. was the studio's first choice for the character of Lennie, with "Big Boy" Williams, Brian Donlevy, and Broderick Crawford being other considerations, Burgess Meredith was actually in eleventh place for the part of George, being preceded in the studio's preference by, among others, Franchot Tone, Humphrey Bogart, and Robert Preston.

Wishing to keep the New York office abreast of the latest news on the completed picture, which was expected to boost the studio into the upper ranks of independent production companies, Roach executive Frank Ross wrote East Coast representative Tom Walker on November 2, 1939, "Our first preview of 'Of Mice and Men' last night in Pasadena was a tremendous success. We have a great picture and one we can all be proud of."[26] The following day, another West Coast executive, Hugh Huber, echoed Ross's sentiments while adding the cautionary note, "How well it will do at the box office, of course, no one can tell, but at least it will be a good prestige picture."[27]

Industry reaction to *Of Mice and Men* was overwhelmingly positive. It became one of the ten films to be nominated for the best-picture Oscar for 1939, a year which, of course, is considered by many to be Hollywood's richest ever. Mary Pickford, whose opinion was perhaps most important of all considering her producer-owner status in United Artists, wired Roach that the picture "is another feather in the cap of United Artists."[28]

Huber's early concerns about the picture's box office viability appeared unfounded during the early limited metropolitan bookings. Ross victoriously wired east on December 26, 1939: "WELL, IT LOOKS LIKE WE'VE GOT IT. 'OF MICE AND MEN' IS DOING SMASH HIT BUSINESS." In the reverie of the moment, the studio even decided to spend additional money on the preparation of theatrical prints so that one hundred, enough for the most prestigious venues, could be printed in sepia.[29] At this point, the United Artists sales force went into action.

Ross's only misgiving about United Artists' plans for *Of Mice and Men's* New York premiere was UA's choice of theater. UA had booked the film at the Roxy; Ross considered this venue undesirable and had unsuccessfully lobbied for the Rivoli.[30] UA's approach to this important premiere run on Broadway was effectively sabotaged by Twentieth Century–Fox, which had just completed its own film version of a Steinbeck novel. Although it was completed after *Mice,* Fox was able to book *The Grapes of Wrath* into the Rivoli while simultaneously postponing the opening of *Mice* at the Roxy, a Fox-controlled theater, by pushing a line of Fox pictures in ahead of it. *Of Mice and Men* was finally permitted to open on Broadway three weeks after the premiere of *The Grapes of Wrath*.[31] By that time *Grapes* had seized considerable press attention and publicity, eclipsing *Of Mice and Men*. Despite the early critical raves and a best-picture Oscar nomination, *Of Mice and Men* was a poor box office performer. For Roach and his staff, the blame for the film's failure lay squarely with United Artists.[32]

Another Roach dramatic production from 1940, *One Million B.C.*, is noteworthy as the film that briefly brought legendary silent-film director D. W. Griffith out of forced retirement. Even though Griffith had not made a film in eight years, Roach believed that Griffith's name would add prestige and financial returns to any picture with which he was associated.[33] Roach had a tendency to cling tenaciously to certain pet ideas, even when they did not pan out after repeated attempts. The strategy of bringing faded talent out of mothballs for whatever marquee value they still held had produced mixed results at best, from the All-Star shorts of the 1920s to the films Roach made with Mabel Normand and Harry Langdon (to whom Roach gave another comeback shot in the late 1930s, to be examined shortly). Undeterred by the track record of the All-Star tactic, Roach wrote Griffith at his home in Kentucky on May 13, 1939. Addressing him as "Dear David," Roach started by reviewing the studio's proposed production schedule for the upcoming 1939–40 movie season, which already included *One Million B.C.*, then continued,

> I need help from the production side to select the proper writers, cast, etc., and to help me generally in the supervision of these [two or three] pictures.[34]

Roach's communication was extremely vague on the exact nature of the services Griffith would render, saying that they would "see how you could work into any capacity into which you would fit."[35] Obviously relishing the opportunity to return to work, Griffith answered Roach by telegram on May 22.

> LETTER RECEIVED TODAY. ACCEPT YOUR OFFER. WILL DISCUSS SALARY WHEN WE MEET. SURE WE CAN AGREE ON TERMS AS OUTLINED IN YOUR LETTER. LET ME KNOW WHEN YOU WANT ME AND I WILL LEAVE ON RECEIPT OF FARE TO AND FROM CALIFORNIA FOR WIFE AND SELF. REGARDS.[36]

Griffith arrived in Los Angeles in mid-June and by mid-August was working on preproduction for *One Million B.C.* Whether or not Roach had this assignment for Griffith in mind from the very beginning, it was a logical vehicle for the director's talents. Since the film was to be set entirely in prehistoric times, before the advent of any recognizable language, it would, in essence, be a silent (or, at least, dialogueless) picture, with the actors communicating almost exclusively through pantomime. Griffith realized that the audience would have to be coaxed into the concept and suggested the addition of a framing narrator sequence to prepare the audience for what would follow.[37] Months later, when the film was previewed, it became apparent that even the narrator wasn't enough, and a full dialogue prologue, with a group of explorers stumbling upon prehistoric cave drawings, was deemed necessary. The film, then, became something of a flashback sequence to the prologue.

In August and October, Griffith directed costume and casting tests for *One Million B.C.,* and during one of the August sessions, he shot a single test for *Of Mice and Men.*[38] Yet, regardless of any hopes that Griffith may have had for a comeback, *One Million B.C.* started under Roach's direction on November 6, 1939, and concluded on December 26, with a process and background photography unit under the direction of Hal Roach Jr. The exact extent of the production assistance Griffith provided Roach continued to be rather ill-defined, and he was stricken from the studio payroll on December 16.[39] Despite Griffith's minimal involvement with the picture, Roach still hoped to cash in on Griffith's name. A full-page ad for *One Million B.C.* in the *Hollywood Reporter* in late 1939 indicated that the film was "A D. W. Griffith Production, Directed by Hal Roach." Griffith objected to the use of his name, and when the film actually went into general release in April 1940, the published credits did not mention Griffith anywhere. Roach listed himself alone as producer and shared the directorial credit with Hal Roach Jr.[40] Like *Of Mice and Men, One Million B.C.* failed to find favor with the mass audience, although in this case the complaints tended to involve lack of any discernible plotline and poor direction. In this one instance, even Roach himself eventually conceded that the film was a dud.[41]

An examination of *Zenobia* turns the discussion to the Laurel and Hardy series, which should have been Hal Roach's most reliable breadwinner during his United Artists period. The United Artists contract had called for up to four Laurel and Hardy features per year, and the trade paper ads from June 1938 that announced the coming season's UA product confirmed Roach's intention to produce all four.[42] However, in August the long-simmering dispute between Roach and Stan Laurel over salary and creative control boiled over. Laurel refused to return to the studio for retakes on *Block-Heads,* the final Laurel and Hardy comedy for MGM, and Roach placed him on four-weeks suspension without pay, "postponing" the start of production on the first Laurel and Hardy film for United Artists.[43] Then, the *Motion Picture Herald* of August 20 carried the story that Roach was suing Laurel for breach of contract and was replacing the Laurel and Hardy films with a series that would team Hardy with Harry Langdon.[44]

While this move seemed reminiscent of Roach's bluff about a Hardy Family series during Laurel's 1935 walkout, all indications were that Roach sincerely meant to carry out his stated intentions this time. Langdon had finally taken to heart the lessons of his fall from stardom and the subsequent decade of appearing in demeaning, low-budget shorts, and had become known by the late 1930s as a cooperative and eager worker, a complete reversal of his reputation of ten years earlier. His cameo at the end of *There Goes My Heart,* his work on the screenplay of *Block-Heads,* and more than a passing resemblance between his screen persona and that of Laurel suggested to Roach that he could simultaneously dispose of the troublesome Laurel situation and give a repentant Langdon another chance at stardom.

That the animosity between Roach and Laurel was mutual was confirmed by a trade press story in mid-September, which announced that Mack Sennett would resume production with a new company, Senate Pictures Corporation, with Laurel as his star. The first film from the new company was to be appropriately entitled *Problem Child,* and in it Laurel would play the son of two midgets. Not coincidentally, the associate producer of *Problem Child* was to be Jed Buell, the producer of the infamous all-midget western *The Terror of Tiny Town.*[45] Unfortunately, given the intriguing premise of the film, the trade story was to be the first and last ever heard of *Problem Child.* As Laurel sat idle, Roach pressed on with the production of *Zenobia,* starring Hardy and Langdon.

When *Zenobia* was ready for theatrical release, Roach booked Hardy for an appearance on Jack Haley's Wonder Bread radio program to plug the new picture. On March 31, 1939, the day of the radio show, Laurel telegraphed Hardy, "Will be listening and wishing you loads of success. Yours as ever."[46] While the sentiment was undoubtedly sincere, Laurel addressed the telegram to the studio rather than to Hardy's home. This may well have been intended as an olive branch for Roach, an indirect message that the "problem child" wanted to come home.

In the meantime, Roach had a new problem child of his own, namely, *Zenobia.* The film was not simply a Laurel and Hardy picture without Laurel. As an elaborate costume piece, it bore little resemblance to most of the Laurel and Hardy vehicles. Hardy's character and appearance as well were quite different from that of "Ollie" (see appendix 2, synopsis 27).

Whether the Hardy and Langdon team would have succeeded with straight Laurel and Hardy material can never be known, but the end result of the *Zenobia* strategy was a box office disaster. United Artists had difficulties even booking the film into theaters.[47] The problem with *Zenobia* was best summed up in England, where the reviewer for the *Daily Mirror* observed that "Hardy without Laurel is like *Hamlet* without the prince."[48]

Fortunately for all concerned, the prince returned. In mid-May, the motion picture trade press carried the announcement that Laurel and Hardy would reunite at Roach in a series of four pictures during the following season.[49] Laurel's period of unemployment had convinced him that he needed Hardy and, for the time being, Roach as well. As for Langdon, despite a charming performance in *Zenobia*, his acting career remained stuck in low gear. Until his death in 1944, he would continue to alternate between starring in cheap short comedies and playing supporting roles in low-budget features. At least Laurel apparently bore him no ill will for having "borrowed" his partner; Langdon contributed to the screenplays of the next three Laurel and Hardy pictures.

Only one slight wrinkle complicated the resumption of Laurel and Hardy pictures at Hal Roach Studios. Ever since Laurel and Hardy began working at the studio, as solo players and at different times, Roach had kept each under contracts as separate performers rather than as a team. Since these contracts invariably came up for renewal at different times, the situation had worked somewhat to Roach's advantage, making it difficult for the team to leave the studio as a unit to seek employment elsewhere, a fact that had been one of the running disagreements between himself and Laurel. By the time of Laurel's suspension, he was on a multiple-picture contract, still owing Roach four films, while Hardy was still on a straight-term contract with several years remaining. Part of Laurel's strategy during his layoff from Roach, which at the time seemed permanent, was to wait out the time remaining in Hardy's contract and reunite with him elsewhere when he was free from Roach. To that end, Laurel began discussions with other producers regarding future Laurel and Hardy films. The conversations with Boris Morros, a former Broadway producer and film composer who had decided to enter independent film production, were so promising that Laurel contracted for the team to appear in Morros's inaugural picture, despite his then impending reconciliation with Roach.

Surprisingly, Roach was not at all resistant to the idea of the reunited Laurel and Hardy doing a film away from his lot. Beyond seeking to placate Laurel and thus, hopefully, secure a long and tranquil association with the team after the Morros picture was finished, Roach stood to profit from the loan-out of several contract employees, including Hardy, screenwriters Charles Rogers and Langdon, and even Laurel and Hardy cameraman Art Lloyd. United Artists, on the other hand, objected strenuously to the deal, protesting that their contract with Roach had assured them exclusive rights to Laurel and Hardy.[50] Undoubtedly making the situation doubly irksome to UA executives was the fact that Morros would release his film through RKO, which was becoming a popular distributor for producers who had defected from United Artists. Roach's response, perhaps taking a page from Goldwyn, was that a good "outside" Laurel and Hardy picture could only enhance the UA-distributed Laurel and Hardys to come. Besides, Roach continued, *A Chump at Oxford,* the first of the Laurel and Hardy films for United Artists, would be ready for distribution before the completion of the Morros picture, entitled *The Flying Deuces.*

While Roach was proved wrong on the last point, with circumstances that delayed the release of *A Chump at Oxford, The Flying Deuces* was a popular success that considerably boosted Laurel and Hardy's stock with the public. Under the direction of A. Edward Sutherland, a veteran comedy director who had been Roach's producer on the unfortunate *Zenobia, Deuces* provided Laurel and Hardy with exactly the vehicle they needed for a return after more than a year's absence from the screen.

The circumstance that had permitted *The Flying Deuces* to beat *A Chump at Oxford* to the theaters had to do with film length. As previously discussed, in his quest of the early 1930s to differentiate his product from the short subjects of other producers, Roach had experimented with comedies that ran three reels, one reel longer than the standard length of short comedies. One Laurel and Hardy film of 1931, *Beau Hunks,* actually ran four reels. While three- and four-reel short subjects were not exactly popular with theater managers, who were seeking to reduce rather than expand the amount of time devoted to shorts so that they could show a second feature, and even though *Beau Hunks* was nobody's idea of the perfect Laurel and Hardy film, Roach was convinced that forty minutes was the ideal length for Laurel and Hardy. At forty minutes, he reasoned, Laurel and Hardy featurettes could be booked as the second half of a double feature for better rental fees than those commanded by shorts, while, at the same time, they would be short enough not to have to resort to dramatic padding, musical numbers, or romantic subplots. The problem with this theory was that it ignored certain realities. The public and exhibitors alike seemed perfectly pleased with Laurel and Hardy at one-hour feature length, and moreover, only a few of the team's features for Roach had resorted to the padding to which Roach took exception.

Nevertheless, as with the All-Star concept, Roach clung to his idea of forty-minute Laurel and Hardy films. In 1935 Roach announced an upcoming four-reel Laurel and Hardy picture that was subsequently shelved when Laurel staged his walkout. Now, in 1939, probably encouraged by the relatively successful MGM reissue of *Beau Hunks* in 1937, and eager to make four Laurel and Hardy films per year rather than the two that had been customary at full feature length, Roach decided that the "reunion" Laurel and Hardy films should be produced as four-reelers.

United Artists was not enthusiastic about the shorter-than-feature Laurel and Hardys but reluctantly agreed to the idea, reasoning that less was better than none at all. They did bring up a potential problem, however. Foreign markets, where Laurel and Hardy were extremely popular, had never been very receptive to short films. Thus several of the foreign-language Laurel and Hardy shorts of the early talkie era had been expanded or combined with other shorts to give them featurette length. United Artists strongly argued that even featurette length would not be adequate for the foreign markets as they existed in 1939 and insisted that Roach pad the new Laurel and Hardys to at least six reels for overseas distribution. Roach agreed, and production commenced accordingly on *A Chump at Oxford*.

By early August, however, with *A Chump at Oxford* and *The Flying Deuces* both racing to completion, each production unit trying to beat the other into distribution, the Roach staff realized that they would not be able to pad the material they had on *Chump* to a full six reels for the foreign version. Roach had little choice but to send the film back before the cameras for additional scenes. The new material, when edited, constituted a prologue that ran a full two reels, which would then be followed by the four-reeler already completed. As disjointed as this result may seem, the two reels contain some of the best material of the film and permit the duo to play a scene with longtime foil James Finlayson, who is absent from the remaining four reels. After the opening two reels, the six-reel version of *Chump* eases into a slightly expanded version of the four-reel edition, with some scenes permitted to play a bit longer than they did in the original featurette edit.

As the editing of the new material began, Roach was faced with an interesting problem. Even though he had lobbied hard for the four-reel concept, and even though the version of *A Chump at Oxford* that was complete and ready for release and for which United Artists had already begun advertising and accepting bookings was a four-reel featurette, the new feature-length foreign version was shaping up to be a much better picture. Regardless of Roach's commitment to Laurel and Hardy four-reelers, it made virtually no sense to release what now amounted to an abridgement to the U.S. domestic market. As *The Flying Deuces* completed postproduction and sailed easily into theaters in October without competition, Roach and United Artists began frantically assessing their options in a series of terse transcontinental wires. These communications also demonstrate the amount of control over the Laurel and Hardy product Roach had granted to Laurel in an effort to keep him in the fold, much as he had done with Harold Lloyd two decades earlier.

- EVERYBODY HERE THINKS FOREIGN VERSION IS TERRIFIC IMPROVEMENT OVER 4 REELER.
- HOLD UP DOMESTIC RELEASE OF LAUREL & HARDY UNTIL WE CAN MAKE A DECISION. HOW MUCH EXTRA GROSS CAN WE GET AS A FEATURE? WHAT ABOUT THE CONTRACTS ALREADY SOLD?
- DON'T RELEASE THE LONGER VERSION OF L&H OR SHOW IT TO CENSORS IN THIS COUNTRY UNTIL WE GET LAUREL'S OK.

And, finally,

HAVE MADE ARRANGEMENTS WITH LAUREL TO RELEASE FOREIGN VERSION DOMESTICALLY. WE ARE DEPENDING ON UNITED ARTISTS TO MAKE THIS ADDED EXPENSE WORTHWHILE.[51]

Although the decision to go with the longer version was made at the end of October, the musical scoring for the new material and the changing of theatrical prints, booking status, and advertising delayed release of *A Chump at Oxford* until January 1940, four months after the debut of *The Flying Deuces*. This time lag prevented direct competition between the two films, the situation United Artists had feared in which one Laurel and Hardy film would have cut into the box office potential of the other. To the contrary, as Roach had suggested, the popularity of *The Flying Deuces* probably helped UA sell *A Chump at Oxford*.[52]

After the outcome of the length debate on *A Chump at Oxford*, Roach decided to make the team's next film a standard (for Laurel and Hardy) one-hour feature. *Saps at Sea*, Laurel and Hardy's second picture for United Artists release, has a particularly nostalgic and retrospective feel. Despite the painfully cheap appearance of most of the sets, critics praised the good, old-fashioned belly laughs derived from things like an explosive stove, a balky Model T (a car that had been out of production for many years by that time), and even a cameo by a star of Mack Sennett silent films, Ben Turpin, in his final film appearance. The sentimental tone of *Saps at Sea* was ironically appropriate; although not planned as such, it would be the last film Laurel and Hardy were to make at the studio that had been their professional home since the beginning of their partnership.

A story and starting date for the production of Laurel and Hardy's third film for UA release seemed firmly set at the end of 1939.[53] However, on February 5, 1940, the *Hollywood Reporter* carried a news item in which the team announced their intention to part with Roach to produce full-length comedies for their own company, Laurel and Hardy Feature Productions.[54]

Roach was not willing to give up his starring attraction so easily and would attempt during the coming years to get the team back on his lot. Despite the Roach-Laurel tiffs of the previous decade and Roach's desire of the late 1930s to upgrade to a more sophisticated product line, his bid to become a major independent producer was already beginning to sour and Roach correctly assessed an urgent need to keep his one consistent breadwinner in the fold. For now, however, the break seemed unavoidable. Laurel was convinced that the team could do better elsewhere. After nearly three months of negotiations with Laurel and Hardy, and stonewalling anxious United Artists executives, Hal Roach Studios finally notified its New York office at the end of April that it was "okay for UA to cancel contracts on third and fourth Laurel and Hardys."[55]

Laurel and Hardy's departure from Roach marked the end of their "classic" era. In 1941, after a year of inactivity, Laurel and Hardy Feature Productions made a nonexclusive contract with Twentieth Century–Fox for the services of Laurel and Hardy, a popular Hollywood tactic of the era that permitted Laurel and Hardy to be paid in the form of capital gains, which were taxed at a lower rate than personal income.[56] After six mediocre features for Fox and two equally dismal films for MGM, Laurel and Hardy decided to call it quits, retiring from the screen in 1945. Aside from a feeble film comeback attempt produced in France in 1950, the team would spend the rest of their careers in a series of stage revues, mostly in Europe. The tragedy for both the team and the Hal Roach Studios during the 1940s is that they were never able to reconcile. Personalities aside, their collaboration had been mutually beneficial, and a reunion could have revived the fortunes of both the comedians and the company.

Trying to Stay Afloat

The year 1940 saw the Hal Roach Studios at the brink of financial ruin. Reviewing the performance of the previous season's pictures, the Roach New York office noted that on *Captain Caution,* a swashbuckler that had been the final film of the 1939–40 year, the figures "are not good. The entire UA organization is scared to death. . . . The company has no theatres of its own where thoughtful consideration is given the producer's investment. . . . *Mice and Men*, although one of the greatest pictures ever produced, encountered difficulties, and [with *One*] *Million B.C.* in many situations we were compelled to accept cash settlements together with the exhibitor's refusal to play it."[57] Even the final Roach–Laurel and Hardy pictures, although ultimately made as features specifically to avoid such a fate, frequently found themselves billed on the bottom half of a double feature, thus receiving a smaller percentage of the box office take.[58]

Roach's unpaid production loans were accumulating faster than the sluggish UA sales force could bring in picture returns. Bills for film stock and laboratory services were past due. On top of this situation, the financial community, apprehensive about the possible outcome of *U.S. v. Paramount Pictures,* was tightening up its lending policies to *all* independent producers.[59]

With characteristic showmanship, Hal Roach announced in May that he would spend $6 million on six feature productions for the 1940–41 season.[60] Behind the scenes, though, he was desperately scrambling to keep his studio afloat. In early August Roach wrote an urgent and personal letter to Will Hays in which he confided that the studio's $2.6 million debt had made it virtually impossible to obtain any further production funding. He implored Hays to use his influence to assist him in obtaining a loan from the Reconstruction Finance Corporation, noting that an RFC loan for $1 million had been arranged to assist Walt Disney in the construction of his new studio in Burbank. Underscoring the gravity of the situation, Roach concluded that such a loan would "enable us to keep in operation a studio with a payroll of approximately $50,000 per week while in production. I feel it would be a shame to close a plant that has been in constant production for 27 years."[61] Despite Hays's intervention on Roach's behalf, the RFC refused the loan on the grounds of "insufficient security."[62] With this news, Roach's supplier of unexposed film stock discontinued Roach's credit line "until such time as an agreement of payment program can be entered into between yourselves and ourselves."[63]

With little hope of obtaining additional financing, Roach turned to his only other alternative short of declaring bankruptcy. He began pressing United Artists anew to do a better job of selling his pictures and, hence, to bring back to the studio money that could be used to pay off the debt and to finance new films.[64]

Realizing that even improved returns from UA would not arrive quickly enough to save his current production schedule, Roach decided by the end of 1940 to curtail his 1940–41 production season after the completion of only three of the six features he had announced in May. In late January 1941, the trade press announced that upon the completion of pickup shots and editing on the last two films, *The Broadway Limited* and *Topper Returns,* the studio would close for a period of six weeks, after which it would begin production for the 1941–42 season.

Had it not been for some eleventh-hour arm twisting by Roach, it is unlikely that the studio ever would have reopened. Oddly enough, the idea that saved the studio was the same one that had never quite jelled with Laurel and Hardy: the production of featurettes. Although Roach's efforts at shorter features had always been directed at his starring comedy team, he had actually opined to a trade press reporter in 1938 that due to problems in double-feature program lengths, all "B" pictures might eventually decline in running time to fifty, forty-five, and even as little as thirty minutes.[65] Now, through circumstances not of his own choosing, he had a chance to put that theory into practice. As stated by Roach's New York office, the "smaller pictures" would not be "top 'A' productions but something that can fit on any program, be playable, and easily sold at fair prices because they can be made very cheaply."[66] Although the major studios were cutting back on "B" production to take full advantage of an improving "A" market, a healthy market demand for "B" pictures still existed. Roach reasoned that even the anemic UA sales force would have little difficulty placing films deliberately intended for the bottom of a double bill.

Roach had already sounded out his idea during the fall of 1940 in a covert attempt to get a new distributor, but none of the companies he approached, which included RKO and Twentieth Century–Fox, wanted anything to do with four-reel pictures.[67] Now, convinced that featurettes were the last hope to keep his studio alive, Roach waged an all-out campaign to convince skeptical United Artists executives that shorter pictures were not just a financial necessity for him but actually the wave of the future in the motion picture business. To this end, the designation used for the new films was changed from the blandly descriptive "four-reeler" to "streamliner," a name that suggested speed, efficiency, and the post-Depression American culture. After a March 1941 Roach publicity release, made without the approval of UA, which announced the changeover in production from conventional features to streamliners, the studio was inundated with telegrams from industry leaders commending Roach for his innovation. While many of these were, no doubt, sincere, the over-the-top zeal with which some writers expressed themselves, particularly considering that no one, including UA, had actually expressed an interest in distributing streamliners, suggests that Roach may have called in a great many personal favors. Typical of the communications was the following from Harry Brandt, an exhibition executive aligned with the studio-controlled, "affiliated" theaters:

> Congratulations to you on your vision in bringing out your streamlined features. Our association has long been an advocate for the elimination of double features and we believe that streamlined features are the first step in the direction of bringing our industry back to a normal presentation of pictures. You have led the industry in many instances in the past.[68]

The same sentiment, that shorter second features would provide a transition away from what many in the industry still referred to as "the double feature evil," was echoed in telegrams from David O. Selznick, John Balaban, Spyros Skouras, and others.

Despite the letters of recommendation, United Artists remained unconvinced. In mid-March the UA line seemed firmly drawn. UA would accept fewer but not shorter pictures from Roach. The UA executives specifically requested that Roach commit to supply two of the remaining three features for the 1940–41 season and one additional feature for the 1941–42 season.[69] This, for Roach, was a financial impossibility.

Under continuing pressure from Roach, United Artists finally capitulated in April and agreed to accept streamliners for distribution provided that they were a bit less streamlined. Specifically, UA wanted the films to be five reels in length rather than four, with standard running times between 45 and 50 minutes, and suggested that an extra sixth reel would be better still.[70] And United Artists would help alleviate Roach's financial plight by sending his way any of their independent producers who needed to rent studio space.[71] While Roach had, on rare occasions, rented his facilities to other producers, the rental business would become a cornerstone of studio operations for the duration of Hal Roach Studios' existence. Although this model of a studio renting its facilities to independent producers was born out of financial necessity rather than any visionary attributes of Roach, it soon would become the industry norm.

The planned production schedule for the streamliners called for five series with four films in each series for a total studio output of twenty streamliners per year. The proposed series breakdown was as follows:

Technicolor musical extravaganzas,
a Miss Polly series with Patsy Kelly and Zasu Pitts as two "old maids,"

collegiate stories, featuring various sporting events,

"Young Love," with Marjorie Woodworth "and a leading man to be
   determined in a Harold Lloydish series," and

a war comedy series, possibly to star Laurel and Hardy, or a series of
   Mr. and Mrs. Topper comedies.[72]

The idea for war, or "service," comedies, as they were more frequently
called, was nothing new. Laurel and Hardy themselves has been cast in the
army twice, in *Pack Up Your Troubles* (1932) and *Bonnie Scotland* (1935), and
had served hitches with the French Foreign Legion in *Beau Hunks* and *The
Flying Deuces*. More significant, however, Universal's hot new team of Abbott
and Costello was set to make its starring debut in 1941 with *Buck Privates*,
to be followed within the year by *In the Navy* and *Keep 'Em Flying*.

There was just one problem with Roach's plan. Only days after Laurel
and Hardy service comedies were proposed to United Artists, the team's
agent informed the Hal Roach Studios that Laurel and Hardy would probably not be interested in returning, due to the low salaries budgeted for the
streamliners.[73] In a similar vein, the suggested alternative to Laurel and
Hardy, the proposed series of *Topper* films, with their requisite special effects and royalty payments to the Thorne Smith estate, seemed beyond the
streamliner series' fiscal constraints.

Roach ultimately decided on service comedies for the fifth series, but
rather than Laurel and Hardy, William Tracy and Joe Sawyer were respectively cast as an eager but naive draftee and his long-suffering career sergeant.
The films of this series, starting with *Tanks a Million* (released September
12, 1941), became the most consistently successful of Roach's streamliners.

The altered nature of Hal Roach Studios' product line required a new
distribution contract with United Artists. While Roach had asked that
United Artists distribute an entire proposed year's output of twenty films,
United Artists, not at all certain about the future of either streamlined
pictures or the Hal Roach Studios, wished only to commit to five of the
films, one from each series. In a compromise, United Artists agreed to
contract for five but to attempt to sell ten. If the first five succeeded, the
second five would be welcomed, and if the first five failed, the second group
would not be produced and UA would cancel any exhibition contracts for
the remainder.[74] The new contract also relieved Roach of any further full-
length feature obligations to UA.

With the distribution contract set, Roach and his staff began happily
calculating anticipated streamliner profits. With the actual budget per
streamliner set at around $110,000, four streamliners could be produced

for the cost of a single Roach feature-length picture but overall would bring in an estimated return 50 percent to 75 percent greater than one feature.[75] While the actual returns were extremely variable and overall a bit lower than projected, all of the streamliners were profitable, with the studio banking anywhere from $17,000 (for *Fiesta*) to $185,000 (for *Tanks a Million*) upon the initial release of the first ten.[76]

Popular and critical reception of the streamliners was mixed. The *Hollywood Reporter* greeted the first release, *Tanks a Million*, with, "The show is a solid howl and a sure hit attraction on any bill. If Roach can hold to the quality of this 50 minutes of screamingly funny farce, his idea of shorter features is certain to prove a winner."[77] Initial entries from the other series drew less than rave reviews, with one disgusted exhibitor dubbing the first of the musical extravaganzas, *Fiesta*, a complete waste of Technicolor (see appendix 2, synopsis 28).[78] Nevertheless, even though critics, exhibitors, and the public perceived most of the nonservice streamliners as substandard fare, they made money for exactly the reason Roach had predicted: the reduced program time for a standard feature and a streamliner permitted theater managers to squeeze in an extra full performance every day. The quality of the streamliner was irrelevant, provided the theater had a strong first feature (see appendix 2, synopsis 29).

With the financial success of the first five streamliners guaranteeing the production of the second five, Roach and United Artists began to evaluate the individual series. With *Fiesta*, the first color film ever produced by Roach, the added expense of color did not increase the film's draw but, rather, merely reduced its profit margin. Thus color was dropped from the musical series. After the production of *Flying with Music*, the musical for the second group of streamliners, the entire musical series was discontinued.

For the Miss Polly series, Roach was unable to obtain the services of Patsy Kelly, so he costarred Zasu Pitts with Slim Summerville, who had appeared with Pitts in several features of the 1930s. After the pair turned up in both *Miss Polly* and *Niagara Falls*, the latter being the first installment in the Young Love series, United Artists requested no more films with the duo, thus terminating both series in one blow. Similarly, the collegiate series was killed after only a single entry, *All American Co-ed*, which featured Harry Langdon in a supporting role. The three canceled series were replaced in the second group of streamliners by a series of comic westerns featuring Noah Beery Jr., a domestic comedy series starring William Bendix, and the production of an extra William Tracy service comedy, providing two such pictures for this group.

By the fall of 1941, the dark days of six months earlier seemed well behind the Hal Roach Studios. The company was still heavily in debt, but the
upswing in business, bolstered by the beginnings of a general economic
surge in the motion picture industry later referred to as the war boom,
virtually guaranteed a return to solvency. A new contract with United Artists called for the production of eight to sixteen streamliners per year, to
be sold in groups of eight. And Roach would be permitted to produce, in
any given year, two to four full-length features in lieu of the streamliners.
This contract was to continue in effect until 1945, the termination date of
Roach's original 1938 UA contract.[79] Roach announced in late 1941 his
intentions to produce sixteen of what the *Hollywood Reporter* dubbed
"preshrunk films" for the 1942–43 season. The Tracy, Bendix, and Beery Jr.
series would continue, along with a new series that would parody the misadventures of Adolf Hitler and Benito Mussolini (to be played by doubles,
of course).

While riding the crest of this new wave of success, the fortunes of the
Hal Roach Studios suddenly took yet another bizarre twist. The initial entry
in the second group of five streamliners had not yet reached theater screens
at the time of the attack on Pearl Harbor. As America mobilized for wartime industrial production, the Film Conservation Committee, reporting
in July 1942, recommended that

> a certain percentage of "B" product be made as four-reel streamlined
> productions. Hal Roach is already doing this with eminent success,
> and it is felt by a number of screen writers that such tabloids, while
> saving an enormous amount of film, would be ideal for Musicals,
> Westerns, Documentaries and other dramatic subjects.[80]

However, Roach was hardly in a position to enjoy any accolades for his
accomplishments with the streamliners. On June 26, 1942, shortly after
completing production on the second film of the third series, Hal Roach,
at age fifty, was called into active military duty. For the first time in its
twenty-eight-year history, the Hal Roach Studios would have to function
without its namesake.

Although trite, the term *roller coaster ride* seems a perfect description of
life at the Hal Roach Studios in the years from 1938 to 1942. The studio's
entry into the first ranks of prestige independent production à la Selznick
and Goldwyn crashed due to a weakened market and the studio's inability, either creatively or financially, to consistently produce a truly quality
feature product. Ruin was averted at the last moment by the resurrection

of Roach's pet theory about the commercial viability of "featurettes" (proving that sometimes tenacity pays off), and the studio was well on its way to recovery when Roach, well past the normal age for military service, was called into active duty. The roller coaster ride wasn't over yet; for the remainder of the 1940s, the downhill run would be rather steep.

8

Fort Roach, 1943-48

The Second World War produced an unprecedented boom for the American film industry. Although the European film market had collapsed, the domestic U.S. market had never been more active. Because of the conversion of most industries to wartime production, employment was high but the availability of consumer goods was low. Precious little in the way of raw materials or factory space could be spared for the production of items not essential to the war effort. Recreational travel became difficult. Gasoline and rubber tires were rationed, and train travel was discouraged, since the railroad system was needed for movement of troops and war materials. Thus the movies presented the U.S. population with one of the few remaining leisure activities.

The Hal Roach Studios were not to participate in this wartime bonanza. Instead, Roach was called into military service, removing him from his position as an active studio head, and the studio output was converted from entertainment featurettes to military training films. As a result, the Hal Roach Studios emerged from World War II in greatly weakened condition.

These problems were not insurmountable. Indeed, Walt Disney was successful in surviving a similar set of circumstances. However, Disney enjoyed some advantages not held by Roach. In the first place, Disney himself was not pressed into military duty and thus was able to continue in personal control of his studio's operation. Furthermore, the military's use of the Disney studio came primarily in the form of contracts with Disney to produce military training films; with Roach the studio was leased outright by the government, which brought in its own staff. This difference, combined with Disney's maintenance of an annual release output of twelve animated theatrical shorts, kept his prewar staff on the payroll and "in practice." Although Disney emerged from the Second World War owing $4.3 million to the Bank of America, all indications pointed to his studio being able to return to profitability in the postwar years. His "stars" were as popular as ever and were readily available at the stroke of a brush. Roach, on the other hand, had already lost his most valuable stars, and most of his staff drifted into jobs at other studios during the war. As a result, Disney survived a lean postwar period to continue a successful career as a theatrical producer; the Hal Roach Studios were moribund, producing only four streamliners and some industrial films and surviving primarily on income from reissues of old films and rentals of studio facilities.[1]

Major Hal Roach

Hal Roach and the U.S. Army enjoyed a long and complicated relationship. Roach had barely escaped military service in the First World War, winning a draft exemption only after Rolin employees pleaded in a series of affidavits that the studio workforce of seventy would be idled if Roach were taken from them.[2] Even after the exemption was granted, Dwight Whiting conceded the continuing peril so long as the war lasted when he wrote a friend in December 1917, "Everything is going nicely with the Rolin Film Company, which I suppose will continue until the big draft comes along. So meanwhile we are grinding out as many pictures as possible."[3]

While Roach successfully avoided the draft in World War I, his country would later ask his help in other ways. In 1925 Roach received a letter from Major General Charles Saltzman, chief signal officer of the Army, informing him that the Signal Corps desired to improve its use of motion pictures. To that end, the Corps was extending an invitation to him and to other leaders in the motion picture industry to accept a commission as major in the Signal Reserve Corps. The letter closed by assuring that "this would impose no obligation upon you in time of peace, except as you voluntarily would wish to render."[4] Since the global conflict of seven years earlier had been dubbed "the war to end all wars," Roach seemed to be taking no risk by accepting the commission and, to the contrary, stood to profit politically within the film industry by joining the ranks of Lieutenant

Colonel Will H. Hays, Major Jesse Lasky, Major Robert Rubin, Major Albert Warner, and others. Roach enthusiastically responded that he "would be most honored to accept a commission in the Signal Reserve Corps and will devote such time either in peace or war that your department might desire from me to the best of my ability."[5]

From all indications, Roach took his new commission seriously, leaving the studio in October 1927 for a two-week training session in Washington at the Army's request, despite the fragile state of his young association with MGM at the time, and writing an essay for the Signal Corps entitled "Photographing a War."[6] Still, after this initial service activity in the late 1920s, his duties over the next fifteen years appear to have entailed little more than attending "reserve officers' nights" and participating in the Army golf association.

In late 1941 the Hal Roach Studios was in a rather feeble period of recovery from near bankruptcy. Survival of the debt-laden firm was by no means a certainty under the best of circumstances, and the risk of failure would be greatly increased if Roach had to leave for military service. With that very real likelihood looming, Roach resigned his reserve commission. However, in an enlistment clause not mentioned by Major General Saltzman in 1925, the Army retained the right in times of national emergency to call any ex–reserve officer back into active duty within six months of his leaving the service.[7] On June 26, 1942, the Army chose to exercise its option, sending Roach notification to report for duty.[8] Roach asked for a deferment, citing his age, fifty, and the critical condition of his company. In the event that a complete deferment was not possible, Roach requested a delay in his induction so that he could try to get the studio in a position to function without him.[9] The Army denied both requests, and Roach reported for duty as ordered on July 25, 1942.[10]

Although studio publicity indicated that the twenty-four-year-old Hal Roach Jr. would take over the studio reigns while his father was in the service, in reality the responsibility was split between two studio executives: Hugh Huber, who received Roach's power of attorney, and C. W. "Ted" Thornton.[11] In point of fact, however, there was little to oversee. Despite a November 7, 1942, trade ad in which studio employees pledged to carry on in "Major Hal's" absence, the eighth streamliner for the 1942–43 season had wrapped production in August, only weeks after Roach left for the Signal Corps. Eight streamliners being enough to satisfy his minimum annual obligation to United Artists, Roach decided to temporarily suspend production at his studio until he was able to better peruse his options. At this point, of course, no one knew how long the war would last; if it turned out to be a short conflict, Roach could reasonably make it back to his studio in time for the 1943–44 production season. And there was always the chance that Roach could obtain an early discharge, permitting him to return to work for the upcoming season. On a less positive note, if the latest set of eight streamliners proved box office failures, there would likely be no 1943–44 season for the Hal Roach Studios, and any urgency for an early release from the service would cease to exist.

With these considerations in mind as he settled into military life at the Signal Corps' photographic center at Astoria, Long Island, Roach continued to run his studio by remote control, receiving periodic updates on the editing progress of the last streamliners and, later, news on preview audience reactions and box office receipts. The sales figures were mixed. While giving every indication of a profit on the last eight streamliners, they nevertheless were somewhat weaker than on the first ten. This was not bad news, but neither was it the kind of thing Roach wanted to hear while considering whether to give the go-ahead to a new group of streamliners to be produced in his absence. Then a seemingly serendipitous opportunity arose.

In 1940 the U.S. government had seriously considered purchasing the studios of Roach's old rival, the bankrupt Educational Pictures, for the production of "national defense pictures." The deal fell through when Electrical Research Products, Inc., Western Electric's motion picture sound subsidiary, foreclosed on the $250,000 mortgage it held on the lot.[12] As war became an ever-approaching reality, and with it the promise of record numbers of draftees who required highly organized and accelerated indoctrination, the need for military training films became even more pressing. At the request of the Academy of Motion Picture Arts and Sciences, the Hal Roach Studios had produced three training short subjects for the Army in 1941.[13] The Army, knowing that the studio was idle and was fully capable of serving its needs—and, in all probability, lobbied intensively by Roach himself—offered in October 1942 to rent, on a month-by-month basis, one-half of the studio facilities for the Army Air Force's first motion picture unit. The rental shortly was expanded to a long-term lease that covered the entire studio property (fourteen acres with six sound stages), with the exception of certain administrative offices that would remain occupied by studio executives and clerical staff. The rental fee, minus interest that accrued owing to slow government payments during the first year, was $11,500 per month, or $138,000 per year.[14]

Whether Roach had improperly used his Signal Corps connections to swing the rental deal came under immediate scrutiny of the Special Senate

Committee Investigating the War Program, which, after hearing much testimony, quietly dropped the matter. Ironically, Major Roach was never able to arrange a transfer to his own studio, nicknamed "Fort Roach," and spent the war working at other film facilities in the eastern United States.

Regardless of its origin and whatever machinations caused it to happen, the Army rental seemed an ideal answer to Roach's dilemma. The government's lease payments, combined with the studio's other sources of revenue, would permit the Hal Roach Studios to tread water financially until the end of the war without having to produce any new films. As a bonus, the Army would be finished with the studio at the end of the war, the same time as it would be through with Roach's services, permitting Roach to resume production literally where he left off.

Only one loose end complicated an otherwise neat package: the unfulfilled two years of the United Artists contract. The 1942 agreement had given Roach the option of producing a minimum of two feature-length pictures in lieu of the minimum eight streamliners. Roach telegraphed his intentions of going the feature route in the November 1942 "Major Hal" ad. In addition to listing the final eight streamliners as the Roach studio product for 1942–43, the ad also announced a pair of upcoming features to star William Bendix: *Yanks Down Under* and *The Tennessee Tornado.* When it became apparent that he would be unable to return for any new productions for the 1943–44 season, Roach struck a deal whereby *Yanks Down Under* would be financed by UA producer Edward Small, produced by longtime Roach employee Fred Guiol, and released as a Hal Roach production. Roach would sell Small the script, the services of Bendix, the major percentage of the "producer's share" of the profits, and use of the Hal Roach Studios, if the film could be shot so as not to disrupt the Army's productions. Before the film was completed, United Artists agreed, under the wartime circumstances, to release Roach from his 1943–44 obligations. *Abroad with Two Yanks,* as the final picture was titled, was ultimately released as an Edward Small production, and *The Tennessee Tornado* was shelved.[15] Hal Roach Studios formally requested the cancellation of its distribution contract with United Artists in October 1944, and United Artists agreed.[16]

Beyond the rental paid by the Army, the Hal Roach Studios' income during the Second World War was supplemented by a couple of meager but noteworthy sources. The first of these was the "loaning out" of long-term contract talent to other studios. *Lease-out* would have been a more accurate name for the process, since the producer who held the talent's contract charged the borrowing studio a sum in excess of the talent's actual salary. The talent received his or her normal salary for the period of the loan, and the lending producer pocketed the overage. This practice was extremely profitable for other producers, particularly Roach's fellow UA producer David O. Selznick, whose inactivity as a filmmaker in the 1940s was largely offset by the loaning of a rather high-profile group of contract talent, including director Alfred Hitchcock. Roach himself had profited handsomely in the early 1940s by loaning out the services of contract players Victor Mature and Carole Landis. In 1941, Mature's weekly salary was $450, yet Roach was able to lend him out for three thousand dollars per week to UA producer Arnold Pressburger for *The Shanghai Gesture*.[17] Unfortunately, by the time Roach was inducted into the military, he had already sold the contracts of Mature and Landis to Twentieth Century–Fox, leaving only a single marketable player under exclusive contract: William Bendix. Loan-outs of Bendix from the war era through the early 1950s brought thousands of dollars into the Roach coffers.[18]

Another source of revenue was from reissues of the studio's older films, both in theatrical and nontheatrical, or "substandard," venues. Theatrical reissues of old films would become increasingly important to the entire movie industry as the 1940s wore on, to the point that Paramount Pictures in 1948 refused to rent or lease its library to television for fear of reducing its theatrical reissue value.[19] An ongoing program of theatrical reissues of older Roach product, particularly overseas, had been part of the standard mode of operation at MGM and UA, but in 1943 the Hal Roach Studios contracted with a distributor called Film Classics for a major theatrical reissue of much of the Roach-MGM work, including many of the features and most of the talkie shorts.[20] A major omission from the Film Classics package was the Roach-produced Our Gang series, which was blocked from re-release by MGM, since it was still producing new Our Gang one-reelers in 1943. Film Classics continued its reissues until 1951, when it went out of business.

Although it distributed Hal Roach films for only eight years, Film Classics left an indelible mark on studio history. The opening title sequences of most of the Roach short subjects from the early 1930s featured very elaborate background artwork that usually related in some way to the subject matter of the film to follow. Unfortunately, these same title sequences generally featured the MGM lion logo at the bottom of the screen throughout their entirety, and MGM demanded that its logo, a registered trademark, be removed from the Film Classics reissues. Rather than go to the expense of optically reprinting the credits in such a way as to remove the lion but retain the rest of the artwork intact, Film Classics simply removed the original credits entirely from the picture negatives and replaced them with its own significantly blander title sequences, sometimes misspelling cast and crew names in the process. As a result, generations of moviegoers and television viewers have seen much of the classic Hal Roach product in a form slightly different from the way it was originally presented. Sixty years after the initial Film Classics–Hal Roach contract, film preservationists are still trying to undo the damage and locate the original title sequences, some of which have survived in poorly labeled film cans and others of which are apparently long gone.

Hal Roach Studios' involvement in substandard distribution, primarily eight- and sixteen-millimeter film prints for rental or outright sale to non-theatrical (e.g., academic, church) and home situations, dated back to the 1920s, when both Pathé and the Kodascope Library (a division of Kodak) reissued much of the studio's silent product, frequently in abridged form that ran five minutes or less to avoid competition with theatrical showings. Pathé believed that the "Pathex" home versions might actually have promotional value and released some of the Roach abridgements concurrently to the theatrical run of the complete picture. In the words of J. A. Berst, the quarrelsome former head of Pathé Exchange, Inc., who had been demoted to the Pathex division by the mid-1920s, people who bought a Pathex print would probably then want to view the entire film in a theater "to see the difference and have a better inkling of the complete story."[21] Some Kodascope releases amounted to little more than three-minute excerpts, issued under different titles from the full original film. Miniature versions of Laurel and Hardy's *Do Detectives Think?* and *With Love and Hisses* became, respectively, *Graveyard Nights* and *Right Dress.*[22] These and subsequent name changes have led to a bit of confusion over the years, with the titles sometimes being included in theatrical filmographies of individual series.

In 1935 Frederick Gerke bought the nontheatrical world reissue rights to a number of Hal Roach silent comedies.[23] He then resold the rights to fifteen of the Our Gang comedies in this package to Exclusive Movie Studios of Chicago. These silent Our Gang pictures remained in nontheatrical distribution even after Roach sold the Our Gang series to MGM, but in an attempt to comply at least partially with the terms of that agreement, the name "Our Gang" was removed from many of the prints. In subsequent years, the Roach Our Gang films would be known by names ranging from the unimaginative Famous Kids to the too imaginative Those Lovable Scalawags and Their Gangs. In the early television era, someone apparently noticed that the main title card on most of the silent Our Gang films had read, "Hal Roach presents His Rascals in [picture title]. An Our Gang Comedy." Thus, from the very beginning of television distribution of this series to the present day, the Hal Roach Our Gang pictures have been known as the Little Rascals. As examples of the manner in which even some of the features were confusingly retitled, four Roach features with Laurel and Hardy from the 1930s, *The Devil's Brother, Babes in Toyland, Bonnie Scotland,* and *Pick a Star,* were all reissued theatrically (and subsequently to television and home video) under the titles *Bogus Bandits, March of the Wooden Soldiers, Heroes of the Regiment,* and *Movie Struck,* respectively. Additionally, in the late 1940s Roach routinely took pairs of entries from the streamliner series and reedited them into "new" features for theatrical and television release. Hence two of the William Bendix "McGuerins from Brooklyn" films returned to theater screens in 1949 as *Two Knights from Brooklyn,* and even the soon-to-be-discussed new "kid" pictures were recycled as *The Adventures of Curley and His Gang.*

In 1940 the motion picture industry, prodded by angry exhibitors complaining of unfair competition, attempted to clamp down on the sixteen-millimeter nontheatrical industry. At the heart of the issue were "gypsy showmen," itinerant exhibitors who roamed the countryside with a tent, a projector, and a crate full of sixteen-millimeter nontheatrical film prints. These wandering minstrels would set up shop in a town, in direct competition with local theaters, and would remain until the inventory of films had been used up. Then they would pack up and move on. Although their films were usually not as current as those being played in the legitimate theaters, their admission charges were considerably lower.[24] And although the exhibition of sixteen-millimeter prints under these circumstances was a violation of the nontheatrical film rental and purchase agreements, there was no practical way of enforcing individual contract stipulations with thousands of sixteen-millimeter prints in circulation.

The motion picture industry was still pondering what to do about the "gypsies" when the Second World War erupted. As part of its mission to help the war effort, the film industry sent its processing laboratories into overtime, cranking out sixteen-millimeter prints of current features for distribution to the armed forces worldwide. The glut of film prints and sixteen-millimeter projection equipment returning to "civilian life" after the war, combined with the outcome of *U.S. v. Paramount* in May 1948, which divorced the theater chains from the rest of the industry and, at the same time, made the exhibitors' worries of less concern to the producer-distributors, guaranteed for sixteen-millimeter nontheatrical distribution a healthy, unmolested place in the postwar motion picture industry.

With his company's financial distress overriding his sympathy for the regular exhibition sector's worries about competition, Roach continued to make nontheatrical agreements with multiple distributors. In 1941 he signed a contract with Post Pictures, which distributed sixteen-millimeter prints of much of his MGM sound product until 1953.[25] In 1949 he entered into a similar agreement for both theatrical and nontheatrical rights on most of his United Artists pictures with Favorite Films.[26] Still later, the Hal Roach Studios granted Blackhawk Films the right to sell eight- and sixteen-millimeter prints of much of its work. The result of having multiple nontheatrical distribution contracts going all the way back to the 1920s produced considerable confusion as to who owned precisely what rights to which pictures. The situation was to become even more complicated when the studio started selling television rights in the 1950s.

Though the Army rental and supplemental income would prevent Hal Roach Studios from having major financial troubles during the war, those sources of revenue would not be sufficient to permit the company to pay off any of its preexisting and substantial debt. Thus Roach was not absolutely sure that his company would escape bankruptcy in his absence. As a precautionary move, to protect the company's library of twenty-six feature-length films from being attached by a creditor, Roach dug into his personal savings to buy it from Hal Roach Studios, Inc., for $497,858.50 in June 1944. This purchase would also assure Roach of a postwar personal income for himself from theatrical reissue and television sales of the films, regardless of the fate of the Hal Roach Studios. Once back from the war and more optimistic about the studio's future, he sold the films back to Hal Roach Studios in 1946.[27]

Before this relatively brief period of optimism in 1946, however, Roach began to consider seriously whether he actually wanted to return to his old, debt-laden business at the war's end. In April 1945, shortly before the end of the fighting in Europe, Roach granted former employee Milton Bren the authority to sell the entire studio property, excluding the film library, for $1.5 million. The proposed sale was a very limited-time offer; Bren was given from April 5 to April 15 to close a deal. He was unable to do so, and no sale occurred. Nevertheless, the failed transaction suggests that Roach considered closing his company and possibly leaving active film production at this point in his life.[28]

The Postwar Era

Although the war years had been a period of unprecedented profit for Hollywood, 1947 marked the beginning of a deep recession for the film industry that would last well into the 1950s. A population shift to the sub-urbs (away from the first-run downtown theaters) and a loosening of the wartime restrictions on consumer purchasing and leisure-time activities (such as travel) caused box office receipts to plummet, resulting in the clos-ing of theaters and a cutback in film production.[29]

At war's end, however, most industry insiders anticipated a continua-tion of the war boom. By August 1945 Roach had determined that the best course, for the present, was to gear the studio back up for streamliner production. As the Army Air Force did not anticipate vacating the studio until the end of the year, Roach and his executives had several months to chart their reactivation strategy.[30] They decided to resume production without a distribution contract, the first time since the earliest days at Rolin that the studio had produced without a distributor. The belief was that a new contract with United Artists would be easy to obtain, but that firm would be considered as a last resort because of its poor performance in the past and its deteriorating standing within the industry.[31]

While other distribution options were being considered, Roach and his staff began planning their new films. In a departure from previous stream-liner procedure, Roach wanted to make all of the new films in color and to release them in a way to better fit the postwar marketplace. The major studios had cut back on their production of "B" pictures during the war, and many of the more prestigious first-run theaters had reverted to show-ing single, rather than double, features. Roach's plan for the new stream-liners was to release them in pairs under a single "umbrella" title, then break them into component units for subsequent runs in theaters that still showed multiple features. This way, the films could be handled as hundred-minute "A" pictures in initial release before assuming the traditional fifty-minute bottom-of-the-double-bill role later.[32]

As to content of the new films, Roach wanted one series to feature Wil-liam Tracy, the star of the studio's most popular service comedies. These pictures would follow Tracy's character as he attempted to readjust to ci-vilian life. A second series would come close in tone, perilously close in MGM's eyes, to Our Gang. Though MGM had discontinued production of the Our Gang one-reelers in 1944 and the 1938 sale of the series had given Roach first rights to repurchase and resume the series if MGM dropped it, Metro was vigorously opposed to a new Our Gang–like series by Roach, stating that it might desire to reactivate the series itself at a future date. Ultimately, MGM reluctantly gave Roach permission to produce a new "kid" series, so long as the name "Our Gang" was not used and no com-parison was drawn in studio publicity between Roach's new pictures and his old "Gangs."[33] Other streamliners in the new group would be one-shot productions, with a series of sequels always a possibility if one of the films proved particularly successful.

With production plans under way, the next step was to arrange financing for the new films. A serious disadvantage of going into production without a distributor was that the studio would have to seek its own bank loans rather than rely on a distributor's production advances. As noted earlier, during the initial phase of the UA relationship, Roach had arranged his own financing, a situation that led directly to the massive studio debt of the early 1940s. Because that debt had precluded Roach from obtaining any more bank loans, United Artists advanced him $105,000 per picture on the streamliners of 1941–43.

Resuming production without guaranteed distribution caused the studio debt to mushroom. Plans for a new series of twelve streamliners budgeted at $150,000 each required a total in bank loans of $1.8 million.[34] A series of loans approaching this amount was obtained from the Bank of America in 1946 and 1947.[35] In addition, Hal Roach once again approached the Reconstruction Finance Corporation and, this time, was successful. An RFC loan of $1.5 million was obtained for "rehabilitation of the studio."[36] Commencing its postwar production schedule with more than $3 million in new debt placed an overwhelming burden on the small studio, a burden it was ill-equipped to handle.

The first of the new streamliners, *Curley,* an Our Gang derivative, went into production on April 11, 1946. It was followed in rapid succession through the summer and early fall by three more pictures. Then production suddenly ceased, even though preproduction work had been completed and start dates scheduled for an additional two films.[37] The borrowed money, which was to have covered the production of twelve short features, was virtually gone after only four. Inflated postwar production expenses, combined with studio overhead, had ballooned the actual costs of the first four pictures from the budgeted $150,000 to between $300,000 and $450,000 apiece. A distributor who was willing to handle the completed films and possibly provide advances for future productions had to be found fast.[38]

The cessation of production by Roach did not throw the lot into darkness, as a steady stream of independent producers rented studio space and support services from the Hal Roach Studios. For the remainder of the decade, the majority of studio activity would be by outside producers who rented space. Even in the last studio boom of the 1950s, the rental business would be an extremely important source of income.

The quest for distribution of the new streamliners took more than six months. MGM turned Roach down, saying it was not interested in distributing outside product.[39] Ultimately, Roach determined that his only option was a new contract with United Artists. Signed on May 2, 1947, the agreement called for UA to distribute six to twelve short feature pictures per year for five years. All were to be produced in Cinecolor, with a running time of forty-five to sixty-five minutes.[40] In lieu of the short features, Roach could deliver two to four full-length pictures to satisfy his obligation for any year.

Roach had chosen Cinecolor for his new films because it was less expensive than Technicolor. Unfortunately, this economy was apparent on the screen. While Technicolor was a full-color process, in which separate records of each of the three primary colors were photographed, Cinecolor attempted to produce a complete color palette using only two primary colors. The result was a limited color range that tended toward a cold, blue-green cast.

Alas, poor color rendition was not the worst thing the new films had going against them. Not one of the four films had any star players. This deficit had not been a problem with the original streamliners, which had been designed for the bottom of the bill and which had relied on the major-studio features with which they were booked for drawing power. However, the exhibition of a pair of streamliners as the "A" feature proved to have very little audience attraction, even though use of the word *streamliner* was expressly forbidden by UA sales management for the tandem releases in an effort to avoid any "second-rate feature" stigma. Battling the same preconception about his abbreviated product, Roach issued a press release that repeated verbatim one of his favorite themes from the silent All-Star days of more than twenty years earlier. "We spend as much time, care and money per reel on our comedies as is spent on dramatic features," he said, "and we think we have as much right to make them shorter as David O. Selznick has to make them longer."[41]

The umbrella titles given for the picture pairs were another source of difficulty, being rather confusing to moviegoers. *Curley* (see appendix 2, synopsis 30) and *Fabulous Joe,* the latter about a talking dog (and produced by Harold Lloyd's first leading lady, Bebe Daniels), were released to theaters as *The Hal Roach Comedy Carnival* in August 1947. *Here Comes Trouble,* the Tracy vehicle (see appendix 2, synopsis 31) and *Who Killed Doc Robbin?,* the second of the "kid" pictures, followed in April of 1948 as *Lafftime.* To potential audiences, the tandem titles often sounded like collections of old theatrical shorts from the 1930s rather than new "A" material; in fact, since

1946 Film Classics had released a series of feature-length "festivals" of old Roach shorts under the title Funz-A-Poppin' Comedy Carnival. Adding to this misperception were UA lobby posters that simply featured the umbrella title surrounded by cartoon caricatures of laughing movie patrons, with no hint of the stars, the stories, or the vintage of the new productions. Those who saw the films generally registered satisfaction, but all too few people could be enticed into the theaters to give them a chance.

All four films would have sunk without a ripple had not the Memphis, Tennessee, board of censors banned *Curley* because its biracial cast was shown as a socially integrated group. According to the Memphis censors, "the South does not permit Negroes in white schools nor recognize the social equality between the races even in children."[42] Roach, United Artists, and the Motion Picture Association of America mounted a legal challenge, arguing that the Memphis ban violated constitutionally protected rights of free speech and due process. The censors prevailed through the Tennessee court system, and the U.S. Supreme Court declined to hear the case. When one Memphis theater ultimately did play *Curley* in defiance of the ban, it encountered no resistance or reprisal from the Memphis authorities. *Curley*'s run in Memphis netted two hundred dollars, a paltry sum compared with the five thousand dollars in legal fees incurred by Roach and his coplaintiffs.[43]

Roach blamed United Artists and their sluggish sales force for the poor nationwide performance of *Comedy Carnival* and *Lafftime*. On February 9, 1948, two months before *Lafftime* was even released, UA and Roach terminated by mutual consent the 1947 agreement under which Roach still owed UA two short features. The termination contained the provision that if he wished, Roach could, but was not obligated to, deliver a final full-length feature in lieu of the remaining two films to United Artists prior to February 9, 1949.[44] This final feature was never produced.

Shortly after the early 1948 termination of the UA contract, Roach negotiated a new distribution deal with MGM. Exactly how he was able to accomplish this, given the less than stellar performance of his most recent films, is something of a mystery, explainable perhaps by a new willingness among the big five studios to deal with the "outside" product of independent producers during the late 1940s.

The new contract called for Roach to produce for MGM distribution six films per year to run between forty and fifty-five minutes. Four of the films would be made in color, with either Technicolor or Cinecolor acceptable, on a budget of three hundred thousand dollars apiece, and the remaining two would be in black and white with individual budgets of two hundred thousand dollars.[45] Then the reality of the postwar Hollywood retrenchment hit. Having persuaded MGM to take him back as a producer, Roach was unable to obtain financing for the new series of pictures. MGM, which had made Roach's ability to arrange his own financing a nonnegotiable prerequisite for the new deal, refused to advance the studio any money on the new productions, and the contract was canceled.[46] Roach would try to renegotiate the MGM deal four more times in the coming years, the last attempt being in 1953, but on each occasion he found MGM absolutely unreceptive.

The year 1948 ushered in a new low in the fortunes of the Hal Roach Studios. As the industry-wide recession deepened, the possibilities of Roach reactivating theatrical production became increasingly remote. Commenting on the state of the industry at the time, *Fortune* noted that "independent production . . . is substantially wiped out. If the independent is producing he has cut costs like everyone. But more likely he has suspended operations and is waiting for the market to stabilize."[47] Unlike most independents who operated with little overhead, Roach had a studio facility to maintain. Each day of little or no activity pushed the studio deeper into the red. During this period, Roach had virtually no internally generated production, with the exception of an occasional training or industrial film. The income from the studio rental business was not sufficient to cover studio overhead, and the Bank of America attached what little revenues were coming in from *Comedy Carnival* and *Lafftime* "to liquidate a bank loan which is far from being paid out."[48]

In May, Hal Roach contacted the U.S. Air Force with an offer to sell the entire fourteen-acre studio, fully equipped, for $4.5 million. His sales pitch, that the Air Force needed its own studio to keep pace with the Signal Corps and Navy, each of which already had its own filmmaking facilities, failed to impress the Air Force brass, who declined Roach's offer in June.[49]

Thus, unable to sell his debt-ridden studio or to obtain production funding or distribution for further theatrical films, Hal Roach again found himself with only one option to avoid bankruptcy. This time, that one alternative was television.

9

The Man Who Bet on Television, 1949–60

Having failed to return to theatrical feature production, Hal Roach was forced to define a new product line for the studio. The production of theatrical shorts was generally on the wane in the industry, precluding a return of Hal Roach Studios to the form of production in which it had experienced its greatest success. While the studio produced industrial films and rented its facilities to independent producers, the income derived from these sources was not sufficient even to meet studio overhead, much less cover the studio's massive debts to the Reconstruction Finance Corporation, the Bank of America, and numerous other creditors. The successful postwar launch of television broadcasting in the United States, however, appeared to offer real production prospects for the studio.

Most early television shows were produced via live video from cramped studios in New York City. The production-value and logistical constraints on these productions, plus the restriction that the live shows could be recorded only in the form of low-quality kinescopes, which were unsuitable for repeat broadcast, made the television production field ripe for the entry of West Coast film studios. Production of series on film would permit the devotion of more time and care to each episode, as well as the rebroadcast of the programs, dubbed "telefilms."

The only snag was that the major film studios were withholding their product from broadcast television. The Federal Communications Commission (FCC) moved slowly in considering whether to grant television station licenses to film studios. The Commission had broadly hinted that the major producers would likely be barred from broadcasting because Hollywood's antitrust practice of vertical integration, that is, controlling production, distribution, and exhibition, could be duplicated all too easily in television if the studios produced programming, operated television networks, and owned local television stations. The FCC failed to address the apparent contradiction that its favored custodians of the television airwaves, the radio networks, engaged in much the same vertical practice.

In retaliation for being locked out of substantial television station ownership, and despite a recession in the theatrical film industry that began in 1948 and had forced retrenchment and layoffs, the major studios decided not to produce any new material for television and were even withholding the release of their old movies to the new medium. The industry leaders opted, instead, to pursue other forms of nonbroadcast television, such as theater TV and pay TV, which lay generally beyond the control of the FCC. Thus the telefilm production field fell to new independent producers, such as Desilu, and older, marginal theatrical producers, such as Roach and Republic.

In June 1955, *TV Guide* ran a profile of Hal Roach Jr. entitled "The Man Who Bet on Television." It basically related a typical rags-to-riches Hollywood story of a young man who, though born into the film industry, had been permitted by his father to "get his experience on someone else's payroll."[1] After a rigorous apprenticeship elsewhere, Roach Jr. returned to the family business in 1948 brimming with ideas about the new medium of television. Roach Sr. acquiesced to his son's plans and now, seven years later, Roach Jr. was running the studio, having bought it from his father, and was "the most prolific film producer in the world,"[2] topping "the combined footage of Metro-Goldwyn-Mayer, 20th Century–Fox and Warner Bros."[3] His importance in the hierarchy of television producers was confirmed by his having been one of the founding members of the Academy of Television Arts and Sciences and served as that body's second president.

Actually, the part about Roach Jr.'s difficult climb to success in the industry seems to have been embellished by both the elder and younger Roach for the *TV Guide* reporter. The fact is, from the time Roach Jr. graduated from Culver Military Academy in 1937 until the early 1940s, when the studio shifted into military production, he appears to have had no shortage of prestigious positions on the films produced by his father. Among other things, Roach Jr. is listed as the associate producer of the 1938 Laurel and Hardy film *Block-Heads* and was the second unit director on *One Million B.C.* and *The Broadway Limited*. Roach Jr. went on to produce a number of the streamliners, three of which he also directed. By the late 1940s, after years of grooming for the position of studio head, Roach Jr. was ready to play a major role in the company's transition to television production. Official confirmation of his rise came in September 1949, when Hal Roach Sr. sent him to New York to try to promote television production business for the ailing studio. Underscoring the gravity of the situation, the fifty-seven-year-old Roach Sr. sent his thirty-year-old son east with this charge:

> This is the most important situation you have ever been asked to handle for our company and what you can or cannot do on this trip will certainly have a great bearing on the future of both of us.
>
> Use your good judgment and the best of luck to you, and please keep me posted on things as they develop.[4]

While the Roaches agreed on the importance of television to the future of the firm, they disagreed on the matter of approach. Senior saw the televised future residing in the realm of one-hour television programs to be scheduled as individual events (i.e., "specials").[5] Junior, on the other hand, was a firm believer in series programming—that is, assembly-line-produced half-hour police, adventure, and comedy programs. "It's like the auto business," he explained to *Time* in 1954.[6]

Initially and not surprisingly, the company pursued Roach Sr.'s television strategy, which encompassed far more than program length. Roach Sr. envisioned splitting his one-hour shows into smaller components, generally stated as two fifteen-minute shorts and a thirty-minute "feature." Although Roach would maintain his enthusiasm for subdividing a one-hour block well into the early 1950s, he was never able to sell anyone on the concept.

Some of Roach's other ideas were a bit more visionary. As he saw it, quality television programs could not be produced under the single-sponsor system that television had carried over from radio.[7] In a letter to Roach Jr. in 1949, he explained his alternative.

> The answer for television will be better shows and this can only be accomplished by spending more money per show. Therefore, multiple sponsors is the only answer to the problem now, then the commercial for each sponsor will be like a page in a magazine and the best commercial will sell the most goods.[8]

Not only did multiple sponsorship eventually become standard practice, it was actually referred to as "magazine" advertising, although the term was never credited to Roach Sr.

Sharing the motion picture industry's belief that control over distribution was the key to profitability, Roach Sr. also favored the idea of syndicating his programs and selling them directly to local television stations nationwide, rather than going through the established television networks. Once it successfully entered the television production field, Hal Roach Studios would produce several series for syndication.

However, studio fortunes in this area rose and fell with the syndication market itself. After a promising start in the early 1950s, the first-run syndication market fell on hard times when the major television networks consolidated their domination over choice programming hours and national advertising budgets. The "made for syndication" market languished from the late 1950s until the 1970s, when satellite distribution and the rise of independent television stations and cable made it a profitable alternative to traditional network distribution. In addition to direct sales of programs to television stations, Roach believed that the studio should employ its nontheatrical distribution channels to circulate sixteen-millimeter film prints of its television productions to schools, churches, and civic organizations in areas of the country not yet reached by television signals.[9]

On the matter of production practice, Roach Sr. anticipated a coming trend, albeit one that would be implemented by others before the Roach Studios' financial quagmire permitted Roach to test it. Writing to Roach Jr. in 1949, he stated, "I believe by changing our production technique in photographing straight on instead of cuts as we do in motion pictures and thereby minimize light changes, and try and effect other economies, we can cut our costs considerably below our present budgets."[10] This suggestion of filming "straight on," shooting continuous action with multiple cameras rather than breaking the action into individual camera setups and takes, although actually an old industry practice employed during the transition to synchronized sound, would be hailed as a revolutionary technique in dramatic program production when employed by Desilu on *I Love Lucy* in 1951.

Two months into his 1949 mission to New York City, Roach Jr. had lined up few concrete production prospects. Roach Sr. could barely contain his frustration at his son's inability to produce, but neither could he pass up the chance to propose yet another grandiose scheme in a letter to his son. With the particular brand of brashness and daring that had characterized his entire career, Roach Sr., with his company on the verge of financial ruin, suggested that if they could not sell programming to the existing networks, perhaps Hal Roach Studios should set up a network of its own.[11] Needless to say, this idea didn't get very far, although Roach Sr. was not wrong in understanding the need for vertical integration to be a success.

In a second letter written to Roach Jr. on the same day, Roach explained his use of the term *casuals* in connection to advertisements.

> [W]here we mention "casuals" I have reference to a remark such as "Give me a Lucky Strike" instead of saying "Give me a cigarette." A man carrying a carton of Coca-Cola, mention the name of a television set, a gas range, a refrigerator, etc., or have someone say "A Buick gives you a good automobile ride," etc.[12]

While this type of "casual" mention of a sponsor's product was employed to a certain limited degree in the earliest days of television, as it had been for years in radio, it proved a major liability when programs with such mentions went into reruns or syndication with different sponsors. Because of this difficulty, the practice of integrating commercials into program content was limited largely to live shows, which would be telecast only once. Virtually the only form of casual advertising practical on filmed programs was the exclusive use of a particular brand of automobiles on some shows.

However, financial conditions at the studio in 1949 rendered any discussion of future television production purely academic. Virtually the only result of Roach Jr.'s and Sr.'s trips to New York was an increase in the number of independent television producers who rented space at Hal Roach Studios, including the Groucho Marx series *You Bet Your Life* and Apex Productions' *The Lone Ranger*.[13]

By mid-1949, even before Roach Jr.'s first trip to New York, a "creditors committee" was, in Roach Sr.'s words, overseeing "every expenditure, and our income is only sufficient . . . to pay taxes and insurance, and a skeleton crew to keep the studio in operation."[14] In 1950 a major turnover in the studio's board of directors saw four of the five directors, including Roach Jr., replaced by representatives of the creditors. Roach Sr. remained on the board but was barred from attending meetings of an executive committee formed by three of the new board members.[15] Before the year was out, the fourth new board member, H. R. P. Lytle, who also had been excluded from the executive committee, was replaced by a reinstated Roach Jr.[16]

The executive committee immediately addressed the creditors' claims against the studio. The first item of business was to trim studio overhead so that it could be covered by operating income, mainly rental of space, allowing income from reissues of old films to be used solely to satisfy the debt.[17] Next the committee explored options for increasing studio revenue. While the studio's financial straits precluded the production of any theatrical features, streamliners, or television series (with the exception of the Magnavox pictures to be discussed shortly), a less expensive form of production in which the studio did engage during this period was the making of television commercials, including a 1950 Union Oil spot featuring Marilyn Monroe, and industrial public relations films.[18] A much more drastic method of liquidating the studio's debt, selling the studio and all of its assets, was also pursued. As he had done before, Roach Sr. approached the U.S. Air Force with an offer to sell and again was rejected. However, Roach advised the executive committee not to lose hope in the matter, since the rapidly escalating Cold War might cause the Air Force to reconsider.[19] If sale of the studio to the government was doubtful, other prospects were even more remote. The major studios were cutting back on theatrical production and had excess capacity of their own. They certainly were not interested in purchasing more studio space. The young telefilm industry was too early in its development for any producers to consider buying their own studios.

In the midst of the studio's financial crisis of 1950, Roach Sr. obtained board approval to embark on a single major television production project. In August 1950, Hal Roach Studios began negotiations with Magnavox for the production of two one-hour television "movies." These productions, *The Three Musketeers* and *Hurricane at Pilgrim Hill,* were promoted by Magnavox both in advertising and as part of the network presentation as the first motion pictures produced exclusively for television. They received a strongly favorable reception upon their late 1950 airings on CBS as part of the normally live, New York–based *Magnavox Theater.* Though they were filmed with budgets and shooting schedules even more modest than those of the streamliners, these productions did much to restore the faltering reputation of the Hal Roach Studios within the entertainment industry, proving, at the very least, that the company was still capable of creating productions more ambitious than commercials and industrial films. Unfortunately, the Magnavox shows did little to improve the firm's financial standing. Magnavox decided to cancel the *Magnavox Theater,* so there was no more business from that customer, and other potential sponsors preferred the economies of live production to the more costly concept of made-for-TV movies.

The two films, plus a third, *Tales of Robin Hood,* which was shot at the same time as the other two but not shown on *Magnavox Theater,* received limited television syndication and second-feature *theatrical* releases between 1951 and 1954.[20] The theatrical release hit a snag in the few television markets where the Magnavox films had been syndicated. In some instances, one of the films would turn up on a local station's late show immediately prior to its theatrical run, certainly not a situation conducive to a box office bonanza.[21]

By mid-1951, Hal Roach Studios was busier than it had been in years, yet it continued to inch ever closer to financial extinction. Most of the production on the lot was of a rental nature, capable of meeting the overhead but not of paying off the studio debt. Internally generated production was still limited largely to television commercials and a single syndicated series, *The Children's Hour*. Among the new productions leasing space at Roach were *Amos 'n' Andy, Abbott and Costello* (who were doing an independent feature at Roach in addition to their weekly television series), and a pair of theatrical features being produced by Walter Wanger.[22]

Two other "rental" series produced at the studio were actually made by companies partially owned by Roach Jr. Roach Jr. originally had intended that these programs be solely produced by Hal Roach Studios but found the executive committee of the board of directors unable to part with the money necessary to initiate and cultivate the projects. The first of these two series was to become, as it happened, the single most successful television program that Roach Jr. was ever to produce: *The Stu Erwin Show,* known also at various times in both its original run and in syndication as *Life with the Erwins, The Trouble with Father,* and *The New Stu Erwin Show.*[23] Stu Erwin was a veteran Hollywood comic who had actually appeared in a single Hal Roach silent short in 1928 entitled *A Pair of Tights.* The television series, typical of many family situation comedies at the time, featured Erwin as a bumbling middle-aged, middle-class husband and father. It ran for five years on ABC.

Roach Jr.'s other television venture of 1950 was *Racket Squad,* starring Reed Hadley. In an unusual departure from the norm, this program actually started life as a syndicated series, sold to television on a station-by-station basis and distributed to these stations nationwide on sixteen-millimeter film. In the summer of 1951, the series was picked up by CBS, where it ran with new episodes for the next two years.

Ultimately, economic ruin for the Hal Roach Studios was averted not by sale or rental of the studio to television producers, nor by new production, but rather by the studio's past: the 1951 sale of the Our Gang shorts to television for two hundred thousand dollars.[24] While this sum was pitifully inadequate to permit repayment of the Reconstruction Finance Corporation or Bank of America loans, which together totaled over $3 million, it would permit a settlement with Roach's numerous other creditors, which included other film studios, trade publications and organizations, equipment and film stock suppliers, and the Motion Picture Association of America. Such a settlement would allow the studio to resume production and, if successful, begin to liquidate the major debt. To this end, the Hal Roach Studios' board of directors proposed in August 1951 to settle with its creditors (excluding the Bank of America, the Reconstruction Finance Corporation, and Roach Sr., who had personally lent the company $750,000 between 1946 and 1951) by paying 60 percent of the amount that it owed them, a total of $170,595, to cancel a $284,325 debt.[25]

Realizing that a 60 percent settlement was the best they might ever be able to obtain from Hal Roach Studios, more than 85 percent of the creditors accepted the offer.[26] With their task accomplished, the three studio board members who represented the creditors resigned on September 12, 1951, and were replaced by Roach Sr. appointees. The studio was once again under Roach's control.[27]

The early 1950s became a period of activity and expansion not seen at the Hal Roach Studios since its glory days of the 1920s and 1930s. Speaking in glowing terms in late 1951 about the bonanza that television would bring to Hollywood, Roach Sr. explained, "In television you need five times as many people as you do in motion pictures. Once mass production is really rolling in telepix, there will be a real need for industry workers. The impact of TV is just beginning to be felt in that respect."[28] Roach went on to suggest that television and the movies were completely compatible and complementary, with television providing the sort of talent training ground for the movies that vaudeville once had.[29]

In the summer of 1952, a new hit series came into the Roach fold. After an initial year and a half of instability while it bounced back and forth between CBS and NBC several times, Roach's *My Little Margie* finally found a home on NBC for the final two years of its run. The program ultimately generated 126 episodes, as well as spin-off series for both of its stars, Gale Storm and Charles Farrell, after its demise.[30]

Studio expansion of a different sort occurred on two fronts in 1953. On March 23, the *New York Times* announced the formation of Lincoln Productions, a low-budget theatrical feature firm headed by Roach Jr. and headquartered at Hal Roach Studios. The company revealed a release schedule of six pictures to be produced during the first year with budgets of between $150,000 and $200,000 per film.[31] The enterprise turned out to be short-lived, perhaps the result of declining demand for "B" pictures in the 1950s, although the firm's announced first picture, *Captain Scarface,* did actually reach theater screens.

The other area of expansion yielded more long-term results. In January, Harry Allen, the owner of three Canadian film companies (Cardinal Films, Screen Guild Productions, and the Film Classics estate), merged his interests into a partnership with Hal Roach Studios to form Guild International Films (later Guild Films).[32] The new firm would engage in some production but would be primarily a motion picture and television distributor. The partnership, sought by Roach Sr., represented the first time the Hal Roach Studios had ever directly controlled the distribution of its own product.

In 1954 Laurel and Hardy made an extremely brief and final return to the Hal Roach Studios. The highly successful television distribution of the Our Gang and Laurel and Hardy theatrical shorts had prompted the Roach staff to consider another way to mine the studio's past successes: create new versions of the old series. After reflection, the idea of a new version of Our Gang was shelved. All of the original "Gang" members were grown, of course, and the formula needed to put together a new kiddie troupe had eluded Roach staffers on *Curley* and *Who Killed Doc Robbin?*, even though both had been produced under the supervision of Our Gang's original director, Robert F. McGowan. Laurel and Hardy, however, were still alive, if aging, and were finally receptive to returning to the studio for a new series of films for television. Any doubts about the salability of new Laurel and Hardy films to the television audience were dispelled by a strongly positive reaction to a December 1954 installment of *This Is Your Life* that paid tribute to the two comedians. Roach Sr. declined to attend the program, sending Roach Jr. as the studio representative. The senior Roach did show up for a subsequent ceremony at the Hal Roach Studios to unveil a commemorative plaque for Laurel and Hardy, and he and Roach Jr. posed for photographs with the studio's famous team.

Early in 1955, Roach Jr. signed Laurel and Hardy to a contract for a series of four one-hour specials to be filmed in color under the title of *Laurel and Hardy's Fabulous Fables.* The programs were to be comic opera versions of well-known fairy tales and operettas, similar to *Babes in Toyland;* another Victor Herbert work, *The Red Mill,* was one of the titles considered.[33] Speaking to a *TV Guide* reporter in the spring of 1955, Laurel hinted about the program and, at the same time, added his voice to the live-versus-film debate.

> We're definitely planning a TV show, though we don't want to talk about it yet. But it won't be live. We made a hit in the movies because our pace made slapstick funny. Instead of just hitting someone in the face with a pie, we slowed down and showed our reactions. Reactions make slapstick funny. For that you need film.[34]

Unfortunately, *Laurel and Hardy's Fabulous Fables* was never to be realized. On April 25, 1955, two days after the appearance of the *TV Guide* article and shortly before scheduled commencement of filming on the first episode, Laurel suffered a stroke. While relatively minor, the illness left Laurel with a certain amount of stiffness and slurred speech that took a year of therapy to correct. By mid-1956, when Laurel felt well enough to resume an active partnership with Hardy, the pair barely had time to sit for a joint portrait session before Hardy fell to a massive stroke that left him an invalid until his death on August 7, 1957.

The year 1955 was probably the pinnacle of Roach Jr.'s success as a television producer. In February, at the age of thirty-six, he bought out his father's interests in Hal Roach Studios and became the principal owner of the company, its Culver City facility, and its library of films and television programs.[35] Roach Sr. reportedly had watched his son's progress as a television producer with great pride and now thought that the time had come for him to hand over the studio reigns, although he would retain his office at the studio and hold the positions of board member and studio adviser, with the final say on any major decisions.[36]

The studio staff was informed of the change in management by a memo from Roach Sr. on February 28.

> A public statement is about to be released announcing the fact that the studio facilities have been purchased by Hal Roach Enterprises, a corporation owned by Hal Roach, Jr. I doubt that any words can express my feelings at this moment. . . .
>
> It is with both pride in our past and unlimited confidence in the future of the business that I commend my son to you. With your help I am sure he will build Hal Roach Studios into yet greater dimensions than it has ever known. I cannot wish for him a greater assurance of success than this: that he may enjoy the same wholehearted cooperation which has made me your debtor forever.[37]

On the following day, a letter to all shareholders, creditors, and claimants of the old company announced that "Hal E. Roach Studios, a California corporation, has elected to wind up its affairs and voluntarily dissolve."[38] In April Hal Roach Jr. changed the name of his company, Hal Roach Enterprises, to Hal Roach Studios.

Under the terms of the transfer, Roach Sr. agreed to sell his 75 percent interest in Hal Roach Studios to Roach Jr. for $2,270,805.85 and an additional 7 78/100 percent interest for $255,430.77, payable in equal installments over thirty years. For his part, Roach Jr. had to agree that unless his father's consent was first obtained, he would not "undertake any television production operations as an individual or through any corporation" other than Hal Roach Studios or one of his preexisting production arrangements.

This last stipulation had arisen from the fact that Roach Jr. had become involved in an unwieldy number of television coproduction ventures during the early 1950s—arrangements that forced the studio to split licensing and syndication revenues with Roach Jr.'s various partners. While he had been forced into these outside deals in the earliest days of television production, during the tenure of the tight-fisted executive committee, he had continued the practice even after his father had regained full studio control. In addition to avoiding any more of these coproduction arrangements, Roach Jr. agreed to fold his interests in the earlier ventures into Hal Roach Studios as soon as possible. As examples of the degree of complication of Hal Roach Jr.'s television production affairs, consider the ownership splits on the following programs: *Racket Squad,* produced by Rabco, of which half was owned by Hal Roach Jr. and half by ABC-Paramount; *Life with the Erwins,* 50 percent of which was owned by Sherpen, Inc., which was owned entirely by Hal Roach Jr.; *My Little Margie,* 50 percent of which was held by Rovan Films, which was 90 percent owned by Hal Roach Jr.; *Public Defender,* produced by H-R Productions, which was entirely owned by Hal Roach Jr.; *Duffy's Tavern,* produced by R & M Productions, of which 50 percent was owned by Hal Roach Jr.[39]

In June, only four months after Roach Jr. assumed control of the studio, *TV Guide* proclaimed him "perhaps the most prolific TV film producer in the world."[40] By then, Hal Roach Studios was embarking on one of the most intriguing television projects with which it would ever be involved. As early as 1951, Roach Jr. recognized the battle lines being drawn between the East Coast producers of live drama and the West Coast film group to which he owed allegiance. In an interview with *Time* that year, in which he claimed to be responsible for already turning out "nearly three times" as much footage for television as Hollywood's annual feature film output, Roach Jr. slammed the "high art" nature of East Coast production, particularly the Toscanini concerts and the prestige programming of Pat Weaver at NBC. "On TV, a character must be immediately self-explanatory," Roach noted. "That's why a guy like William Bendix will be great. . . . Like it or not, television is Everyman's entertainment."[41] The *Time* article went on to say,

> The "live" producers of the East Coast don't speak Everyman's language with Roach's facility. He discovered this on a recent trip to

Manhattan, when some TV men tried to sell him on the idea of an hour-long ballet show. Says Roach: "I just told them ballet is not mass entertainment and most likely never will be." His credo: "You can't rationalize the public's taste. It isn't a question of intellectuality. It's the same thing as the public liking football and baseball and not liking polo and jai alai. It's just that we're attuned to that sort of thinking; we realize our audiences' tastes."[42]

It is difficult to imagine any television executives of the period pitching a ballet show, especially to a West Coast film producer, and Roach's story is highly reminiscent of his father's publicity releases in which he tried to depict himself as a visionary with a special feeling for the tastes of the common man. In a 1954 *Time* article that debated the merits of filmed versus live programs, Roach Jr. replied to the argument that live television carried the thrill of spontaneity by saying, "Who wants to see a stagehand in the wrong place, or hear an actor muff his lines? That's what spontaneity means."[43]

With this background, Roach Jr. undoubtedly knew that he was trespassing on East Coast turf when he decided to produce a filmed version of one of the most cherished of live television institutions, the anthology series. In May 1955, Roach and the Screen Directors Guild announced their coproduction of the *Screen Director's Playhouse,* a half-hour anthology series with its episodes, some in color, to be directed by Hollywood's leading directors and featuring the industry's top stars. The program's sponsor was Eastman Kodak, and the Directors Guild's portion of the proceeds, as had been the case with a live radio series of the same title several years earlier, would go to the Guild's educational and benevolent foundation.

The timing of *Screen Director's Playhouse* was no accident. It came at the historical moment at which several of the major Hollywood production companies became actively involved in telefilm production.[44] During the 1955–56 season, *Screen Director's Playhouse* shared the airwaves with three filmed anthology or rotating series from major Hollywood studios: *MGM Parade, The 20th Century–Fox Hour,* and *Warner Brothers Presents.* That Hal Roach Studios was permitted to make *Screen Director's Playhouse,* with its ties to the mainstream feature-production industry, would seem to indicate that the industry chieftains held no grudges against Roach for his early defection into television production. Taken together, the four series represented an all-out Hollywood assault on East Coast dramatic television production.

Screen Director's Playhouse premiered on NBC on October 5, 1955, with a Leo McCarey comedy entitled "Meet the Governor." The East Coast reaction was brutal. *New York Times* critic Jack Gould reviewed the program the next day.

> [T]he Screen Directors Guild of Hollywood should stand with its face to the wall. The organization began its own television program last night . . . with a preposterous film done in the worst possible taste. Leo McCarey wrote and directed the initial film. . . . Patently, he has only contempt for the television audience. He palmed off a piece of abominable rubbish that would never have seen the light of day as a synopsis for the second half of a double bill in a movie theater. . . .
>
> It is perhaps too much to expect that Mr. McCarey would be interested in elevating TV, but he could refrain from trying to push it further down.[45]

Of the two other series entries reviewed by the *New York Times,* "A Midsummer Daydream" won faint praise more on the basis of William Saroyan's script than on John Braham's direction.[46] John Ford's baseball drama "Rookie of the Year," which starred John Wayne, was characterized as having "struck out early in the game."[47] Other episodes, such as George Marshall's "The Silent Partner" with Buster Keaton and an Errol Flynn swashbuckler, "The Sword of Villon," passed virtually unnoticed.

In the end, the initial foray of Hollywood's leading theatrical film producers into television was something of a bust. *MGM Parade* expired after a single season, as did *Warner Brothers Presents,* although one of its rotating elements ("Cheyenne") would continue as an independent series for eight years. *The 20th Century–Fox Hour* managed to last two seasons. *Screen Director's Playhouse,* like the offerings from MGM and Warner Brothers, lasted but one year. The program switched from NBC to ABC in June of 1956 and expired with "High Air," broadcast on ABC on September 12, 1956, starring Hal Roach streamliner stalwart and loan-out property William Bendix and newcomer Dennis Hopper.[48]

Despite the failure of *Screen Director's Playhouse,* production on other series continued to roll at the Hal Roach Studios at an accelerating rate. In August 1956, Roach Jr. commented to a reporter that a 25 percent increase in the cost of a half-hour television script since the previous year was consistent with an increase in "above the line" costs generally.[49] Not only was the studio producing more, but the product also was becoming more expensive.

After only one year under Roach Jr.'s control, the Hal Roach Studios were, once again, approaching a financial crisis. Roach Jr. candidly acknowledged his situation in a confidential letter to the head of ABC film syndication in June 1956.

> We find ourselves in an extremely uncomfortable cash position due, in part, to the large amount for which we are carrying our partnership venture, Rabco TV Productions, Inc. [Rabco was a fifty-fifty partnership venture between Hal Roach Jr. and ABC–United Paramount Theaters formed for the production of *Racket Squad*.][50]
>
> Preproduction costs for next season, and some essential plant improvements, make it necessary for us to seek AB-PT assistance in order to fund Rabco's open account. It is not possible for us to obtain [via normal channels] the measure of relief which we require. . . .
>
> Our situation will correct itself during the course of the season. . . . However, we are under heavy pressure just now and we really need the assistance above requested.[51]

ABC advanced the requested funds in the form of a promissory note for $140,000 issued on August 23, 1956, payable within two years at 5 percent annual interest. However, the Hal Roach Studios financial situation did not "correct itself" during the 1956–57 season.

The studio's fiscal dilemma was not due to poor management by Roach Jr. On the contrary, the fiscal years ending August 31, 1956, and August 31, 1957, would have been profitable had it not been for the large payments required on the still-outstanding Reconstruction Finance Corporation loan and the installment payments to Roach Sr. for the studio purchase. These payments, however, siphoned off more than the studio was able to earn, and it began to sink even more deeply into debt. Roach Jr. attempted to infuse new capital into the studio by offering a public issue of Hal Roach Studios stock, but the necessary minimum number of shares could not be sold and the plan to go public was aborted.[52]

Further complicating the financial situation was that few of the studio's television series enjoyed an extended first run. While these short-lived series could be produced for a modest profit, they did not generate enough episodes for successful subsequent syndication, thus denying the studio the level of residual payments that could have generated capital for new series and plant expansion. This problem became particularly acute for Roach, as it did for many other independent producers, including Desilu, when the major studios entered active television production. After the initial failures of 1955, the studios found their stride when they abandoned the production of anthology series in favor of more conventional weekly series. The majors could actually afford to spend more on their series than they could recoup from the initial network run, a practice known as deficit financing, with the idea of profiting from an extended subsequent syndication life. These big-budget series produced by the majors featured a production polish approaching that of theatrical films. The standard episode length for prime-time dramas expanded to one hour, further increasing production costs while diminishing the total number of series required to fill a network's prime-time schedule (i.e., a single one-hour program took the place of two half-hour shows). The independent producers found it increasingly difficult to compete on this basis, and their product began to look all the more shabby by comparison.

Even with the prevailing industry climate in the late 1950s providing rough sledding for many independent producers, it must have been something of a shock to the industry when, on May 27, 1958, "the man who bet on television" announced that he was selling Hal Roach Studios to the Scranton Corporation, a wholly owned subsidiary of the F. L. Jacobs Company. Headed by Alexander L. Guterma, the Jacobs Company, formerly a manufacturer of auto parts, had been on an acquisition rampage, expanding into several electronics and entertainment enterprises. Roach Jr. insisted that his company was "very much in the black"[53] and that his only reason for selling what had been a family-owned business since the earliest days was to gain capital needed for expansion of studio activities, including "an increase in the present schedules of production of films for television and feature-length motion pictures for theater distribution."[54] Under the terms of the deal, Roach Jr. was to continue as president and executive producer at the studio under a five-year renewable contract and would join the board of directors of the Scranton Corporation.[55]

Although the merger with Scranton seemed to offer exactly the combination of working capital and financial acumen that the Hal Roach Studios needed for the high-stakes television production field of the late 1950s, the results were ruinous. On September 11, 1958, the Hal Roach Studios, in a deal engineered by Guterma, purchased the ailing Mutual Broadcasting System, a long-established radio network that had not attempted the transition to television.[56] At about the same time, it was announced that the Hal Roach Studios, at a cost of around $1 million, was going to purchase television cameras and four Ampex videotape recorders for partial conversion of the studio to videotape production.[57] Guterma and Roach Jr. seemed poised to push the Mutual network into the television age, with Hal Roach Studios as the center of network production.

The company's potential to revive its theatrical production wasn't neglected either. In January 1959, Scranton purchased the Distributors Corporation of America (DCA), a low-budget theatrical distributor that had handled the release of a 1957 Robert Youngson–Hal Roach silent comedy compilation documentary entitled *The Golden Age of Comedy*. Scranton assumed distribution of the sixty-five pictures already in DCA release, including the legendary *Plan 9 from Outer Space*. DCA was renamed Hal Roach Distributing Corporation and promised a new slate of Hal Roach features to come, the first of which would be a teenage musical entitled *Go, Johnny, Go*.[58] Then, suddenly, the budding communications empire collapsed.

The "steady flow of financing" that Guterma promised had never materialized, and production money at the studio became even tighter than before. By the second half of 1958, production at the studio was down to *The Gale Storm Show;* a ten-episode horror anthology series hosted by Boris Karloff entitled *The Veil; Go, Johnny, Go;* a couple of pilots; and a handful of rental tenants. From September 1 to December 20, the studio posted a net loss of $534,568.[59]

During the second week of February 1959, Alexander Guterma was ordered to appear before the U.S. District Court in New York to explain certain business and stock trading irregularities discovered by the Securities and Exchange Commission. On Friday, the thirteenth of February, the F. L. Jacobs board of directors accepted Guterma's resignation as chairman of the board and elected Roach Jr. to replace him. The following day, Guterma was arrested as he attempted to flee the country on a flight to Ankara, Turkey. As the investigation unfolded, it became evident that the Jacobs Company was a huge, complicated, money-losing mess through which Guterma was engaging in multiple forms of fraud.[60] Sales of unregistered stock were common, and the same identical assets were frequently carried on the books of more than one Jacobs subsidiary. Guterma made numerous unauthorized loans in the names of various companies under Jacobs Company control, then spent the money anywhere within his empire and for whatever purpose he saw fit, regardless of the original purpose of the loan. The companies in whose names the money was borrowed rarely saw any of it.[61]

Early in the investigation, Roach Jr. indicated the true state of his studio when Scranton had taken it over in the previous May. Admitting that the widely reported purchase price of $15.5 million was only a "Hollywood dignity" figure, Roach stated that the true purchase price, thirty-five thousand shares of Scranton stock, amounted to $507,000 on the day the deal was closed.[62] To make matters worse, Guterma had subsequently borrowed Roach's Scranton stock, used it as security on a loan, then defaulted on the loan, leaving Roach Jr. with nothing.[63]

To salvage what he could of the F. L. Jacobs empire now under his care, Roach Jr. spun off the Mutual Broadcasting System into Chapter 11 bankruptcy. Amazingly, Mutual was able to survive several years of reorganization and ownership changes and continued as a radio-only network until 1999, when its last owner, Westwood One, finally pulled the plug. Turning his attentions next to the family business, Roach Jr. tried to raise cash for the Hal Roach Studios by selling to partner Guild Films all rights to several of the Roach television series, including *The Veil, Racket Squad, Code 3, Passport to Danger,* and *Telephone Time.*[64]

All of Roach's efforts were to no avail. During the first months of 1959, Hal Roach Studios ceased production, transferring the making of the last fourteen episodes of *Gale Storm* to another company. The support service staff was cut to the bare minimum required to physically maintain the studio, and the last tenants moved out. F. L. Jacobs went into Chapter 10 reorganization on March 18, 1959, followed by Scranton and Hal Roach Studios on April 3. Roach Jr. resigned the chairmanship of the board of F. L. Jacobs on March 19. Roach's partner, Guild Films, filed for bankruptcy on December 28, 1960, and Hal Roach Distributing Corporation reorganized as Valiant Films Corporation in September 1959 under members of its former DCA management, only to cease operation in April 1961. Still the drama involving Roach and Guterma was to take yet one more bizarre twist.[65]

In September 1959, Guterma, Roach Jr., and Garland L. Culpepper, a Scranton Corporation vice president, were charged by a federal grand jury with failing to register themselves and the Mutual Broadcasting System as "agents of a foreign principal." The three were accused of having, in January 1959, accepted a payment of $750,000 from the dictator of the Dominican Republic, Generalissimo Rafael Trujillo, in exchange for favorable coverage of the Dominican Republic on Mutual radio news broadcasts. The arrangement had been reported to federal authorities by the new Mutual Broadcasting System management, who had found themselves accosted by agents of the Dominican Republic who demanded performance on the deal or return of the money.

On January 27, 1960, Guterma was convicted on sixteen counts of a seventeen-count indictment for conspiring to defraud the U.S. government by impeding the efforts of the Securities and Exchange Commission to protect investors and for willfully failing to file financial reports with the SEC.[66] The man who had credited his business success to the fact that he was "a goddam genius" pleaded nolo contendere to the foreign agency charges several months later.[67]

Roach Jr. pleaded no contest to charges that he had failed to register the Mutual Broadcasting System as a foreign agent. In June 1960, federal judge Joseph R. Jackson imposed a fine of five hundred dollars and told Roach that he was "more sinned against than sinning." After the sentencing, Roach expressed his desire to resume production of motion pictures for TV and theaters.[68]

Since Roach Jr. still owed his father most of the purchase price of the studio, Roach Sr. was, this time, one of the company's principal creditors. Roach Sr. announced characteristically grandiose plans in March 1960 to resume production with "eighty one-hour comedy television shows and four feature-length theatrical features" in the first year of operation, but nothing materialized.[69] The other creditors and the reorganization trustees realized that it was unlikely that sufficient capital could ever be raised to resume production given the heavy mortgages against the studio property and film library. They agreed that the most equitable solution for all concerned was a "plan of orderly liquidation."[70] The studio saw some use as a rental facility during the next few years, with MGM as one of the tenants, while the trustees saw no fewer than four auctions to sell the property halted by restraining orders originating from complainants with claims against F. L. Jacobs. Finally, on December 20, 1962, the studio was sold to the Ponty-Fenmore Realty Fund for $1,323,000.[71] Despite a reputation for buying tracts of land only to clear them for new development, the firm announced in January 1963 that it was going to rename the property the Landmark Studios and keep it open as a rental facility for independent producers.[72] However, on May 22, 1963, the *New York Times* ran the following report:

> Hollywood, May 21—The Hal Roach Studio, where the Laurel and Hardy, "Our Gang," Harold Lloyd and Charlie [*sic*] Chase comedies were filmed, will be torn down and replaced with a commercial development, the new owners said today. Maxwell Fenmore said the decision to raze the 43-year-old studio had been reached after four months of unsuccessful efforts to operate it as a studio.[73]

The studio complex, fifty-two buildings (including seven sound stages) on a 14½-acre tract, was demolished in the summer of 1963, to be replaced by light industrial buildings and businesses, including an automobile dealership. The studio was leveled, in part, by a piece of surplus military equipment routinely used for such jobs, instead of a bulldozer, by the demolition contractor: Fort Roach fell to an M-4 Army tank. A small plot of grass with a commemorative plaque is the only indication of the location's illustrious past.

On March 29, 1962, Roach Jr. filed a petition for bankruptcy. Describing himself as "an unemployed motion picture producer," Roach listed debts totaling $1,050,802 against assets of $39,633. Among his creditors were Charles Farrell and Gale Storm, who claimed that Roach owed them $142,491 and $128,538, respectively, arising from their acting contracts from the 1950s. Roach stated that he had earned only twenty-five hundred dollars in 1961 and five hundred dollars from January to March of 1962.[74]

Roach Jr. spent the next decade trying to get back into motion picture and television production. In March 1972, he entered St. John's Hospital in Santa Monica with the general complaint of not feeling well. Two days later, on March 29, 1972, the tenth anniversary of his bankruptcy filing, he died of pneumonia. He was fifty-three.

Roach Sr. maintained his position as the head of the creditor group controlling the Hal Roach Studios, now nothing more than a film library. Because the 1966 film *One Million Years B.C.* was a remake of one of his old properties, Roach even took an associate producer credit. In 1971 Roach sold his interests to a group of Canadian investors, headed by Earl Glick. Under this regime, Hal Roach Studios developed the film-coloring process patented as "Colorization," a name that has become a generic term. In the late 1980s, Hal Roach Studios merged with Robert Halmi Industries, a made-for-TV movie producer, to form RHI Entertainment.[75] In 1994, RHI Entertainment was purchased by Hallmark Cards.[76]

Hal Roach died of pneumonia on November 2, 1992, at the age of one hundred. Although he had made the most of his retirement years, remaining extremely active socially and engaging in frequent hunting and fishing expeditions, he never completely forgot about the industry in which he had been a pioneer. He continued to consider himself a visionary, planning projects for the future, and had little interest in speaking about studio history, except in the briefest of terms. At the time of his death, he was consulting with Universal Pictures for a new theatrical feature version of the Little Rascals.[77] Roach was buried in his hometown of Elmira, New York, in the Woodlawn Cemetery, the final resting place of Mark Twain. His epitaph reads, "After leaving Elmira he found success in Hollywood and Motion Pictures, but always loved his hometown and has returned." The personal odyssey of Hal Roach was finished.

10

Conclusion

The Hal Roach Studios seems to have functioned best when its chief executive left the fine details of creativity up to his employees. Roach Sr. had a good grasp of the motion picture business and could successfully draw a broad road map for the hired help to follow, but things often went less well when he micromanaged projects. Perhaps worse, his dealings with Stan Laurel in the late 1930s are a classic case of ego trumping business judgment. Although Laurel would have tried the patience of Job during this period of his life,[1] Roach failed to appreciate that he needed Laurel and Hardy as an insurance policy against the failure of the prestige picture program. When he did come to this realization toward the end of 1939 (judging from his efforts to placate Laurel), it was too late to mend the relationship.

At its best, the Roach studio was a place where creative people were allowed to flourish with a minimum of interference from the boss. Hiring people who are good at their work, then trusting them to do their jobs properly, is a valid management style and one Roach seems to have employed most of the time. The happy recollections of most who worked there in the 1920s and 1930s, echoed in the many books about Harold Lloyd, Laurel and Hardy, and Our Gang, reflect a relaxed and productive environment and stand in sharp contrast to reminiscences of the employees of Roach rival

Mack Sennett. In his autobiography, Frank Capra recalls that during his time as a Sennett writer, working on the films of Harry Langdon, Sennett kept the writers in an office above his so that he could see them on the stairway if they tried to sneak out early. Eventually, the writers conspired with the studio carpenter to make one step a bit higher than the rest so that Sennett would trip on his way to check up on them, thus waking them from their naps.

Roach's abilities as a judge of raw talent could be spectacularly unreliable, as the long line of failed series from Toto to Irvin S. Cobb demonstrates. On the other hand, Roach could see ability that was apparently invisible to others, as when he hired Stan Laurel for a third time in 1926, despite the comic's poor eight-year track record for Roach and other studios.

The success or failure of Roach's short-film series, the productions by which the studio is best remembered today, depended on a variety of elements, the most important of which were casting and creative talent. These elements may best be explored through examinations of Roach's two most successful series, Laurel and Hardy and Our Gang, which had markedly different origins.

Shortly before their teaming, both Laurel and Hardy had begun to redefine their screen personae: Laurel slowed his pace from his earlier hyperkinetic slapstick character and Hardy softened the edges of his stock comic villain. Both of these changes allowed the comic duo to better work within the developing Roach house style, which relied more on situation than slapstick. Their new characters allowed Laurel and Hardy, under the supervision of producer Leo McCarey, to find a happy fit when they worked together in the All-Star series. Thus, while not hired specifically to fill roles in a preconceived series built around a pair of fat and skinny blunderers, Laurel and Hardy, once teamed, were allowed to refine their characters and relationships with one another to evolve into one of Roach's biggest successes.

Our Gang, on the other hand, started with the preconceived series idea of presenting a group of "normal" children having "regular" adventures. The novelty of the series, there being no other short-comedy series at the time with all-child casts (although imitations of Our Gang would soon appear), combined with astute casting that emphasized the series dedication to a "realistic" rather than idealized treatment of children, struck a responsive cord with audiences. This notion of realism was, in many ways, merely another form of idealism. While the gang played in sandlots and city streets and frequently misbehaved, they also demonstrated a capitalistic drive (through their many money-making schemes) and an ingenuity and inventiveness (building railroads, dog-powered automobiles, and backyard circuses) in the best tradition of the all-American child.

The cast of Our Gang was painstakingly selected to represent seemingly natural group dynamics: a leader, a bully, a younger child tagging along, a female, a fat kid, and, initially due more to Ernie Morrison's contract than to a representation of social reality, an African American. After the initial cast was assembled and soon thereafter embraced by audiences, Roach and series producer Robert McGowan (and his successors) had a relatively easy time replacing children with the appropriate type as cast members outgrew the gang. This replacement was transitional, with the new child being introduced well in advance of the departure of the outgoing cast member. As a result, audiences were never confronted with an entirely "new" gang; every short contained more veteran members than newcomers.

Beyond filling a specified type, the cast members selected for Our Gang needed engaging personalities. This prerequisite became glaringly apparent when Roach and McGowan tried to rekindle the Our Gang formula with the postwar streamliners Curley and Who Killed Doc Robbin? Considering Roach's perilous financial condition at the time and the need to quickly generate new product, the casting for these films was, in all likelihood, done in great haste. As a result, the children in these films appear to have had the Our Gang types superimposed onto them, rather than having been selected because something about their natural personalities filled the required roles. The spontaneity and apparent realism of the earlier gang was completely lost in the process.

In detailing the history of any human endeavor, one encounters numerous junction points that prompt the question "What would have happened had the other road been taken?" In some cases, a particular choice was the result of carefully reasoned business strategy; in other cases it was pure luck, good or bad. Harold Lloyd won his job at Rolin strictly by virtue of having been in the extra pool with Roach during the latter's acting days. Had Lloyd not possessed the innate ability to become one of the top comics of the silent era, Rolin likely would not have survived its first few years. Similarly, had Pathé insisted on continued production of the marginally popular Lonesome Luke series and not agreed to let Lloyd experiment with the glasses character, Rolin never would have distinguished itself from a host of other small short-comedy studios operating at the time. On the other hand, once Lloyd succeeded, and given Roach's difficulty in starting other successful series, it would have been logical for Roach to simply let his studio become the Harold Lloyd Film Corporation and to do nothing else. Happily, Roach elected not to take this path.

On the downside, Roach's late-1930s decisions to sell the Our Gang franchise to MGM and to allow his relationship with Laurel and Hardy to deteriorate would seem, with the benefit of hindsight, to have been two of a series of poor choices during a critical time in the studio's history. His decision to leave MGM and to produce "A" pictures for United Artists seemed sound, but the industry trend he was following turned out to be a short-lived one and he had no fallback plan. When called away from the studio by military service, Roach elected to cease all internally generated entertainment film activity and lease the studio facility to the government. While the guaranteed rental payments seemed a safer choice than allowing his struggling studio to continue in production without his direct supervision, it prevented the Hal Roach Studios from participating in the wartime box-office bonanza and meant that the postwar reactivation of the studio would have to start virtually from scratch.

Perhaps the biggest point of speculation of all is what might have happened if Alexander Guterma had actually managed to pull off his plan to integrate Roach's telefilm and reactivated theatrical film interests with the Mutual Broadcasting System. Mutual may have become a viable fourth television network, and the Hal Roach Studios might have become the sort of media titan that Walt Disney is today.

Or maybe not. The 1950s and 1960s proved rough sledding for the entire Hollywood film industry. Both RKO (one of the five fully integrated major studios) and Republic Pictures (a minor independent) had participated in the war boom, yet both closed their doors before Roach in the 1950s. Desilu, qualitatively the most successful of the independent telefilm producers of the 1950s, was folded into Paramount Pictures in the mid-1960s. It is entirely possible that no matter which course Roach pursued in the late 1930s and early 1940s, all roads may have led to the same dead end.

Fortunately most of the films survive, and the best of them have stood the test of time. Even people who have never seen a silent film are familiar with the image of Harold Lloyd hanging off the oversized clock in *Safety Last*. Laurel and Hardy still have a large and devoted following in the Sons of the Desert, an international fan organization. The Laurel and Hardy and Our Gang films continue to receive frequent television exposure, and the Our Gang franchise was revisited in the feature *The Little Rascals* (1994). In the end, the enduring popularity of the Roach output has earned this little studio, which rarely rose above the status of minor-league niche player in the grand Hollywood scheme, a significant spot in the hearts of the generations it has entertained.

Filmography: The Films of Hal Roach

Silent Films

1914

The following one-reel comedies were produced by Rolin but never received theatrical distribution. The titles and descriptions were contained in a letter from Dwight Whiting to Samuel Cummins on January 11, 1918, in answer to an inquiry from the latter requesting information about any unreleased films that might be available for sale. No action was taken, and the films were scrapped prior to February 16, 1920, according to a letter of that date from Warren Doane to Samuel Cummins.

Willie Runs the Park. "This picture deals with Lloyd's adventures with a park policeman. Slapstick."
A Smell There Was. "Lloyds [*sic*] plays the lead in this and it deals with the troubles of a traveling man with three pet skunks which get loose in a residence. Slapstick."
A Dusty Romance. "This is a tramp picture with Lloyd playing the lead. Slapstick."
Troubles of the Work Family. "This is a Lloyd comedy showing his hard home life. Slapstick."
A Duke for a Day. "Subject matter is a bogus count." Neither this film nor the three that followed featured Harold Lloyd.
Two Bum Heroes. "Features Danny Linthicum and Dickie Rawson. Slapstick."
Powder Monkeys. "Featuring George Whiting, the eccentric vaudeville headliner. Slapstick."
A Daubbo. "A slapstick featuring unknown comedian. Poorest picture of the lot by far."

At least five other films were produced during this speculative period: the one-reel comedies *Why the Boarders Left* (released by General Film in 1915) and *Just Nuts* (released by Pathé in 1915) and three two-reel dramas, *From Italy's Shore, The Greater Courage,* and *The Hungry Actors,* starring Jane Novak and Roy Stewart and featuring Harold Lloyd as a supporting player. Two of the dramas eventually were released.

1915

All films produced between 1915 and 1927 were released by Pathé. Where supplemental information (i.e., an exact release date) has been obtained from a secondary source about this filmography and subsequent ones, the author's name is noted. All secondary sources are listed in the bibliography.

All films released in 1915 were one reel in length. All films are believed to feature Harold Lloyd.

Just Nuts. April 19—Willie Work
Lonesome Luke. June 7—Reilly
Once Every Ten Minutes. July 12—Reilly
Spitball Sadie. July 31
Soaking the Clothes. August 9
Pressing His Suit. August 23
Terribly Stuck Up. August 28
A Mixup for Mazie. September 6—Lonesome Luke

Some Baby. September 20
Fresh from the Farm. October 4
Giving Them Fits. November 1—Lonesome Luke
Bughouse Bellhops. November 8—Lonesome Luke
Tinkering with Trouble. November 17
Great While It Lasted. November 22—Lonesome Luke
Ragtime Snap Shots. November 29—Lonesome Luke
A Foozle at the Tee Party. December 8—Lonesome Luke
Ruses, Rhymes, and Roughnecks. December 15—identified in the trades as the first official entry in the Lonesome Luke series
Peculiar Patients' Pranks. December 22—Lonesome Luke
Lonesome Luke, Social Gangster. December 29

1916

All films feature Harold Lloyd as Lonesome Luke. All films are one reel in length.

Lonesome Luke Leans to the Literary. January 5
Luke Lugs Luggage. January 12
Lonesome Luke Lolls in Luxury. January 19
Luke, the Candy Cut-Up. January 31
Luke Foils the Villain. February 14
Luke and the Rural Roughnecks. March 1
Luke Pipes the Pippens. March 15
Lonesome Luke, Circus King. March 29
Luke's Double. April 12
Them Was the Happy Days. April 26
Luke and the Bomb Throwers. May 8
Luke's Late Lunchers. May 22
Luke Laughs Last. June 5
Luke's Fatal Flivver. June 19
Luke's Society Mixup. June 26
Luke's Washful Waiting. July 3
Luke Rides Roughshod. July 10
Luke—Crystal Gazer. July 24
Luke's Lost Lamb. August 7
Luke Does the Midway. August 21
Luke Joins the Navy. September 4
Luke and the Mermaids. September 18
Luke's Speedy Club Life. October 1
Luke and the Bang Tails. October 15
Luke and the Chauffeur. October 29
Luke's Preparedness Preparations. November 5
Luke, Gladiator. November 12
Luke, Patient Provider. November 19
Luke's Newsie Knockout. November 26
Luke's Movie Muddle. December 3
Luke, Rank Impersonator. December 10
Luke's Fireworks Fizzle. December 17
Luke Locates the Lute (*Loot* in a later *MPW* listing). December 24
Luke's Shattered Sleep. December 31

1917

All films are one reel unless otherwise noted. *LL* indicates a Lonesome Luke film. *HL* indicates a "glasses character" Harold Lloyd film.

Luke's Lost Liberty. January 7—LL
Schemer Skinny's Schemes. January 14—Dee "Skinny" Lampton
Luke's Busy Day. January 21—LL
Drama's Dreadful Deal. January 28—Dee "Skinny" Lampton
Luke's Trolley Troubles. February 4—LL
Skinny's Love Tangle/Schemer Skinny's Scandal—February 11—a pair of half-reel Dee Lampton comedies released together on a single reel
Lonesome Luke—Lawyer. February 8—LL
Luke Wins Ye Ladye Faire. February 25—LL
Lonesome Luke's Lively Life. March 18—the first LL two-reeler.
Skinny Gets a Goat. March 25—a Dee Lampton half-reel comedy released on the second half of a full reel after a Max Linder half-reel reissue, *Max's Feet Are Pinched*
Skinny's False Alarm/Skinny's Ship Wrecked Sand-Witch. April 1—a pair of half-reel Dee Lampton comedies released together on a single reel.
Lonesome Luke on Tin Can Alley. April 15—LL—two reels.
Lonesome Luke's Honeymoon. May 20—LL—two reels.
Lonesome Luke, Plumber. June 17—LL—two reels—Reilly
Stop! Luke! Listen! July 15—LL—two reels—Reilly
Lonesome Luke, Messenger. August 5—LL—two reels
Lonesome Luke, Mechanic. August 19—LL—two reels
Lonesome Luke's Wild Women. September 2—LL—two reels
Over the Fence. September 9—The first "glasses character" film—HL
Lonesome Luke Loses Patients. September 16—LL—two reels
Pinched. September 23—HL
By the Sad Sea Waves. September 30—HL
Lonesome Luke in "Birds of a Feather." October 7—LL—two reels
Bliss. October 14—HL
Lonesome Luke from London to Laramie. October 21—LL—2 reels
Rainbow Island. October 28—HL
Lonesome Luke in Love, Laughs, and Lather. November 4—LL—two reels
The Flirt. November 11—HL
Clubs Are Trumps. November 18—LL—two reels
All Aboard. November 25—HL
We Never Sleep. December 2—the last Lonesome Luke film—two reels
Move On. December 9—HL
Bashful. December 23—HL
Step Lively. December 30—HL

1918

All films are one reel unless otherwise noted.

The Tip. January 6—HL
The Movie Dummy. January 13—Toto—two reels
The Big Idea. January 20—HL
The Lamb. February 3—HL
Hello Teacher. February 10—pilot for a proposed series starring Snub Pollard

Hit Him Again. February 17—HL

A One Night Stand. February 24—Toto—two reels—This title is dropped from released title listings in subsequent issues of *MPW,* so it actually may not have been released at this time.

Beat It. February 24—HL

A Gasoline Wedding. March 3—HL

Look Pleasant Please. March 10—HL

Fare Please. March 17—Toto—two reels

Here Come the Girls. March 17—HL

Let's Go. March 24—HL

On the Jump. March 31—HL

Follow the Crowd. April 7—HL

Pipe the Whiskers. April 14—HL

It's a Wild Life. April 21—HL

Hey There. April 28—HL

His Busy Day. April 28—Toto—two reels

Kicked Out. May 5—HL

The Non-Stop Kid. May 12—HL

Two Gun Gussie. May 19—HL

The Junkman. May 26—Toto—two reels—originally announced for release on February 17 but withheld until this time

Fireman Save My Child. May 26—HL

The City Slicker. June 2—HL

Sic 'Em Towser. June 9—HL

Somewhere in Turkey. June 16—HL

Cleopatsy. June 23—Toto—two reels

Are Crooks Dishonest? June 23—HL

The Furniture Movers. June 30—This film was listed as Rolin in *MPW* and in copyright registration but did not appear in the Roach records.

An Ozark Romance. July 7—HL

Fire the Cook. July 14—the first Toto one-reeler

Kicking the Germ Out of Germany. July 21—HL

Beach Nuts. July 28—Toto

That's Him. August 4—HL

Do Husbands Deceive? August 11—Toto

Bride and Gloom. August 18—HL

Nipped in the Bud. August 25—Toto

Two Scrambled. September 1—HL

The Dippy Daughter. September 8—Toto

Bees in His Bonnet. September 15—HL—Dardis

The Great Water Peril. September 22—Toto

Swing Your Partners. September 29—HL

No Place Like Jail. October 1—Stan Laurel

Why Pick On Me? October 13—HL

The next four comedies initially were announced for release between mid-October and mid-November but were rescheduled as indicated below, creating a one-month period during which no Hal Roach comedies were released.

Nothing but Trouble. November 17—HL

An Enemy of Soap. November 24—Toto
Hear 'Em Rave. December 1—HL
Just Rambling Along. December 8—Stan Laurel
Take a Chance. December 15—HL
Check Your Baggage. December 22—Toto
She Loves Me Not. December 29—HL

1919

All films are one reel unless otherwise noted.

Do You Love Your Wife? January 5—Stan Laurel
Wanted—$5000. January 12—HL
Love's Young Scream. January 19—Director Alf Goulding subs for HL while latter temporarily walks out on studio in dispute with Roach.
Going! Going! Gone! January 26—HL
Hustling for Health. February 2—Stan Laurel
Ask Father. February 9—HL
Toto's Troubles. February 16—Toto
On the Fire. February 23—HL
Hoot Mon! March 2—Stan Laurel
I'm on My Way. March 9—HL
Look Out Below. March 16—HL
The Dutiful Dub. March 23—HL
Next Isle Over. March 30—HL
A Sammy in Siberia. April 6—HL
Just Dropped In. April 13—HL
Crack Your Heels. April 20—HL
Ring Up the Curtain. April 27—HL
Young Mr. Jazz. May 4—HL
Si Senor. May 11—HL
Before Breakfast. May 18—HL
The Marathon. May 25—HL
Back to the Woods. June 1—HL
Pistols for Breakfast. June 8—HL
Swat the Cook. June 15—HL
Off the Trolley. June 22—HL
Spring Fever. June 29—HL
Billy Blazes, Esq. July 6—HL
Just Neighbors. July 13—HL—the last HL one-reeler produced
At the Old Stage Door. July 20—HL
Never Touched Me. July 27—HL
A Jazzed Honeymoon. August 3—HL
Count Your Change. August 10—HL
Chop Suey & Co. August 17—HL
Heap Big Chief. August 24—HL
Don't Shove. August 31—HL
Be My Wife. September 7—HL
The Rajah. September 14—HL
He Leads, Others Follow. September 21—HL
Soft Money. September 28—HL

Count the Votes. October 5—HL
Pay Your Dues. October 12—HL—Reilly
His Only Father. October 19—HL—Dardis
Start Something. October 26—a Rolin Comedy starring Snub Pollard
All at Sea. November 2—Snub Pollard (H series no. 1)
Bumping into Broadway. November 2—HL—two reels
Call for Mr. Cave Man. November 9—Snub Pollard
Giving the Bride Away. November 16—Snub Pollard
Order in the Court. November 23—Snub Pollard
It's a Hard Life. November 30—Snub Pollard
Captain Kidd's Kids. November 30—HL—two reels
How Dry I Am. December 7—Snub Pollard
Looking for Trouble. December 14—Snub Pollard
Tough Luck. December 21—Snub Pollard
From Hand to Mouth. December 28—HL—two reels
The Floor Below. December 28—Snub Pollard

In addition to the Snub Pollard films listed above, number 8 in the series, untitled, was abandoned before completion.

1920

All films are one reel unless otherwise noted. *HL* indicates a comedy starring Harold Lloyd. *SP* indicates a comedy starring Snub Pollard.

Red Hot Hottentots. January 4—SP
Why Go Home? January 11—SP
Slippery Slickers. January 18—SP
The Dippy Dentist. January 25—SP
All Lit Up. February 1—SP
Getting His Goat. February 8—SP
His Royal Slyness. February 8—HL—two reels
Waltz Me Around. February 15—SP
Raise the Rent. February 22—SP
Find the Girl. February 29—SP
Fresh Paint. March 7—SP
Flat Broke. March 14—SP
Cut the Cards. March 21—SP
The Dinner Hour. March 28—SP
Haunted Spooks. March 31—HL—two reels
Speed to Spare. April 4—SP
Shoot on Sight. April 11—SP
Don't Weaken. April 18—SP
Cracked Wedding Bells. April 25—SP
An Eastern Westerner. May 2—HL—two reels
Drink Hearty. May 2—SP
Trotting Through Turkey. May 9—SP
Merely a Maid. May 16—Beatrice La Plante
All Dressed Up. May 23—SP
Grab the Ghost. May 30—SP
You're Pinched. June 6—SP

High and Dizzy. June 13—HL—two reels
Start the Snow. June 13—Beatrice La Plante
All in a Day. June 20—SP
Any Old Port. June 27—SP
Don't Rock the Boat. July 4—SP
Hello Uncle. July 11—Beatrice La Plante
The Home Stretch. July 18—SP
Call a Taxi. July 25—SP
Live and Learn. August 1—SP
Little Miss Jazz. August 8—Beatrice La Plante
Run 'Em Ragged. August 15—SP
A London Bobby. August 22—SP
Money to Burn. August 29—SP
A Regular Pal. September 5—Beatrice La Plante
Get Out and Get Under. September 12—HL—two reels
Go as You Please. September 12—SP
Rock-a-By-Baby. September 19—SP
Doing Time. September 26—SP
June Madness. October 3—Vanity Fair Girls (with Eddie Boland)
Fellow Citizens. October 10—SP
Alias Aladdin. October 17—Vanity Fair Girls (with Eddie Boland)
When the Wind Blows. October 24—SP
Mamma's Boy. October 31—Vanity Fair Maids (with Eddie Boland)
Insulting the Sultan. November 7—SP
The Sandman. November 14—Vanity Fair Girls (with Eddie Boland)
The Dear Departed. November 21—SP
Queens Up. November 28—Vanity Fair Girls (with Eddie Boland)
Cash Customers. December 5—SP
Vanity Fair Girls Comedy. December 12
Park Your Car. December 19—SP
Number Please! December 26—HL—two reels
Greek Meets Greek. December 26—Vanity Fair Girls (with Eddie Boland)

1921

All films are one reel unless otherwise noted. *VFG* indicates Vanity Fair Girls comedy (also starring Eddie Boland). *EB* indicates an Eddie Boland comedy without the Vanity Fair Girls. *HLR* indicates Harold Lloyd reissue. *GL* indicates Gaylord Lloyd comedy.

The Sleepy Head. January 1—VFG
The Morning After. January 16—SP
Burglars Bold. January 16—VFG
Whirl of the West. January 23—SP
Pinning It On. January 30—VFG
Oh, Promise Me. February 6—VFG
Open Another Bottle. February 13—SP
Prince Pistachio. February 20—VFG
His Best Girl. February 27—SP
Paint and Powder. March 6—VFG
Make It Snappy. March 13—SP
Running Wild. March 20—VFG

Fellow Romans. March 27—SP

The Love Lesson. April 3—EB

Rush Orders. April 10—SP

Hobgoblins. April 17—EB

Bubbling Over. April 24—SP

Hurry West. May 1—EB

Now or Never. May 5—HL—three reels—distributed by Associated Exhibitors—Dardis

No Children. May 8—SP

A Straight Crook. May 15—EB

Big Game. May 22—SP

Save Your Money. May 29—SP

The Killjoys. June 5—SP (alternate title, *Blue Sunday*)—Anthony and Edmonds

Where's the Fire? June 12—SP

Own Your Home. June 19—SP

The High Rollers. June 26—SP

You're Next. July 3—SP

Among Those Present. July 3—HL—three reels—distributed by Associated Exhibitors—Dardis

The Bike Bug. July 10—SP

At the Ring Side. July 17—SP

Bliss. July 17—HLR

No Stop-Over. July 24—SP

The Flirt. July 24—HLR

What a Whopper. July 31—SP

All Aboard. July 31—HLR—two-thirds reel

Teaching the Teacher. August 7—SP

The Tip. August 7—HLR

Spot Cash. August 14—SP

Rainbow Island. August 14—HLR

Name the Day. August 21—SP

Move On. August 21—HLR

Stop Kidding. August 28—EB

By the Sad Sea Waves. August 28—HLR

By the Jail Bird. September 4—SP

Over the Fence. September 4—HLR

I Do. September 11—HL—two reels—distributed by Associated Exhibitors—Dardis

On Their Way. September 11—EB

One-Quarter Inch. September 11—HLR—This mysterious title does not show up in the initial group of HL one-reelers and is not in the Roach records. It is either a film that was not previously released, a retitled version of an earlier film, or, most likely, an *MPW* mistake.

Late Lodgers. September 18—SP

Bashful. September 18—HLR

The Chink. September 25—EB

Rough Seas. September 25—Gaylord Lloyd

Gone to the Country. October 2—SP

The Lucky Number. October 2—GL

Sweet By and By. October 9—EB

A Zero Hero. October 9—GL

Law and Order. October 16—SP
Dodge Your Debts. October 16—GL
Never Weaken. October 22—HL—three reels—distributed by Associated Exhibitors—
  Dardis
Late Hours. October 23—EB
Trolley Troubles. October 23—GL
Fifteen Minutes. October 30—SP
Pistols for Breakfast. October 30—HLR
On Location. November 6—SP
Just Dropped In. November 6—HLR
Hocus Pocus. November 13—SP
Crack Your Heels. November 13—HLR
Penny-in-the-Slot. November 20—SP
The Marathon. November 20—HLR
The Joy Rider. November 27—SP
Back to the Woods. November 27—HLR
The Hustler. December 4—SP
The Pickaninny. December 4—Sunshine Sammy Morrison—two reels
Somewhere in Turkey. December 4—HLR
Sink or Swim. December 11—SP
Look Pleasant, Please. December 11—HLR
Shake 'Em Up. December 18—SP
Two Gun Gussie. December 18—HLR
The Corner Pocket. December 25—SP
Fireman Save My Child. December 25—HLR
A Sailor-Made Man. December 25—HL—four reels—distributed by Associated Exhibitors—Dardis

1922

All films are one reel unless otherwise noted. In addition to previous codes used, *WE* designates the Ruth Roland serial White Eagle. The episodes of this serial, all two-reelers, will be designated by episode number rather than episode title. *PP* indicates a Paul Parrott comedy. *OG* indicates an Our Gang comedy.

Try, Try Again. January 1—C series—either Sunshine Sammy Morrison or Paul Parrott
WE no. 1. January 1
Before Breakfast. January 1—HLR
Lose No Time. January 8—SP
Take a Chance. January 8—HLR
WE no. 2. January 8
WE no. 3. January 15
Loose Change. January 15—PP
The Non-Stop Kid. January 15—HLR
WE no. 4. January 22
Call the Witness. January 22—SP
That's Him. January 22—HLR
WE no. 5. January 29
Years to Come. January 29—SP
She Loves Me Not. January 29—HLR
WE no. 6. February 5

The Lamb. February 5—HLR
Blow 'Em Up. February 5—SP
WE no. 7. February 12
Stage Struck. February 12—SP
Look Out Below. February 12—HLR
WE no. 8. February 19
Rich Man, Poor Man. February 19—PP
The Big Idea. February 19—HLR
WE no. 9. February 26
Down and Out. February 26—SP
Here Comes the Girls. February 26—SP
WE no. 10. March 5
Pardon Me. March 5—SP
On the Jump. March 5—HLR
WE no. 11. March 12
The Bow Wows. March 12—SP
On the Fire. March 12—HLR
WE no. 12. March 19
High Tide. March 19—Sunshine Sammy Morrison
Hey There. March 19—HLR
WE no. 13. March 26
Hot off the Press. March 26—SP
Hit Him Again. March 26—HLR
WE no. 14. April 2
The Anvil Chorus. April 2—SP
Beat It. April 2—HLR
WE no. 15. April 9
Jump Your Job. April 9—SP
Next Aisle Over. April 9—HLR
Stand Pat. April 16—PP
An Ozark Romance. April 16—HLR
Full o' Pep. April 23—SP
Bride and Gloom. April 23—HLR
Kill the Nerve. April 30—SP
Pipe the Whiskers. April 30—HLR
Days of Old (*Days of Gold* according to Anthony and Edmonds). May 7—SP
Follow the Crowd. May 7—HLR
Light Showers. May 14—SP
Swing Your Partners. May 14—HLR
Do Me a Favor. May 21—SP
Why Pick on Me? May 21—HLR
In the Movies (*The Movie* according to Anthony and Edmonds). May 28—SP
Ask Father. May 28—HLR
Punch the Clock. June 4—SP
Nothing but Trouble. June 4—HLR
Good Morning Judge. June 4—EB
Strictly Modern. June 11—SP
The Non-skid Kid. June 11—EB—produced in 1921 as VFG no. 18
Hale and Hearty. June 18—SP

Be My Wife. June 18—HLR
Many Happy Returns. June 25—Eddie Boland
Some Baby. June 25—SP
Wanted—$5,000. June 25—HLR
Friday the 13th. July 2—PP
Just Neighbors. July 2—HLR
The Man Haters. July 2—VFG—produced in 1920 as VFG no. 6
A Bed of Roses. July 9—PP
The Stone Age. July 9—SP—produced late 1921
The Late Lamented. July 9—Eddie Boland
A Jazzed Honeymoon. July 9—HLR
The Timber Queen. A Ruth Roland Serial
Spring Fever. HLR
The Dumb Bell. July 16—SP
The Sleuth. July 16—PP
The Bride-to-Be. July 23—PP
Going! Going! Gone! July 23—HLR
Busy Bees. July 23—possibly Sunshine Sammy Morrison—first of the C series to be
    produced after the departure of Eddie Boland
Take Next Car. July 30—PP
A Gasoline Wedding. July 30—HLR
The Stone Age. August 6—SP—Anthony and Edmonds
The City Slicker. August 6—HLR
Touch All the Bases. August 13—PP
Let's Go. August 13—HLR
The Truth Juggler. August 20—PP
It's a Wild Life. August 20—HLR
Rough on Romeo. August 27—PP
Hear 'Em Rave. August 27—HLR
Grandma's Boy. September 3—HL—five reels—distributed by Associated Exhibitors—
    Dardis
Wet Weather. September 3—PP
Off the Trolley. September 3—HLR
Si Senior. September 10—HLR
One Terrible Day. September 10—OG—two reels
The Landlubber. September 10—PP
365 Days. September 17—SP—two reels
Bone Dry. September 17—PP
Count the Votes. September 17—HLR
Soak the Sheik. September 24—PP
Two Scrambled. September 24—HLR
Face the Camera. October 1—PP
Pay Your Dues. October 1—HLR
Fire Fighters. October 8—OG—two reels
Never Touched Me. October 8—HLR
The Uppercut. October 8—PP
The Old Sea Dog. October 15—SP—two reels
Out on Bail. October 15—PP
Chop Suey and Co. October 15—HLR

Shiver and Shake. October 22—PP

The Rajah. October 22—HLR

The Golf Bug. October 29—PP

At the Old Stage Door. HLR

Shine 'Em Up. November 5—PP

Our Gang. November 5—OG—two reels

Hale and Hearty. November 5—SP—This film previously had been assigned a release date of June 18, 1922.

His Only Father. November 5—HLR

Hook, Line, and Sinker. November 12—SP—two reels

Kicking the Germ Out of Germany. November 12—HLR

Washed Ashore. November 12—PP

Harvest Hands. November 19—PP

I'm on My Way. November 19—HLR

Young Sherlocks. November 26—OG—two reels

The Flivver. November 29—PP

Don't Shove. November 26—HLR

Blaze Away. December 3—PP

Saturday Morning. December 3—OG—two reels

Soft Money. December 3—HLR

Newly Rich. December 10—SP—two reels

I'll Take Vanilla. December 10—PP

Young Mr. Jazz. December 10—HLR

Fair Week. December 17—PP (Anthony and Edmonds list a PP release at this time entitled *Leave It to Me.*)

Dr. Jack. December 19—HL—five reels—Pathé

White Blacksmith. December 24—PP

Sic 'Em Towser. December 24—HLR

Fire the Fireman. December 31—PP

A Quiet Street. December 31—OG—two reels—Maltin and Bann

A Sammy in Siberia. December 31—HLR

1923

All films are one reel unless otherwise indicated. In addition to the previous codes, *DDD* indicates Dippy Doo Dads, *SL* indicates Stan Laurel, *Spat* indicates Spat Family, and *WR* indicates Will Rogers.

Watch Your Wife. January 7—PP

Dig Up. January 7—SP

Paste and Paper. January 14—PP

Mr. Hyppo. January 21—PP

The Champeen. January 28—OG—two reels

Don't Say Die. January 28—PP

A Tough Winter. February 4—SP—two reels

Once Over. February 11—PP

Jailed and Bailed. February 18—PP

The Cobbler. February 18—OG—two reels—Maltin and Bann

A Loose Tight Wad. February 18—PP

Tight Shoes. February 25—PP

The Big Show. February 25—OG—two reels

Before the Public. March 4—SP—two reels
Shoot Straight. March 11—PP
Do Your Stuff. March 11—PP
For Safe Keeping. March 18—PP
A Pleasant Journey. March 18—OG—two reels
Bowled Over. March 25—PP
Where Am I? April 1—SP—two reels
Safety Last. April 1—HL—seven reels
Get Your Man. April 1—PP
The Smile Wins. April 8—PP
Boys to Board. April 8—OG—two reels
Good Riddance. April 15—PP
Speed the Swede. April 22—PP
California or Bust. April 29—SP—two reels
The Noon Whistle. April 29—Stan Laurel
Sunny Spain. May 6—PP
White Wings. May 13—SL
Giants vs. Yanks. May 13—OG—two reels
Don't Flirt. May 20—Dippy Doo Dads
Sold at Auction. May 27—SP—two reels
For Art's Sake. May 27—PP
Under Two Jags. June 3—SL
Back Stage. June 3—OG—two reels
The Watch Dog. June 10—DDD
Pick and Shovel. June 17—SL
Fresh Eggs. June 24—PP
Courtship of Miles Sandwich. June 24—SP—two reels
Collars and Cuffs. July 1—SL
Dogs of War. July 1—OG—two reels
The Uncovered Wagon. July 8—PP
Kill or Cure. July 15—SL
Jack Frost. July 22—SP—two reels
Her Dangerous Path. July 22—ten-chapter serial starring Edna Murphy
For Guests Only. July 2—PP
Lodge Night. July 29—OG—two reels
Gas and Air. July 29—SL
The Green Cat. August 5—SP—two reels
Post No Bills. August 5—PP
Oranges and Lemons. August 12—SL
The Mystery Man. August 19—SP—two reels
Be Honest. August 19—DDD
Live Wires. August 26—PP
July Days. August 26—OG—two reels
Short Orders. September 2—SL
Call of the Wild. September 2—dramatic feature—seven reels
Take the Air. September 9—PP
Why Worry? September 16—Harold Lloyd's last film for Hal Roach—six reels
Let's Build. September 16—Spat Family—two reels
The Walkout. September 16—SP—two reels

A Man about Town. September 16—SL

Finger Prints. September 23—PP

No Noise. September 23—OG—two reels

Roughest Africa. September 30—SL—two reels

Stepping Out. September 30—DDD

No Pets. October 7—PP

Heavy Seas. October 7—Spat—two reels

Jus' Passin' Thru. October 14—Will Rogers—two reels

It's a Gift. October 14—SP—This film was cut from two reels to a single reel for release. Subsequent films in the Pollard series were shot as one-reelers.

Winner Take All. October 21—PP—produced in 1922

Stage Fright. October 21—OG—two reels

Frozen Hearts. October 28—SL—two reels

The Knockout. October 28—PP or DDD

The Whole Truth. November 4—SL

Roughing It. November 4—Spat—two reels

Dear Ol' Pal. November 11—Snub Pollard and Paul Parrott

Hustlin' Hank. November 11—WR—two reels

Derby Day. November 18—OG—two reels

Save the Ship. November 18—SL

Go West. November 25—DDD

The Soilers. November 25—SL—two reels

The Great Outdoors. December 2—Spat—two reels

Join the Circus. December 2—Pollard and Parrott

Uncensored Movies. December 9—WR—two reels

Scorching Sands. December 9—SL

Sunday Calm. December 16—OG—two reels

Fully Insured. December 16—SP

Mother's Joy. December 23—SL—two reels

Lovey-Dovey. December 23—DDD

It's a Boy. December 30—SP

1924

All films are two reels in length unless otherwise noted. In addition to previous codes,
CC indicates a Charley Chase comedy.

The Darkest Hour. January 6—Spat

Two Wagons—Both Covered. January 6—WR

At First Sight. January 6—Charley Chase—one reel

Handle 'Em Rough. January 6—one reel

Tire Trouble. January 13—OG

The Big Idea. January 13—SP—one reel

Smithy. January 20—SL

The Bar-Fly. January 20—DDD—one reel

One of the Family. January 27—CC—one reel

Help One Another. January 27—Spat

Just a Minute. February 3—CC—one reel

The Cowboy Sheik. February 3—WR

Big Business. February 10—OG

Powder and Smoke. February 10—CC—one reel

The Man Pays. February 17—DDD—one reel
Postage Due. February 17—SL
Political Pull. February 24—Spat
A Perfect Lady. February 24—one reel
Hard Knocks. March 2—CC—one reel
The Cake Eater. March 2—WR
The Buccaneers. March 9—OG
Love's Reward. March 9—DDD—one reel
Love's Detour. March 16—CC—one reel
Zeb Versus Paprika. March 16—SL
Hunters Bold. March 23—Spat
Don't Forget. March 23—CC—one reel
The King of Wild Horses. March 30—Rex, the Wonder Horse—five reels
Big Moments from Little Pictures. March 30—WR
Fraidy Cat. March 30—CC—one reel
Seein' Things. April 6—OG
Friend Husband. April 6—SP—one reel
Our Little Nell. April 13—one reel
Brothers under the Chin. April 13—SL
Hit the High Spots. April 20—Spat
One at a Time. April 20—Earl Mohan—one reel
Get Busy. April 27—SP—one reel—produced in 1923
High Brow Stuff. April 27—WR
Commencement Day. May 4—OG
Publicity Pays. May 4—CC—one reel
Near Dublin. May 11—SL
North of 50-50. May 11—DDD—one reel
April Fool. May 18—CC—one reel
Bottle Babies. May 18—Spat
Going to Congress. May 25—WR
Position Wanted. May 25—CC—one reel
Cradle Robbers. June 1—OG
Before Taking. June 1—Earl Mohan—one reel
Rupert of Hee-Haw. June 8—SL
Up and at 'Em. June 8—DDD—one reel
Fast Black. June 15—Mohan and Engle—one reel
Suffering Shakespeare. June 15—Spat
Young Oldfield. June 22—CC—one reel
Don't Park There! June 22—WR
Stolen Goods. June 29—CC—one reel
Jubilo, Jr. June 29—OG
Jeffries, Jr. July 6—CC—one reel
The Wide Open Spaces. July 6—SL
Why Husbands Go Mad. July 13—CC—one reel
Radio Mad. July 13—Spat
Our Congressman. July 20—WR
A Ten Minute Egg. July 20—CC—one reel
It's a Bear. July 27—OG
Seeing Nellie Home. July 27—CC—one reel

Short Kilts. August 3—SL
A Hard-Boiled Tenderfoot. August 10—Spat
A Truthful Liar. August 17—WR
Sweet Daddy. August 17—CC—one reel
The Battling Orioles. August 24—Glenn Tryon—five reels
High Society. August 24—OG
Why Men Work. August 31—CC—one reel
South o' the North Pole. September 7—Spat
Outdoor Pajamas. September 14—CC—one reel
The Sun Down Limited. September 21—OG
Gee Whiz, Genevieve. September 28—WR
Should Landlords Live? September 28—Arthur Stone
Sittin' Pretty. September 28—CC—one reel
Lost Dog. October 5—Spat
Too Many Mamas. October 12—CC
The Goofy Age. October 12—Glenn Tryon
Every Man for Himself. October 19—OG
Bungalow Boobs. October 26—CC—one reel
Sky Plumber. October 26—Arthur Stone
Hot Stuff. November 2—Spat
Accidental Accidents. November 9—CC—one reel
Hot Heels. November 9—Arthur Stone
Fast Company. November 16—OG—produced in the fall of 1923, between *Lodge Night* and *Stage Fright,* as "A#16."
Are Blond Men Bashful? November 23—Arthur Stone
All Wet. November 23—CC—one reel
Deaf, Dumb, and Daffy. November 30—Spat
White Sheep. December 7—Glenn Tryon—six reels
Meet the Missus. December 7—Glenn Tryon
The Poor Fish. December 7—CC—one reel
The Mysterious Mystery. December 14—OG
Just a Good Guy. December 21—Arthur Stone
Royal Razz. December 21—CC—one reel
The Rubber-Neck. December 28—Spat

In addition to the above, number 8 in the Will Rogers series, untitled, was abandoned before completion and was not released.

No release dates are indicated in the Roach records for number 1, *Hoss and Hoss,* and number 9, *Hard Working Loafers,* in the Arthur Stone, or E, series, nor were these films registered for copyright, suggesting that they never were finished. Additionally, number 4 and number 11 in the series, untitled, evidently were abandoned before completion.

1925

All films are two reels unless otherwise noted. In addition to previous codes, *GT* indicates Glenn Tryon and *AS* indicates Arthur Stone.

Wages of Tin. January 4—GT
The Rat's Knuckles. January 4—CC—one reel

The Big Town. January 11—OG

Hello Baby. January 18—CC—one reel

Laugh That Off. January 25—Spat

Fighting Fluid. February 1—CC—one reel

Circus Fever. February 8—OG

Change the Needle. February 15—AS

Family Entrance. February 15—CC—one reel

The Fox Hunt. February 22—Spat

Plain and Fancy Girls. March 1—CC—one reel

Haunted Honeymoon. March 1—GT

Dog Days. March 8—OG

Should Husbands Be Watched?—March 15—CC—one reel

Hard Boiled. March 15—the first Charley Chase two-reeler

Excuse My Glove. March 22—Spat

Is Marriage the Bunk? March 29—CC—one reel

Sailor Papa. March 29—GT—produced fall 1924.

The Love Bug. April 5—OG

Bad Boy. April 12—CC

Are Husbands Human? April 12—James Finlayson—one reel

Black Hand Blues. April 19—Spat

Hold My Baby. April 26—GT

Big Red Riding Hood. April 26—CC—one reel

The Black Cyclone. May—Rex, the Wonder Horse, feature

Shootin' Injuns. May 3—OG

Looking for Sally. May 10—CC

Grief in Bagdad. May 10—one reel—produced in 1924

Wild Papa. May 17—Spat

Tell It to a Policeman. May 24—GT

Sure-Mike. May 24—Martha Sleeper—one reel

Ask Grandma. May 31—OG

What Price Goofy?—June 7—CC

Royal Four-Flush. June 14—Spat

Riders of the Kitchen Range. June 13—a "Hunky" Dorrey comedy with Earl Mohan and
     Billy Engle—one reel—produced in 1924

Thundering Landlords. June 21—GT

In the Grease. June 21—James Finlayson—one reel

Official Officers. June 28—OG

Isn't Life Terrible?—July 5—CC

Chasing the Chaser. July 5—James Finlayson—one reel

Sherlock Sleuth. July 12—AS

Daddy Goes a' Grunting. July 19—GT

Yes, Yes, Nannette. July 19—James Finlayson—one reel—the last silent Hal Roach one-
     reeler produced, although between the backlog of unreleased films and reissues,
     the studio continued releasing one-reelers through 1926

Boys Will Be Joys. July 26—OG

Innocent Husbands. August 2—CC

The Bouncer. August 2—Mohan—one reel—produced 1924

Tame Men and Wild Women. August 16—AS

Mary, Queen of Tots. August 23—OG

No Father to Guide Him. September 6—CC
Unfriendly Enemies. September 13—James Finlayson—one reel
Madame Sans Jane. September 13—GT
Somewhere in Somewhere. September 20—All-Star no. 3
Your Own Back Yard. September 27—OG
The Big Kick. September 27—Kelly—one reel—produced 1924
Moonlight and Noses. October 4—Clyde Cook
The Caretaker's Daughter. October 11—CC
Cuckoo Love. October 18—GT
Solid Ivory. October 25—one reel—produced 1924
All Wool. October 25—Earl Mohan—one reel—produced 1924
There Goes the Bride. October 25—All-Star no. 4
Better Movies. November 1—OG
Are Parents Pickles? November 8—PP—one reel
Should Sailors Marry? November 8—Clyde Cook
The Uneasy Three. November 15—CC
Papa, Be Good! November 22—GT
Whistling Lions. November 22—PP—produced 1922
Laughing Ladies. November 29—Lucien Littlefield, Katherine
Grant, Gertrude Astor
Hold Everything. December 6—Eddie Borden—one reel
One Wild Ride. December 6—OG
Starvation Blues. December 13—Clyde Cook
His Wooden Wedding. December 20—CC
Tol'able Romeo. December 20—Frank Butler—one reel
Flaming Flappers. December 27—GT

1926

All films are two reels unless otherwise noted. By this time, Roach's All-Star series was under way. Specific stars for this series are indicated where known.

A Punch in the Nose. January 3—All-Star no. 2—Lucien Littlefield, Al St. John, James
    Finlayson
Good Cheer. January 10—OG
Between Meals. January 10—Sunshine Sammy Morrison—one reel—produced 1921
What's the World Coming to? January 17—Clyde Cook
The Roustabout. January 17—PP—one reel—produced 1921—According to Anthony
    and Edmonds, the title of this film was changed to *Don't Butt In* before release.
Charley, My Boy. January 24—CC
Long Pants. January 24—GT
Soft Pedal. January 30—PP—one reel—produced 1921
Your Husband's Past. February 7—All-Star
Buried Treasure. February 14—OG
Pay the Cashier. February 14—PP—one reel—produced 1921
Wandering Papas. February 21—Clyde Cook (with Oliver Hardy; director, Stan Laurel)
Mama Behave. February 28—CC
The Only Son. February 28—PP—one reel—produced 1921–22
Hug Bug. March 7—GT
Do Your Duty. March 7—SP—one reel—produced 1922
Hired and Fired. March 14—PP—one reel—produced 1921–22

Dizzy Daddies. March 14—All-Star—James Finlayson
Monkey Business. March 21—OG
Wife Tamer. March 28—Clyde Cook, Lionel Barrymore
Dog Shy. April 4—CC
The Old War Horse. April 11—Snub Pollard and Paul Parrott—one reel—produced 1923
Ukulele Sheiks. April 11—GT
Madame Mystery. April 18—Theda Bara (All-Star)
Baby Clothes. April 25—OG
Uncovered Wagon. April 25—PP—reissue
Scared Stiff. May 2—Clyde Cook
Mum's the Word. May 9—CC
Say It with Babies. May 16—GT
Don Key—Son of Burro. May 23—All-Star no. 1
Uncle Tom's Uncle. May 30—OG
He Forgot to Remember. June 6—Clyde Cook
The Big Idea. June 6—SP—one reel—reissue
The Golf Bug. June 13—PP—one reel—reissue
Long Fliv the King. June 13—CC
Cow's Kimono. June 20—GT
Take the Air. June 20—PP—one reel—reissue
Never Too Old. June 27—Claude Gillingwater (All-Star)
Thundering Fleas. July 4—OG (with Charley Chase, Oliver Hardy)
Man about Town. July 4—SL—one reel—reissue
Are Crooks Dishonest? July 11—HLR—one reel—reissue
Mighty Like a Moose. July 18—CC
It's a Gift. July 18—SP—one reel—reissue
Along Came Auntie. July 25—GT
Merry Widower. August 1—Ethel Clayton (All-Star)
Harvest Hands. August 1—PP—one reel—reissue
Shivering Spooks. August 8—OG
Count Your Change. August 8—HLR—one reel—reissue
Under Two Jags. August 15—SL—one reel—reissue
Bumping into Broadway. August 15—HLR—two reels—reissue
Crazy Like a Fox. August 22—CC
Ring Up the Curtain. August 22—HLR—one reel—reissue
Fully Insured. August 29—SP—one reel—reissue
Should Husbands Pay? September 5—All-Star
The Devil Horse. September 12—Rex, the Wonder Horse—feature
The Fourth Alarm. September 12—OG
Bromo and Juliet. September 19—CC
The Valley of Hell. MGM release—western feature—five reels
The Desert's Toll. MGM release—western feature—six reels
Wise Guys Prefer Brunettes. October 3—All-Star
Tell 'Em Nothing. October 17—CC
Get 'Em Young. October 31—Harry Myers (All-Star)
Raggedy Rose. November 7—Mabel Normand—three reels
Be Your Age. November 14—CC
War Feathers. November 21—OG
On the Front Page. November 28—Lillian Rich (All-Star)

The Nickel Hopper. December 5—Mabel Normand—three reels
Many Scrappy Returns. December 12—CC
Telling Whoppers. December 19—OG
Forty-five Minutes from Hollywood. December 26—Glenn Tryon and the Hal Roach
 All-Stars—This film started production in late 1925 as a Glenn Tryon comedy. It
 was shelved upon completion, then went back into production with a drastically
 altered second half that included cameos by Our Gang, Theda Bara, Stan Laurel,
 and Oliver Hardy (not teamed).

1927

All films are two reels, unless otherwise noted, and, until September 1927, were distributed by Pathé. For films released between September 1927 and February 1928, a distributor (either Pathé or MGM) is indicated beside the film title. After February 1928,
all films were distributed by MGM. By the beginning of the 1927–28 movie season, the
All-Star series centered on Stan Laurel, Oliver Hardy, and James Finlayson. In some
of these films, Laurel and Hardy appeared as a team; in others they were cast as adversaries or one or both were relegated to minor supporting roles. The actors are listed
below as "Laurel and Hardy" in films in which they play as a team and as "Stan Laurel, Oliver Hardy" in the others.

Anything Once. January 2—Mabel Normand
There Ain't No Santa Claus. January 9—CC
Bring Home the Turkey. January 16—OG
Two-Time Mama. January 27—GT
Should Men Walk Home? February 6—Creighton Hale (All-Star)
Are Brunettes Safe? February 6—CC
Seeing the World. February 13—OG (with Stan Laurel)
Why Girls Say No. February 20—Marjorie Daw (All-Star)
One Hour Married. February 27—Mabel Normand (All-Star)
A One Mama Man. March 6—CC
Ten Years Old. March 13—OG
Duck Soup. March 20—Laurel and Hardy (All-Star)
Hon. Mr. Buggs. March 27—Matt Moore (All-Star)
Forgotten Sweeties. April 3—CC
Love My Dog. April 10—OG
Slipping Wives. April 17—All-Star (Priscilla Dean, Herbert Rawlinson, Stan Laurel,
 Oliver Hardy)—Skretvedt
No Man's Law. April 24—Rex, Barbara Kent, James Finlayson, Oliver Hardy—fourth
 adventure feature in the Rex series
Jewish Prudence. May 8—Max Davidson
Bigger and Better Blondes. May 15—CC
Tired Business Men. May 21—OG
Eve's Love Letters. May 28—Agnes Ayres, Forrest Stanley, Stan Laurel
Baby Brother. June—OG—Maltin and Bann
Love 'Em and Weep. June 12—All-Star (Mae Busch, Stan Laurel, Oliver Hardy)
Fluttering Hearts. June 19—CC
Don't Tell Everything. July 2—Max Davidson
Why Girls Love Sailors. July 23—Stan Laurel, Oliver Hardy (All-Star)
The Glorious Fourth. July 30—OG
What Women Did for Me. August 14—CC

With Love and Hisses. August 28—Stan Laurel, Oliver Hardy, James Finlayson (All-Star)

The Sting of Stings (the first MGM release). September 3—CC

Sugar Daddies (MGM). September 10—James Finlayson, Stan Laurel, Oliver Hardy (All-Star)

Olympic Games (Pathé). September 10—OG—Maltin and Bann

What Every Iceman Knows (MGM). September 17—Max Davidson—tinted sequences

Sailors, Beware! (Pathé). September 24—Stan Laurel, Oliver Hardy (All-Star)

Yale vs. Harvard (MGM). September 24—OG

The Lighter That Failed (MGM). October 1—CC

The Second Hundred Years (MGM). October 8—Laurel and Hardy (All-Star)—tinted sequences

Call of the Cuckoo (MGM). October 15—Max Davidson (with Charley Chase, James Finlayson, Laurel and Hardy)

The Old Wallop (MGM). October 22—OG

The Way of All Pants (MGM). October 29—CC

Now I'll Tell One (Pathé). October 29—CC (with Stan Laurel, Oliver Hardy)

Hats Off (MGM). November 5—Laurel and Hardy (All-Star)

Chicken Feed (Pathé). November 6—OG—Maltin and Bann

Do Detectives Think? (Pathé). November 12—Laurel and Hardy (All-Star)

Love 'Em and Feed 'Em (MGM). November 12—Max Davidson

Heebie Jeebies (MGM). November 19—OG

Us (MGM). November 26—CC

Putting Pants on Phillip (MGM). December 3—Laurel and Hardy (All-Star)

Assistant Wives (Pathé). December 4—CC—Anthony and Edmonds

Fighting Fathers (MGM). December 10—Max Davidson

Dog Heaven (MGM). December 17—OG

Never the Dames Shall Meet (MGM). December 24—CC

The Battle of the Century (MGM). December 31—Laurel and Hardy (All-Star)

Flaming Fathers (Pathé). 1927—All-Star

Galloping Ghosts (Pathé). 1927—Clyde Cook

1928

All films are two reels in length unless otherwise noted. In addition to the previous codes, *L and H* indicates Laurel and Hardy, *MD* indicates Max Davidson, and *(SS)* indicates that a film was released with a synchronized music and effects sound track.

Playin' Hookey (Pathé). January 1—OG—Maltin and Bann

Pass the Gravy (MGM). January 7—MD

Spook Spoofing (MGM). January 14—OG

All for Nothing (MGM). January 21—CC

Should Tall Men Marry? (aka *Cowboys Cry for It*) (Pathé). 1928—Stan Laurel (All-Star)

Leave 'Em Laughing (MGM). January 28—L and H (All-Star)

Dumb Daddies (MGM). February 4—MD

Rainy Days (MGM). February 11—OG

Flying Elephants (Pathé). February 12—Stan Laurel, Oliver Hardy (All-Star)

Family Group (MGM). February 18—CC

The Finishing Touch (MGM). February 25—L and H (All-Star)

The Smile Wins (the last Pathé release). February 26—OG—Maltin and Bann

Came the Dawn. March 3—MD

Edison, Marconi and Co. March 10—OG

Aching Youth. March 17—CC (*Aching Youths* according to Anthony and Edmonds)
Blow by Blow. March 21—MD
From Soup to Nuts. March 24—L and H (All-Star)
Barnum and Ringling, Inc. (SS). April 7—OG
Limousine Love. April 14—CC
You're Darn Tootin'. April 21—L and H (All-Star)
Tell It to the Judge. April 28—MD
Fair and Muddy. May 5—OG
The Fighting Pest. May 12—CC (*The Fight Pest* according to Anthony and Edmonds)
Their Purple Moment. May 19—last All-Star to feature L and H
Should Women Drive? May 26—MD
Crazy House. June 2—OG
Imagine My Embarrassment (SS). September 1—CC
Should Married Men Go Home? September 8—first in "official" L and H series
That Night. September 15—All-Star—tinted sequences
Growing Pains. September 22—OG
Is Everybody Happy? (SS). September 29—CC
Early to Bed. October 6—L and H
Do Gentlemen Snore? October 13—All-Star—tinted sequences
The Ol' Gray Hoss (SS). October 20—OG
All Parts (SS). October 27—CC—Anthony and Edmonds
Two Tars. November 3—L and H—three reels
The Boy Friend. November 10—All-Star
School Begins (SS). November 17—OG
The Booster (SS). November 24—CC
Habeas Corpus (SS). December 1—L and H
Feed 'Em and Weep. December 8—All-Star
The Spanking Age (SS). December 15—OG
Chasing Husbands. December 22—CC
We Faw Down (SS). December 29—L and H

1929

All films are two reels in length. This is the year that the Hal Roach Studios began to make full talking pictures. The first of these for each series were rushed through production in the spring and distributed as quickly as possible. The last silents were completed before the first talkies were produced, but the silents were temporarily shelved, being released alternately with the talkies through the end of the year. This list includes only the silent films.

Going Ga Ga. January 5—All-Star (Edgar Kennedy, Max Davidson, Marion Byron)
Election Day. January 12—OG
Ruby Lips (SS). January 19—CC
Liberty (SS). January 26—L and H
A Pair of Tights. February 2—All-Star (Edgar Kennedy, Stu Erwin)
Noisy Noises (SS). February 9—OG
Off to Buffalo. February 16—CC
Wrong Again. (SS). February 23—L and H—Skretvedt
Loud Soup (SS). March 16—CC
When Money Comes. March 2—All-Star
The Holy Terror. March 9—OG

That's My Wife (SS). March 23—L and H
Why Is a Plumber? March 30—All-Star
Wiggle Your Ears (SS). April 6—OG
Thin Twins (SS). April 13—CC
Big Business. April 20—L and H
Unkissed Man. April 27—All-Star
Fast Freight. May 4—OG
Movie Night (SS). May 11—CC
Double Whoopee. May 18—L and H
Thundering Toupees. May 25—All-Star
Little Mother. June 1—OG
Cat, Dog, and Co. (SS). September 14—OG
Bacon Grabbers (SS). October 19—L and H
Saturday's Lesson (SS). November 9—OG
Angora Love (SS). December 14—L and H

Sound Short Subjects

1929

All films are two reels unless otherwise noted.

Small Talk. April 18—OG
Unaccustomed as We Are. May 4—L and H
Hurdy Gurdy. May 11—All-Star
The Big Squawk. May 25—CC
Berth Marks. June 1—L and H
Madame "Q". June 8—All-Star
Railroadin'. June 15—OG
Leaping Love. June 22—CC
Men o' War. June 29—L and H
Dad's Day. July 7—All-Star
Snappy Sneezer. July 29—CC
The Perfect Day. August 10—L and H
Hotter Than Hot. August 17—Langdon (All-Star)
Crazy Feet. September 7—CC
Boxing Gloves. September 9—OG
They Go Boom. September 21—L and H
Sky Boy. October 5—Langdon (All-Star)
Bouncing Babies. October 12—OG
Lazy Days. October 24—OG
Stepping Out. November 2—CC
The Hoosegow. November 11—L and H
Skirt Shy. November 30—Langdon (All-Star)
Moan and Groan, Inc. December 7—OG
Great Gobs. December 28—CC

1930

All films are two reels unless otherwise noted. Footages are given for foreign-language versions to provide a comparison with the length of the English-language original (two reels equal to approximately two thousand feet, three reels equal to approximately three thousand feet). *BF* indicates a film in the Boy Friends series.

Night Owls. January 4—L and H
Lardones. Spanish version of *Night Owls*—3,306 ft.
Italian version of *Night Owls*. 3,306 ft.
The Head Guy. January 11—Langdon (All-Star)
Shivering Shakespeare. January 25—OG
The Real McCoy. February 1—CC
Blotto. February 8—L and H—three reels
La vida nocturna. Spanish version of *Blotto*—3,635 ft.
French version of *Blotto*. 3,571 ft.
The Fighting Parson. February 22—Langdon (All-Star)
The First Seven Years. March 1—OG
Los pequenos papas. Spanish version of *The First Seven Years*—1,945 ft.
Whispering Whoopee. March 8—CC
Brats. March 22—L and H.
German version of *Brats*. 1,910 ft.
The Big Kick. March 29—Langdon (All-Star)
La estacion de gasolina. Spanish version of *The Big Kick*—1,839 ft.
When the Wind Blows. April 5—OG
Las fantasmas. Spanish version of *When the Wind Blows*—1,865 ft.
All Teed Up. April 19—CC
El jugador de golf. Spanish version of *All Teed Up*—3,403 ft.
Le jouer de golf. French version of *All Teed Up*—4,065 ft.—Anthony and Edmonds
Below Zero. April 26—L and H
Tiemba y titubea. Spanish version of *Below Zero*—2,591 ft.
The Shrimp. May 2—Langdon (All-Star)
Pobre infeliz. Spanish version of *The Shrimp*—1,637 ft.
Bear Shooters. May 17—OG
Los cazadores de osos. Spanish version of *Bear Shooters*—1,867 ft.
Fifty Million Husbands. May 24—CC
No 'ume de pipe. French version of *Fifty Million Husbands*—3,349 ft.—Anthony and
    Edmonds
Hog Wild. May 31—L and H—This film was originally entitled *Hay Wire*, and many
    trade press references continued to use this title.
Radio mania. Spanish version of *Hog Wild*—1,900 ft.
French version of *Hog Wild*. 1,870 ft.
The King. June 14—Langdon (All-Star)
Der Konig. German version of *The King*—1,801 ft.
A Tough Winter. June 21—OG
Winter Wetter. German version of *A Tough Winter*—1,859 ft.
Semps d'hiver. French version of *A Tough Winter*—1,824 ft.
Fast Work. June 28—CC
Locuras d'amour. Spanish version of *Fast Work*—4,174 ft.
Girl Shock. August 23—CC
Huye faldas. Spanish version of *Girl Shock*—1,885 ft.
Timide malgre lui. French version of *Girl Shock*—1,764 ft.—Anthony and Edmonds
Pups Is Pups. August 30—OG
The Laurel-Hardy Murder Case. September 6—L and H—three reels
Noche de duendes. Spanish version of *The Laurel-Hardy Murder Case*—4,628 ft. Incor-
    porated dubbed original footage and newly photographed Spanish footage of much
    of the 1929 Laurel and Hardy short *Berth Marks*.

German version of *The Laurel-Hardy Murder Case*. 4,665 ft. Also incorporated much of *Berth Marks*.

French version of *The Laurel-Hardy Murder Case*. 4,681 ft. Also incorporated much of *Berth Marks*.

Doctors Orders. September 13—BF (All-Star)

Lo ordeno el doctor. Spanish version of *Doctor's Orders*. This film used the English original with full-frame "cut-in" titles. It was not accepted by MGM for release in this format. 2,493 ft.

Dollar Dizzy. October 4—CC

El principle del dolar. Spanish version of *Dollar Dizzy*—4,103 ft.

Les chercheuses d'or. French version of *Dollar Dizzy*—3,834 ft.—Anthony and Edmonds

Teacher's Pet. October 11—OG

Comenzo la escuela. Spanish version of *Teacher's Pet*. This film used the English original with full-frame "cut-in" titles. It was not accepted by MGM for release in this format. 3,199 ft.

Bigger and Better. October 25—BF (All-Star)

Looser Than Loose. November 15—CC

Una cana al aire. Spanish version of *Looser Than Loose*—3,798 ft.

Gare las bomb! French version of *Looser Than Loose*—3,939 ft.—Anthony and Edmonds

School's Out. November 22—OG

Another Fine Mess. November 29—L and H—three reels

Ladies Last. December 6—BF (All-Star)

High C's. December 27—CC—three reels

French version of *High C's*

1931

All films are two reels unless otherwise noted. *TP* indicates a film in the Thelma Todd–Zasu Pitts series.

Helping Grandma. January 3—OG

Blood and Thunder. January 17—BF (All-Star)

Thundering Tenors. February 7—CC

El alma de la fiesta. Spanish version of *Thundering Tenors*—3,475 ft.

Be Big. February 7—L and H—three reels

Los calaveras. Spanish version of *Be Big*—incorporated a Spanish-language version of *Laughing Gravy*

Les carottiers. French version of *Be Big*—incorporated a French version of *Laughing Gravy*

Love Business. February 14—OG

Chickens Come Home. February 21—L and H—three reels

Politquerias. Spanish version of *Chickens Come Home*

High Gear. February 28—BF (All-Star)—three reels

The Pip from Pittsburgh. March 21—CC

La Senorita de Chicago. Spanish version of *The Pip from Pittsburgh*

Little Daddy. March 28—OG

Laughing Gravy. April 4—L and H. This film was previewed as a three-reeler but was cut to two reels for U.S. domestic release. An English-language copy of the deleted third reel was discovered in the early 1990s. (A Spanish-language version of the expanded film, combined with *Be Big*, previously had been uncovered in the 1980s.)

Love Fever. April 11—BF (All-Star)

Rough Seas. April 25—CC—three reels
Monerias. Spanish version of *Rough Seas*
Bargain Day. May 2—OG
Air Tight. May 9—BF (All-Star)
Our Wife. May 16—L and H
One of the Smiths. May 23—CC
Fly My Kite. May 30—OG
Let's Do Things. June 6—TP—three reels
The Panic Is On! August 15—CC
Tiempos de crises. Spanish subtitled version of *The Panic Is On!*—1,871 ft.
Catch as Catch Can. August 22—TP
Enganchalo. Spanish subtitled version of *Catch as Catch Can*—1,872 ft.
Big Ears. August 29—OG
Orejas de burro. Spanish subtitled version of *Big Ears*—1,923 ft.
Call a Cop. September 12—BF (All-Star)
Llama a un policía. Spanish subtitled version of *Call a Cop*—1,794 ft.
Come Clean. September 19—L and H
Skip the Maloo! September 26—CC
Esquiva el balon. Spanish subtitled version of *Skip the Maloo*—1,914 ft.
The Pajama Party. October 3—TP
Gente al agua. Spanish subtitled version of *The Pajama Party*—1,875 ft.
Shiver My Timbers. October 10—OG
Piratas infantiles. Spanish subtitled version of *Shiver My Timbers*—1,908 ft.
Mama Loves Papa. October 24—BF (All-Star)
One Good Turn. October 31—L and H
Diselo a las mujeres (Save the Ladies!). Spanish subtitled version of *One Good Turn*
     combined with *Come Clean*—3,811 ft.
What a Bozo! November 7—CC
El director de orquesta. Spanish subtitled version of *What a Bozo*—1,922 ft.
War Mamas. November 14—TP
Dogs Is Dogs. November 21—OG
The Kickoff. December 5—BF (All-Star)
Futbol extraordinario. Spanish version of *The Kickoff*—1,887 ft.
Beau Hunks. December 12—L and H—four reels
Heroes de Trachuela. Spanish subtitled version of *Beau Hunks* combined with *Help-
     mates*—5,585 ft.
Hasty Marriage. December 19—CC
Casamiento fulminante. Spanish subtitled version of *Hasty Marriage*—1,898 ft.
On the Loose. December 26—TP

1932

All films are two reels unless otherwise noted. *TB* indicates a film in the Taxi Boys
series.

Readin' and Writin'. January 2—OG
Helpmates. January 23—L and H
The Tabasco Kid. January 30—CC
Seal Skins. February 6—TP
Love Pains. February 13—BF (All-Star)
Free Eats. February 18—OG

Any Old Port. March 5—L and H
The Knockout. March 5—BF (All-Star)
The Nickel Nurser. March 12—CC
Red Noses. March 19—TP
Spanky. March 26—OG
The Music Box. April 16—L and H—three reels
You're Telling Me. April 16—BF (All-Star)
In Walked Charley. April 23—CC
Strictly Unreliable. April 30—TP
Choo Choo. May 7—OG
Too Many Women. May 14—BF (All-Star)
The Chimp. May 21—L and H—three reels
First in War. May 28—CC
The Pooch. June 4—OG
The Old Bull. June 4—TP
Wild Babies. June 18—BF (All-Star)
County Hospital. June 25—L and H
What Price Taxi? August 13—TB (All-Star)
Show Business. August 20—TP
Hook and Ladder. August 27—OG
Young Ironsides. September 3—CC
Scram. September 10—L and H
Strange Innertube. September 17—TB (All-Star)
Alum and Eve. September 24—TP
Free Wheeling. October 1—OG
Girl Grief. October 8—CC
Hot Spot. October 22—TB (All-Star)
The Soilers. October 29—TP
Their First Mistake. November 5—L and H
Birthday Blues. November 12—OG
Now We'll Tell One. November 19—CC
Taxi for Two. December 3—TB (All-Star)
Sneak Easily. December 10—TP
A Lad an' a Lamp. December 17—OG
Mr. Bride. December 24—CC
Towed in a Hole. December 31—L and H
Hopping Off. Unreleased—BF (All-Star). Some footage from this film was used in the
   released version of *Wild Babies.*

1933

All films are two reels unless otherwise noted. *TK* indicates a film in the Thelma Todd–
Patsy Kelly series.

Bring 'em Back a Wife. January 14—TB (All-Star)
Asleep in the Feet. January 21—TP
Fish Hooky. January 28—OG
Fallen Arches. February 4—CC
Twice Two. February 25—L and H
Maids a la Mode. March 4—TP
Forgotten Babies. March 11—OG

Nature in the Wrong. March 18—CC
Taxi Barons. April 1—TB (All-Star)
The Bargain of the Century. April 9—TP
Kid from Borneo. April 15—OG
Me and My Pal. April 22—L and H
His Silent Racket. April 29—CC
Call Her Sausage. May 13—TB (All-Star)
One Track Minds. May 20—TP
Mush and Milk. May 27—OG
Arabian Tights. June 3—CC
The Rummy. June 10—TB (All-Star)
Thundering Taxis. June 24—TB (All-Star)
Wreckety Wrecks. 1933—TB (All-Star)
The Midnight Patrol. August 3—L and H
Sherman Said It. September 2—CC
Bedtime Worries. September 9—OG
Beauty and the Bus. September 16—TK
Busy Bodies. October 7—L and H
Midsummer Mush. October 21—CC
Wild Poses. October 28—OG
Yeast Is West. November 11—All-Star
Backs to Nature. November 14—TK
Dirty Work. November 25—L and H
Luncheon at Twelve. December 9—CC
Air Fright. December 23—TK
Twin Screws. December 30—All-Star
Keg o' My Heart. Musical—Scheduled for a November 11 release, evidence suggests that
this film was scrapped as a lost cause during the editing phase.

1934

All films are two reels unless otherwise noted.

Rhapsody in Brew (initially titled *Symphony in Suds*). January 6—musical
Oliver the Eighth. January 13—L and H—three reels
The Cracked Iceman. January 27—CC
Babes in the Goods. February 10—TK
Mixed Nuts. February 17—All-Star
Jail Birds of Paradise. February 24—musical
Mike Fright. February 25—OG
Hi Neighbor. March 3—OG
Four Parts. March 17—CC
Soup and Fish. March 31—TK
Nest Week-End. April 7—All-Star
Apples to You. April 14—musical
For Pete's Sake. April 14—OG
I'll Take Vanilla. May 5—CC
The First Round-Up. May 5—OG
A Duke for a Day. May 12—musical
Maid in Hollywood. May 19—TK
Benny from Panama. May 28—musical

Music in Your Hair. June 2—musical
Honky Donkey. June 2—OG
Another Wild Idea. June 16—CC
Going Bye Bye. June 23—L and H
I'll Be Suing You. June 23—TK
It Happened One Day. July 7—CC
Three Chumps Ahead. July 14—TK
Them Thar Hills. July 21—L and H
Movie Daze. 1934—All-Star
Mrs. Barnacle Bill. 1934—All-Star
Roamin' Vandals. 1934—Musical
Crooks Tour. 1934—All-Star
The Caretaker's Daughter. All-Star
One Horse Farmers. September 1—TK
Something Simple. September 8—CC
Washee Ironee. September 29—OG
Opened by Mistake. October 6—TK
You Said a Hatful! October 13—CC
The Ballad of Paducah Jail. October 20—Irvin S. Cobb (All-Star)
Mama's Little Pirate. November 3—OG
Done in Oil. November 10—TK
Fate's Fathead. November 17—CC
You Bring the Ducks. November 23—Irvin S. Cobb (All-Star)
Shrimps for a Day. December 8—OG
The Live Ghost. December 8—L and H
Bum Voyage. December 15—TK
The Chase of Pimple Street. December 22—CC
Speaking of Relations. 1934—Irvin S. Cobb (All-Star)
Nosed Out. Unreleased—Irvin S. Cobb

1935

All films are two reels unless otherwise noted.

Anniversary Trouble. January 1—OG
Tit for Tat. January 5—L and H
Treasure Blues. January 26—TK
Okay, Toots! February 2—CC
The Fixer-Uppers. February 9—L and H
Beginners Luck. February 23—OG
Sing, Sister, Sing. March 2—TK
Poker at Eight. March 9—CC
Thicker Than Water. March 16—L and H
The Tin Man. March 30—TK
Southern Exposure. April 6—CC
The Misses Stooge. April 20—TK
The Four-Star Boarder. April 27—CC
Teacher's Beau. April 27—OG
Sprucin' Up. June 1—OG
Lucky Beginners. 1935—This "amateur night" short was directed by Hal Roach (although on-screen credit went to Gordon Douglas) and was released by MGM as a

special. It was one of two films produced by Roach to fill out his release commitment to MGM after the cancellation of the Irvin S. Cobb series.

The Infernal Triangle. August 17—This was the second film made to complete the Cobb contract. Inexplicably, this film was released to theaters as the first short of the Charley Chase series for the 1935–36 season. The absence of Chase or any other recognizable star in this film drew outrage from the exhibitors.

Slightly Static. September 7—TK
Little Papa. September 21—OG
Nurse to You. October 5—CC
Twin Triplets. October 12—TK
Little Sinner. October 26—OG
Manhattan Monkey Business. November 9—CC
Hot Money. November 16—TK
Our Gang Follies of 1936. November 30—OG
Public Ghost No. 1. December 14—CC
Top Flat. December 21—TK

1936

All films are two reels unless otherwise noted.

Pinch Singer. January 4—OG
Life Hesitates at 40. January 18—CC
All-American Toothache. January 25—TK
Divot Diggers. February 8—OG
The Count Takes the Count. February 22—CC
Pan Handlers. February 29—Patsy Kelly and Pert Kelton
The Lucky Corner. March 14—OG
Vamp Till Ready. March 28—CC
At Sea Ashore. April 4—Patsy Kelly and Lyda Roberti
Second Childhood. April 11—OG
On the Wrong Trek. April 18—CC
Hill Tillies. April 24—Patsy Kelly and Lyda Roberti
Arbor Day. May 2—OG
Neighborhood House. May 9—CC. This film, Charley Chase's final one for Hal Roach, was previewed as a one-hour feature but was reedited into a two-reeler for release.
Bored of Education. August 29—OG—one reel
Two Too Young. September 26—OG—one reel
Pay as You Exit. October 24—OG—one reel
Spooky Hooky. December 5—OG—one reel

1937

All films are one reel unless otherwise noted.

Reunion in Rhythm. January 9—OG
Glove Taps. February 20—OG
Three Smart Boys. March 13—OG
Hearts Are Trumps. April 3—OG
Rushin' Ballet. April 24—OG
Roamin' Holiday. June 12—OG
Night 'n' Gales. July 24—OG
Fishy Tales. August 28—OG

Framing Youth. September 11—OG
Pigskin Palooka. October 23—OG
Mail and Female. November 13—OG
Our Gang of Follies 1938. December 18—OG—two reels. This film was marketed by MGM as a "special" short subject, independent of and not included in the general Our Gang package of one-reel releases for 1937–38.

1938

All films are one reel unless otherwise noted.

Canned Fishing. February 12—OG
Bear Facts. March 5—OG
Three Men in a Tub. March 26—OG
Came the Brawn. April 16—OG
Feed 'em and Weep. May 7—OG
The Awful Tooth. May 28—OG
Hide and Shriek. June 18

Hal Roach–MGM Sound Features

Men of the North (1930). Directed by Hal Roach—produced by MGM at its Culver City studio
Pardon Us (August 15, 1931). Laurel and Hardy—McCabe—*Pardon Us* also had versions filmed in Spanish *(De bote en bote)*, French *(Sous les verrous)*, Italian *(Muraglie)*, and German *(Hinter Schloss und Riegel)*. Skretvedt
Pack Up Your Troubles (September 17, 1932). Laurel and Hardy—McCabe
The Devil's Brother (May 5, 1933). Laurel and Hardy—McCabe
Sons of the Desert (December 29, 1933). Laurel and Hardy—McCabe
Babes in Toyland (November 30, 1934). Laurel and Hardy—McCabe
Vagabond Lady (1935). Robert Young
Bonnie Scotland (August 23, 1935). Laurel and Hardy—McCabe
The Bohemian Girl (February 14, 1936). Laurel and Hardy—McCabe
Kelly the Second (1936). Patsy Kelly, Charley Chase
Mr. Cinderella (1936). Jack Haley
Our Relations (October 30, 1936). Laurel and Hardy—McCabe
General Spanky (December 11, 1936). Spanky McFarland, Billie Thomas—Maltin and Bann
Nobody's Baby (1937). Patsy Kelly, Lyda Roberti
Way Out West (April 16, 1937). Laurel and Hardy—McCabe
Pick a Star (May 21, 1937). Patsy Kelly, Jack Haley, Laurel and Hardy—McCabe
Topper (1937). Cary Grant, Constance Bennett
Merrily We Live (1938). Constance Bennett, Brian Aherne
Swiss Miss (May 20, 1938). Laurel and Hardy—McCabe
Block-Heads (August 19, 1938). Laurel and Hardy—McCabe

Hal Roach–United Artists Sound Films

Copyright dates on features, release dates on streamliners.

Features

There Goes My Heart (October 6, 1938). Virginia Bruce, Fredric March
Topper Takes a Trip (1939). Constance Bennett, Roland Young

Zenobia (April 11, 1939). Oliver Hardy, Harry Langdon
Captain Fury (May 25, 1939). Brian Aherne
The Housekeeper's Daughter (November 9, 1939). Joan Bennett, John Hubbard
A Chump at Oxford (January 19, 1940). Laurel and Hardy
Of Mice and Men (February 2, 1940). Burgess Meredith, Lon Chaney Jr.
One Million B.C. (April 12, 1940). Victor Mature, Carole Landis
Saps at Sea (April 26, 1940). Laurel and Hardy
Turnabout (May 21, 1940). John Hubbard, Carole Landis
Captain Caution (September 3, 1940). Victor Mature
Road Show (January 9, 1941). John Hubbard, Carole Landis
Broadway Limited (June 4, 1941). Marjorie Woodworth, Patsy Kelly, Victor McLaglen, Zasu Pitts
Topper Returns (1941). Roland Young, Joan Blondell

Streamliners

Tanks a Million (September 12, 1941). William Tracy
Niagara Falls (October 17, 1941). Zasu Pitts, Slim Summerville
All American Co-Ed (October 31, 1941). Harry Langdon
Miss Polly (January 14, 1941). Zasu Pitts, Slim Summerville
Fiesta (November 28, 1941). Technicolor
Hay Foot (December 12, 1941). William Tracy
Brooklyn Orchid (February 20, 1942). William Bendix
Dudes Are Pretty People (March 13, 1942). Noah Beery Jr.
About Face (April 17, 1942). William Tracy
Flying with Music (May 22, 1942). Marjorie Woodworth
The Devil with Hitler (November 20, 1942). Bobby Watson
The McGuerins from Brooklyn (December 31, 1942). William Bendix
Calaboose (January 29, 1943). Noah Beery Jr.
Fall In (March 5, 1943). William Tracy
Taxi, Mister? (April 16, 1943). William Bendix
Prairie Chickens (May 21, 1943). Noah Beery Jr.
Yanks Ahoy (June 25, 1943). William Tracy
Nazty Nuisance (August 8, 1943). Bobby Watson
Hal Roach Comedy Carnival (1947). Cinecolor
    Part 1—*Curley*
    Part 2—*The Fabulous Joe*
Lafftime (1948). Cinecolor
    Part 1—*Here Comes Trouble*—William Tracy
    Part 2—*Who Killed Doc Robbin?*

DCA–Hal Roach Distributing Corporation Feature

Go, Johnny, Go! (1958). Alan Freed, Jimmy Clanton, Sandy Stewart, Chuck Berry, Jackie Wilson, Ritchie Valens

Appendix I: Television Series at the Hal Roach Studios

Programs by the Hal Roach Studios

Much of this information was obtained from *The Encyclopedia of Television, Television Drama Series Programming,* and *The Complete Directory to Prime Time Network TV Shows.* Programs are listed in alphabetic order. In addition to series, six unsold pilot programs are included.

Alias Mike Hercules—A pilot, produced in 1954, aired on ABC July 31, 1956; thirty minutes. Hugh Beaumont played a tough San Francisco detective.

Blondie—NBC, January 4, 1957, to September 27, 1957; thirty minutes. This television version of the popular comic strip featured Arthur Lake reprising his screen role as Dagwood Bumsted.

The Charlie Farrell Show—CBS, 1956. This summer replacement for *I Love Lucy* featured semiretired actor-turned-Palm-Springs-resort-owner Charlie Farrell as a semiretired actor-turned-Palm-Springs-resort-owner named Charlie Farrell. The humorous occurrences at the resort were reportedly drawn from the real-life experiences of Mr. Farrell.

The Children's Hour—Syndicated, 1951; sixty minutes. Films for children hosted by Maureen O'Sullivan.

Code 3—Syndicated, 1956; thirty minutes. A thirty-nine-episode anthology crime series hosted by Richard Travis as an assistant sheriff of L.A. County.

The Count of Monte Cristo—Syndicated, 1956; thirty minutes. A thirty-nine-episode adventure series.

Duffy's Tavern—NBC, April 5, 1954, to September 3, 1954; thirty minutes. An unsuccessful attempt to bring the long-running radio series to TV.

Forest Ranger—1956; thirty minutes. Pilot for a proposed adventure series with stories to be drawn from U.S. Forest Service files.

The Gale Storm Show—CBS, September 29, 1956, to April 11, 1959; ABC, October 1, 1959, to March 24, 1960; thirty minutes. Gale Storm, who had starred in Hal Roach Studios' successful series *My Little Margie,* appeared here as the social director on a luxury ocean liner. Zasu Pitts costarred. 125 episodes.

Hurricane at Pilgrim Hill—1951. A sixty-minute dramatic "movie" for television.

Love That Jill—ABC, January 20, 1958, to April 28, 1958; thirty minutes. Real-life married couple Anne Jeffreys and Robert Sterling, who had costarred in the earlier *Topper* television series, starred in this short-lived sitcom. Thirteen episodes.

McGarry and Me—CBS, July 5, 1960; thirty minutes. Comedy pilot about a kind-hearted police officer.

My Little Margie—CBS, June 16, 1952, to September 8, 1952; NBC, October 1952 to November 1952; CBS, June 1, 1953, to July 10, 1953 (*Complete Directory* indicates that this run was from January to July of 1953); NBC, September 9, 1953, to August 29, 1955; thirty minutes. This series featured Gale Storm and Charles Farrell. 126 episodes.

Passport to Danger—Syndicated, 1954; thirty minutes. An adventure program featuring Cesar Romero as U.S. diplomatic courier Steve McQuinn. *Encyclopedia of Television* indicates thirteen episodes; *Complete Directory* shows thirty-nine episodes.

Public Defender—CBS, March 11, 1954, to June 23, 1955; thirty minutes. Reed Hadley, star of *Racket Squad,* played the title role in this program. Sixty-nine episodes.

Racket Squad—Syndicated, 1950; thirty minutes. CBS, June 7, 1951, to September 28, 1953. Crime drama starring Reed Hadley. Ninety-eight episodes.

Screen Director's Playhouse—NBC, October 1955 to June 1956; ABC, July 1956 to September 1956; thirty minutes. Thirty-five episodes.

Telephone Time—CBS, April 8, 1956, to March 13, 1957; ABC, June 4, 1957, to April 11, 1958; thirty minutes. An anthology series of historical dramatizations featuring "well-known stars in quality productions." Hosted by John Nesbitt and Dr. Frank Baxter. Seventy-eight episodes.

The Three Musketeers—1951. A sixty-minute dramatic "movie" for television.

The Stu Erwin Show—ABC, October 21, 1950, to April 13, 1955; thirty minutes. 130 episodes.

The Veil—Syndicated, 1958; thirty minutes. Horror anthology hosted by Boris Karloff.

Longevity of the Hal Roach Television Series

Less than one season: five series
One season: five series
Two seasons: two series
Three seasons: two series
Four seasons: one series *(The Gale Storm Show)*
Five seasons: one series *(The Stu Erwin Show)*

Programs by Independents Renting Studio Space at the Hal Roach Studios

Beulah 1950–53
Amos 'n' Andy 1951–53
Mystery Theater (Mark Saber) 1951–54
Life of Riley 1953–58
Waterfront 1953–56
You Are There 1953–57
It's a Great Life 1954–56
So This Is Hollywood 1955
Where Were You?

Number of Series in Production at the Hal Roach Studios, 1950–60

Prod.—produced by Hal Roach Studios
Rent.—produced by a company renting space at Hal Roach Studios

Season

1950–51	Prod. 2	Rent. 1
1951–52	Prod. 4	Rent. 3
1952–53	Prod. 3	Rent. 4
1953–54	Prod. 4	Rent. 4
1954–55	Prod. 4	Rent. 5
1955–56	Prod. 3	Rent. 4
1956–57	Prod. 5	Rent. 2
1957–58	Prod. 3	Rent. 1
1958–59	Prod. 2	Rent. 0
1959–60	Prod. 1	Rent. 0

Appendix 2: Film and Series Synopses

This section explores selected films from series discussed in the text. In most instances, short subjects and features that were produced as part of a series are examined under their series title (e.g., Skinny Series). Feature-length "A" pictures and short subjects of special significance are discussed under individual film titles.

1. Lonesome Luke Series. *Luke's Movie Muddle* (1916), one of the few surviving Lonesome Luke films, reveals that the Chaplin imitation went beyond makeup and costume. Luke's movements and gestures were clearly patterned after Chaplin's. In the film, Luke is the manager, ticket seller-taker, and usher at a small movie theater. Snub Pollard is the projectionist, and Bebe Daniels is an audience member. While Luke flirts with Bebe and other female patrons, Snub's inept projection repeatedly disrupts the show. One of the patrons is smoking a pipe as he enters the theater. He extinguishes the pipe (he thinks) and puts it in his coat pocket. The pipe sparks up during the show, ignites the coat, and the patron runs around wildly, spreading smoke through the theater. The rest of the audience, believing that the theater is on fire, flees in panic, and the film ends with Luke and Snub fighting one another.

2. Skinny Series. At least one of the split-reel Skinny comedies, *Skinny Gets a Goat* (1917), is available for review today. While it doesn't stand out as particularly awful, it isn't very original or entertaining either. Derivative of Mack Sennett's many rural-based comedies, the story is set in a small farming community. The railroad station baggage master and the town constable are fighting for the affections of the same woman, who promises to marry the one who brings her the most unusual gift. She receives a goat and a pig, which promptly run amok. Skinny, who is only marginally involved in the early action, helps to recover the animals and wins the affection of the new general store cashier in the process.

3. Toto Series. One of only two known surviving Toto films, *Do Husbands Deceive?* (1918) shows Toto to be a skilled acrobat and mime but lacking a screen persona or presence. He comes off as a rather vacuous individual, incapable of eliciting audience sympathy. In the film (which, as it exists, is missing its second half), Toto plays a policeman on the trail of a burglar.

4. Stan Laurel Series. Two surviving Stan Laurel comedies from the 1918–19 period actually seem a bit better than one would assume from Laurel's short tenure. In *Just Rambling Along* (1918), a penniless Stan tries to "promote" a meal at a cafeteria. In *Hustling for Health* (1919), Stan's hope of escaping the hustle and bustle of the city for a quiet weekend with a friend

in the suburbs is dashed when the friend's family and neighbors turn out to be rather dysfunctional.

5. Harold Lloyd One-Reel Series: An example of Lloyd's later one-reelers is *Ring Up the Curtain* (1919), in which Harold is a stagehand in a small vaudeville house playing host to a traveling troupe. He falls for the show's leading lady (Bebe Daniels), then disrupts her act by fighting over her with another member of the troupe (Snub Pollard). When the show folds, Harold gives the destitute actress some money, only to have her leave with Snub. Harold is appalled at his naïveté, and the film ends with him engaging in a rather over-the-top suicide attempt by inhaling from a gas lamp. While some of the plot elements may seem Chaplinesque, the film is played with hyperkinetic energy and no pathos.

6. Snub Pollard–Ernie Morrison Series. A typical Pollard-Morrison outing is *Rush Orders* (1921), in which the pair ride into town on a railroad handcar (with Morrison providing the locomotive muscle). Having no money, they split up to forage for food. After numerous unsuccessful attempts to hustle a free meal at a café owned by Marie Mosquini (the future wife of radio pioneer Lee DeForest), Pollard eventually wins sustenance and Marie's hand. A flash forward of twenty years shows the now gray couple still flipping pancakes, with an adult Morrison as a restaurant employee.

7. Harold Lloyd Two-Reel Series. *Bumping into Broadway* (1919) has Harold, a struggling playwright, in love with aspiring actress Bebe Daniels. After evading the landlady, who wants her past-due rent, the pair winds up at an illegal gambling den. They hit the jackpot just as the place is raided. Eluding the police and with their money woes behind them, they embrace and the film ends.

8. Vanity Fair Girls–Eddie Boland Series. In *On Their Way* (1921), Boland buys a junk heap of a used car, and he and his wife take a disastrous motor vacation. The Vanity Fair Girls appear briefly in the opening scenes as the wife's luncheon guests who witness the arrival of Boland and his rattletrap, much to the wife's humiliation.

9. Glenn Tryon Features. In *The Battling Orioles,* Tryon plays a rural youth whose misadventures in the big city reinvigorate the elderly members of his father's baseball team when they have to assist him in rescuing his sweetheart from the clutches of the villain. In *The White Sheep,* which borrows more than a little from 1921's *Tol'able David,* Tryon plays a weakling in a macho family. He is able to save the day (and his father from the gallows) literally by resorting to prayer. While these may have made good Harold Lloyd pictures (indeed, Lloyd reworked the plot of *The White Sheep* for his own independently produced *The Kid Brother* [1927]), Tryon lacked

both Lloyd's on-screen charm and his physical comedy abilities. He simply comes off as a weak and annoying lead. He would appear to better effect in comedies at Universal at the very end of the silent era. Hal Roach took story credit on both of the Tryon features and directing credit on *The White Sheep* (although the film lists two codirectors as well: Roy Clements and Hampton Del Ruth). *The Battling Orioles* was codirected by Ted Wilde (a Lloyd writer, who would later direct *The Kid Brother*) and Fred Guiol. The problem with Glenn Tryon was well summarized by W. B. Frank writing to Warren Doane on December 4, 1924: "[I]f he can change his attitude from more or less of a repulsive one to a sympathetic one, he might get over well."

10. Rex, the Wonder Horse, Features. *King of Wild Horses* (1924) was directed by Fred Jackman from a story by Hal Roach. A sickly, cantankerous banker has acquired a ranch out west and, hoping to improve his health, moves there with his weak, spoiled son (Charley Chase) and his virtuous daughter Mary. The ranch has a dishonest foreman who soon has the son deeply indebted to him for losses at the card table. The foreman coerces the son to help him raid the father's herd and blame the losses on a group of wild horses headed up by the titular character. A neighboring rancher, who is infatuated with Mary, befriends the wild horse and exposes the true thieves.

11. *Madame Mystery* (1926). All that seems to exist of *Madame Mystery* today is a five-minute Pathex 9.5-millimeter abridgement that was prepared for the home-movie market. In this frantically paced version, Bara evades thieves and spies as she transports a top-secret explosive aboard an ocean liner.

12. Mabel Normand series. *Raggedy Rose* (1926) is a Cinderella story. A waifish junk collector's assistant (Normand) wins a rich suitor after he accidentally hits her with his car and allows her to convalesce in his mansion.

13. Western Short Comedy Series. A pilot film was shot at Victorville, California, in April 1927. After watching some of the early dailies, Doane instructed the director that rotund comic Eugene Paulette appeared to be straining too hard to be funny, that the corrals looked too empty, and that the film generally needed more western atmosphere. On the other hand, Doane "thought the interior film of Finlayson was very good indeed, and we all think that Holmes is okay as the other partner." Ultimately the film was revamped and released as *Should Tall Men Marry?* (1928), an All-Star short without Oliver Hardy but with, ironically enough, Stan Laurel in the lead. It would be the last film of his career without Hardy.

14. *Hats Off* (1927). Sadly, considering the importance of *Hats Off* in the development of the team of Laurel and Hardy, it has not been seen for

decades. It is the only Laurel and Hardy film to be completely missing, with no known surviving copies. Another pivotal step in Laurel and Hardy's career, the MGM Technicolor feature-length operetta *The Rogue Song* (1930) exists only in the form of a complete soundtrack and a brief scene or two of the picture.

15. Harry Langdon Series. One of Langdon's films of the period is *The Head Guy* (1930). On a stormy night at the train depot at Elmira, New York (Hal Roach's hometown), stationmaster Edgar Kennedy is called away for the birth of twin children, leaving janitor Harry in charge. A rowdy theatrical troupe on a layover and an escaped duck from the freight room make Harry's flustered attempts to keep order impossible.

16. The Boyfriends Series. In the Boyfriends' short *High Gear* (1931), Mickey takes the gang out for a ride in his father's newly repainted car. After several minor collisions and encounters with traffic cop Edgar Kennedy, the car becomes stuck in the mud during a driving rainstorm that washes off dad's paint job. The gang takes refuge from the storm in a house that is a criminal hideout, and mayhem ensues.

17. Taxi Boys Series. Although some of the Taxi Boys shorts featured large casts of humans (including silent comic Clyde Cook) and crashing taxicabs, many were on a much smaller scale, with Ben Blue and Billy Gilbert doing what sometimes amounted to a thinly veiled Laurel and Hardy imitation. Typical was *Taxi Barons* (1933) in which the duo, fleeing from the police, are mistaken for royalty at a swank dinner party. Although their poor table manners do not tip off their true identities to the other guests, the arrival of the real royalty, and the police, blows their cover, and the pair flees.

18. All-Star Short Comedy Series. In *Mixed Nuts* (1934), a group of out-of-work chorus girls are sent to a proper finishing school courtesy of a National Recovery Administration grant. The well-endowed young women intimidate the effeminate male staff, played by Wakefield, Nelson, and Barclay.

19. *Pardon Us* (1931). The Prohibition-era plot of *Pardon Us* has Stan and Ollie landing in prison after trying to sell home-brewed beer to a detective. The film deals with their adventures in prison: mixing with tough convicts, escaping (mainly by accident), being recaptured, then being paroled after thwarting (again, accidentally) a major prison break.

20. Charley Chase Series. The perception of a qualitative decline in the Chase series is admittedly a highly subjective evaluation by the author, albeit one that is backed up by Roach Studios correspondence of the 1930s. While much of Chase's work, both silent and sound, was based on comedy of errors, with mistaken identity leading to a string of comic situations

and ultimate resolution, Chase's silent films seem to better build toward that resolution. The complications become deeper and develop complications of their own. Often, in the talkies, one gets the feeling of watching a string of events unfolding at a flat pace, with no real gathering of momentum. In the silent film *Limousine Love* (1928), Charley runs out of gas on his way to his own wedding. While he is getting gasoline, a young woman who has fallen into one of those marvelously deep Hal Roach mud puddles uses the curtained rear passenger compartment of his car as a dressing room, removing every stitch of clothing and placing it on an impromptu clothesline outside the car. Chase returns, gasses up, and drives off, causing the clothes to fall into a conveniently placed storm drain before the woman is able to get his attention. He picks up a hitchhiker, the woman's husband (who is unaware of his wife's presence because of the curtains), then arrives at his wedding with a naked woman in the back seat, her potentially homicidal husband in the front seat, and Chase's fiancée (who is already angry at his late arrival), her family, and the wedding party waiting at the curb. For the remainder of the film, a masterpiece of comic timing and construction, Chase is generally successful in his attempts to untangle the mess without letting the wrong parties meet. Contrast this to the sound short *The Pip from Pittsburgh* (1931), which is a favorite among Chase fans. Although Charley has had a bad experience on previous blind dates, he grudgingly accepts one to help a friend (whose own date will only go out if Charley will date her friend). He decides to make himself as disagreeable as possible, wearing a tired, ill-fitting suit (while lending his good suit to his friend), eating garlic, not shaving, and so forth. When the blind date turns out to be the vivacious Thelma Todd, Chase has a change of heart and spends the rest of the film trying to undo the damage, including getting his suit back from his uncooperative friend, one piece at a time. There are no layers of complexity here, and the film ends when Chase, trying to improve his breath, causes a machine full of gumballs to spread its contents across a dance floor. Slapstick mayhem ensues, and the film fades out.

21. Musical Short Series. Despite its short run, the musical series took two distinctly different tracks. One track featured Eddie Foy Jr. in shorts like *A Duke for a Day* (1934), in which a temperamental singing star (Jeanette Loff) bullies her press agent (Foy) into arranging her marriage to royalty. In the other track, Billy Gilbert and Billy Bletcher (the voice of Disney's Big Bad Wolf) played a pair of Dutch brothers attempting to run a beer garden with a live musical stage show.

22. Todd-Pitts-Kelly Series. In *The Soilers* (1932) Pitts and Todd are door-to-door magazine saleswomen. Tired of having doors slammed in their

faces, they resolve to take a more aggressive approach with their next prospect. Unfortunately, he happens to be a judge who has been receiving death threats. He assumes the overzealous pair are crazed assassins and spends most of the film's running time unsuccessfully attempting to elude them. In *Maid in Hollywood* (1934) Todd is about to abandon her dream of a Hollywood career. Kelly engineers a screen test by abducting the actress for whom the test was actually intended. Kelly then proceeds to all but ruin Todd's test with her oafish behavior on the set.

23. Mack Sennett's silent features included *Tillie's Punctured Romance* (1914), *The Extra Girl* (1923), and *His First Flame* (1926).

24. *Nobody's Baby* (1937). The studio did attempt one feature-length incarnation of the Kelly-Roberti partnership. *Nobody's Baby* is a rather hodgepodge affair in which Patsy and Lyda first meet at a radio audition (each ruins the other's act), then become accidental roommates (Patsy's landlady takes in Lyda as a new boarder), *then* inexplicably wind up in nursing school together. At times the film seems little more than a vehicle for unused Todd-Kelly short film story ideas.

25. *Pick a Star* (1937). Yet another Hollywood Cinderella story, with Rosina Lawrence, mainly known to audiences at the time for her role as the late-1930s schoolteacher in Our Gang, as an all-American girl trying to break into the movies.

26. *There Goes My Heart* (1938). While Roach's comedy "A" features generally fared better than its dramatic efforts, the results were never in the same league as the Goldwyn or Selznick productions. Typical was *There Goes My Heart,* the studio's initial UA release. Little more than a slight variation of *It Happened One Night,* the film featured Virginia Bruce, on loan from MGM where she was nearing the end of her brief starring career, as a madcap runaway heiress who is pursued professionally and romantically by a cynical newspaper reporter played by Fredric March, who essentially repeated his similar portrayal from Selznick's successful *Nothing Sacred* of the previous year. In a departure from the basic *It Happened One Night* theme but not from the overall recycled nature of the material, Bruce's character, while on the run, shares an apartment and many scenes with Roach alum Patsy Kelly, scenes that Kelly could well have played with Thelma Todd in their costarring short series of several years earlier. Considering its lack of originality and its generally retrospective tone, the film concludes on an appropriately nostalgic note with an unbilled cameo by Harry Langdon. Overall, *There Goes My Heart* is pleasant enough, but there is little to distinguish it from Roach's non–Laurel and Hardy features for MGM, most of which had been admittedly "B" pictures, even if the admission usually came only after the fact.

27. *Zenobia* (1939). Oliver Hardy plays Dr. Henry Tibbitt, the revered physician of the fictitious town of Carterville, Mississippi, in 1870. His wife is played by the fluttery Billie Burke (the good witch in *The Wizard of Oz* and Mrs. Topper in all three of Roach's Topper films). On the day his daughter is engaged to the son of one of the town's leading citizens, Tibbit is called to attend the ailing elephant (Zenobia) of a medicine show hawker, Professor J. Thorndyke McCrackle (Harry Langdon, in a role that might have been better suited to W. C. Fields). Tibbit is too successful in his work; the grateful pachyderm follows him home, disrupting a high society reception for the engaged couple, threatening the engagement, and prompting a lawsuit by McCrackle for the alienation of Zenobia's affections. It should come as no surprise that all eventually works out for the best. The film is quite charming, and Hardy and Langdon each give commendable and credible performances in roles that deviate from their normal personae. *Zenobia* does not present Hardy and Langdon as a team. Hardy dominates the picture, with Langdon clearly in a subordinate supporting role. This may have actually worked against the film's chances of success: on the basis of the publicity, the public may have been expecting more characteristic Laurel and Hardy material.

28. *Fiesta* (1941). Technicolor was really the only thing *Fiesta* had going. It featured an unknown cast (with the exception of aging silent-film heartthrob Antonio Moreno) in a minimal plot that strung together a series of mediocre musical numbers. The sets and costumes, however, were vividly hued to squeeze every last drop of dye out of the Technicolor process.

29. Streamliner Series. Despite being designed as forty-five-minute films, some of the streamliners seem oddly rushed. Scenes end virtually in mid-sentence. In *Hay Foot* (1941), one of the popular "service comedies," mention is made throughout the entire film of an upcoming national pistol championship match in which the film's characters are to participate. The film fades out on the night before the big competition and fades in on "The End." One almost gets the impression of watching an abridged version of a longer feature.

30. *Curley* (1947): Although it (like *Who Killed Doc Robbin?*) was produced by veteran Our Gang producer-director Robert F. McGowan from his own original story, this feels more like the flaccid Our Gang imitations that have been attempted through the years by other producers. It is basically an expanded version of the Our Gang classic *Teacher's Pet* (1930), in which the gang loses a beloved teacher to marriage, mistakenly believes the new teacher to be an ogre, then has to un–booby trap the classroom when they find out otherwise. Scenes that had approached a poetic beauty in the

original, with Jackie Cooper as the ringleader of the gang and June Marlowe as the new teacher, Miss Crabtree, fall painfully flat in this reincarnation.

31. *Here Comes Trouble* (1948). One of the last directing credits for Fred Guiol, a Roach staffer since the silent days. Home from the war, Doubleday (Tracy) is grudgingly given a job at the newspaper of his girlfriend's father. The newspaper is running a series of stories that expose the workings of a local criminal gang. In a scene straight out of Laurel and Hardy, the gang sends a burlesque dancer to blackmail the editor. Doubleday whisks her into the editor's washroom to keep her quiet and out of sight when the editor's wife pays an unexpected visit. The film concludes at a burlesque theater with a scene curiously reminiscent of Fritz Lang's *Spies* (1929). The criminal kingpin, disguised as a clown, is chased back and forth across the stage by Doubleday and the police to the delight of the audience, who think it is all part of the show, and the consternation of the orchestra leader (Roach veteran Eddie Dunn), who knows it is not.

Appendix 3: The Financial Side of the Hal Roach Studios

Due largely to the chaos between the Hal Roach Studios' entry into bankruptcy and demolition of the studio facilities, the Roach records available to the researcher today are far from complete. Many fascinating "whys" go unanswered because of massive holes in documentation. Regarding the studio's finances, it is difficult to create a precise profit-loss statement for Roach's films because so much of the paperwork is missing. As an alternative, this section provides a series of snapshots of different periods in the studio's operations from the earliest days through the late 1940s, snapshots that allow a glimpse into the business side of early moviemaking.

Payroll
Pay Ledger, 1918

Harold Lloyd, $150/wk
"Toto" Novello, $200/wk
Snub Pollard, $50/wk
Hal E. Roach, $200/wk
Dwight Whiting, $125/wk
Alf Goulding, $35/wk

Weekly Payroll Summaries, November 5, 1921

Administration, $2,353.50 ($1,000 per week for Roach)
Technical, $2,306.73
Lloyd Company, $2,425
Roland Company, $1,826.67
Pollard Company, $1,005
Parrott Company, $805
Extras, $855

Our Gang Salaries at the End of 1937

Darla, $150 per week
Spanky, $200 per week
Alfalfa, $175 per week
Buckwheat, $80 per week
Porky, $150 per week

Contract Salaries in 1937–38

Brian Aherne—four-picture contract over two years: $55,000 for the first, $60,000 for the second, $65,000 for the third, $70,000 for the fourth—each to be completed within eight weeks.
Constance Bennett, $50,000 per picture—ten weeks
Oliver Hardy, $2,500 per week
Patsy Kelly, $1,350 per week
Stan Laurel, $2,500 per week plus $25,000 per picture (for acting) and $5,000 per picture (for creative input)
Alan Mowbray, $1,500 per week
Roland Young, $2,500 per week for not less than six weeks nor more than six months per year

T. Marvin Hatley (composer), $200 per week
Roy Seawright (special effects), $250 per week
Norman McLeod (director), $2,750 per week
John G. Blystone (director), $1,500 per week
Gordon Douglas (director), $250 per week
Milton Bren (producer), $500 per week for forty weeks per year
James W. Horne (director), $300 per week
James Parrott (writer), $250 per week
Edward Sedgwick (director), $1,000 per week

Rolin and Pathé

Rolin signed a new contract with Pathé in 1916 in which Pathé agreed to pay Rolin a lump sum of $5,200 per two-reeler (to cover Rolin's production or "negative" cost) plus 50 percent of the net. The net was defined as that left over after the gross had the following deducted: 30 percent for advertising, $5,200 for the negative cost, $38 for each reel of positive print placed into distribution.

On the Toto films, Pathé agreed to pay a negative cost of $8,000 for each of the first three Toto two-reelers with a bonus of $6,000 upon acceptance by Pathé of the third. Pathé would then pay a negative cost of $10,000 for each subsequent two-reeler.

For each of the initial one-reel Lloyd "glasses" films, Pathé agreed to pay a $2,200 negative cost. For the last four Lloyd one-reelers, Pathé would increase its negative payment to $3,300 per film.

Film Costs and Returns

Gross Earnings for Harold Lloyd Pictures

Film Title	Release Date	Gross as of 12/31/21
Bumping Into Broadway	11/2/19	$113,425.79
Captain Kidd's Kids	11/30/19	102,730.76
From Hand to Mouth	12/28/19	102,766.18
His Royal Slyness	2/8/20	97,318.99
Haunted Spooks	3/21/20	99,772.82
An Eastern Westerner	5/2/20	86,012.16
High and Dizzy	7/11/20	125,759.56
Get Out and Get Under	9/12/20	114,859.98
Number Please	12/26/20	83,521.46
		Gross as of 12/17/21
Now or Never	3/27/21	$161,386.52
Among Those Present	5/29/21	129,856.08
I Do	7/24/21	106,564.61
Never Weaken	10/9/21	74,880.88
A Sailor Made Man	12/10/21	18,464.60

The Snub Pollard one-reelers cost between $8,000 and $9,000 per film from the series inception until mid-1920. At that time, beginning with *Call a Taxi,* the budgets increased to the $10,000–$11,000 range. The most expensive of the Pollard one-reelers was *His Best Girl* at $13,711.

Pollard's salary at the beginning of the series in 1919 was $200 per week plus 12 percent of the producer's profits on his films. His salary increased to $300 per week in 1920, $500 per week in 1922, and $600 per week in 1923.

Ruth Roland Serials: Grosses as of September 8, 1923

	Negative Cost	U.S. Gross	Foreign Gross	Total
White Eagle	$239,483.13	$386,448.98	$58,835.13	$445,284.11
Timber Queen	170,891.54	391,909.72	47,868.97	439,778.69

Gaylord Lloyd Comedies

All of the Gaylord Lloyd comedies lost money. Pathé claimed there were no profits on the films, meaning that Roach received only Pathé's advance.

	Negative Cost	Pathé Advance	Loss
Trolley Trouble	$9,831.91	$5,000	$4,831.91
Rough Seas	6,583.92	5,000	1,583.92
Dodge Your Debts	12,897.67	5,000	7,897.67

The Stan Laurel two-reel comedies of 1923–24 averaged a $38,000 gross per picture. The Our Gang comedies of 1923–24 averaged a gross of $49,444 per picture.

During the 1924–25 movie season, Mack Sennett's Ben Turpin comedies averaged a per-picture gross of $60,000, Mack Sennett Comedies (ensemble cast) averaged $50,000 per picture, and Mack Sennett's Harry Langdon comedies averaged $45,000, shooting to $75,000 once Langdon became established. By comparison, Roach's Arthur Stone and Glenn Tryon short comedies averaged $22,500 per picture and the Spat Family series averaged $18,000.

Costs of Late Silent, Early Sound Shorts

	Total Cost	Studio Cost	MGM Advances	Victor (Sound Recording)
Silent films with synchronized scores				
Laurel and Hardy				
Bacon Grabbers	$39,387.84	$18,008.39	$17,336.39	$4,043.06
Angora Love	38,570.25	16,555.45	18,000.54	4,014.26
Our Gang				
Cat, Dog, & Co.	42,929.63	21,413.53	17,079.22	4,436.88
Saturday's Lesson	39,695.34	21,955.07	14,242.88	3,497.39
Full talking pictures				
Charlie Chase				
Big Squawk	42,861.42	23,807.28	10,500.00	8,554.14
Leaping Love	43,617.97	24,083.39	10,500.00	9,034.58
Snappy Sneezer	39,910.37	22,800.78	10,500.00	6,609.59
Our Gang				
Small Talk	60,752.53	34,612.35	10,500.00	15,640.18
Railroadin'	47,957.29	29,475.40	10,500.00	7,981.89
Boxing Gloves	44,907.43	25,833.79	10,500.00	8,573.64
Laurel and Hardy				
Unaccustomed as We Are	45,692.58	23,697.81	11,436.85	10,557.92
Berth Marks	39,536.61	19,185.57	10,724.53	9,626.51
Men o' War	43,145.17	24,035.41	10,676.20	8,433.56
All Star				
Hurdy Gurdy	36,981.46	17,501.58	10,500.00	8,979.88
Madame "Q"	37,549.71	18,926.44	10,500.00	8,123.27
Dad's Day	38,551.84	20,652.57	10,500.00	7,399.27

MGM's Experience Table for Computing
Probable Gross of Two-Reel Comedies

Weeks on Market	Percentage of Total Gross
1	3
2	4
3	5
4	6
5	7
6	8
7	10
8	12

and so on, adding 2 to the percentage until

27	50
28	51

and so on, adding 1 to the percentage until

57	80
58	80
59	81
60	81

and so on until

87–89	95

until 100% reached at 102 weeks

MGM's advances in the early 1930s were $25,000 per two-reeler, $30,000 when needed, and $40,000 per two-reeler on Laurel and Hardy. This figure was averaged out and deposited weekly.

Arrival of the Depression in Culver City:
Hal Roach Studios' Earned Surplus Account

Parentheses around monetary values indicate a loss.

4/3/26–7/31/26:	$55,953.27
8/1/26–1/29/27:	$100,124.47
1/30/27–7/30/27:	$81,423.20
7/31/27–1/28/28:	$83,793.39
1/29/28–7/28/28:	$18,810.10
7/29/28–1/26/29:	$42,372.89
1/27/29–11/30/29:	$29,245.15
12/1/29–7/26/30:	$36,053.93
7/27/30–8/29/31:	$87,085.34
8/30/31–3/12/32:	($41,875.77)

Roach Picture Performance for the 1930–31 and 1931–32 Seasons

	1930–31	1931–32	Change
Bookings, U.S. and Canada	$2,331,235.45	$2,290,152.01	−$41,083.44
Gross, U.S. and Canada	546,470.78	601,812.71	55,341.93
Gross, foreign	15,034.16	8,546.56	−6,487.60
Total gross	561,504.94	610,359.27	48,854.33
Average collection per week	1,859.28	2,034.53	175.25
Average collection per picture	28,075.25	29,064.72	989.47
Negative costs	982,345.89	891,374.41	−90,971.48
Average income per picture	49,117.29	42,446.40	−6,670.89

Series Income and Contracts per Picture, 1931–32 to 7/16/32

	Total	Average per Picture
Laurel and Hardy	$733,527.90	$91,690.99
Charley Chase	571,894.16	71,486.77
Our Gang	538,755.02	67,344.38
Boy Friends	510,614.16	63,826.77
Pitts-Todd	570,783.24	71,347.90
All Series	2,925,574.48	73,139.36

	Average No. of Contracts per month	Average Rental
Laurel and Hardy		
1931–32	4,633	$11.83
1932–33	4,430	12.74
Charley Chase		
1931–32	4,623	9.70
1932–33	4,396	9.72
Our Gang		
1931–32	4,601	9.17
1932–33	4,384	9.42
Pitts-Todd		
1931–32	4,582	9.68
1932–33	4,397	10.15
Boy Friends, 1931–32	4,561	8.97
Taxi Boys, 1932–33	4,348	9.30
All series		
Total, 1931–32	184,008	1,817,382.38
Total, 1932–33	175,477	1,772,400.51

Negative Costs on Selected Short Subjects

1933
Maids a la Mode	$24,934.23
Bargain of the Century	22,702.58
One Track Minds	22,676.39
His Silent Racket	21,179.28
Arabian Tights	24,047.92
Mush and Milk	20,682.55
Me and My Pal	36,128.91
Thundering Taxis	26,565.05
Call Her Sausage	17,955.12
The Rummy	20,108.89

1938
Follies of '38	60,544.36
Hide and Shriek	19,093.14
Awful Tooth	17,760.59
Feed 'em and Weep	18,860.49
Came the Brawn	21,529.52
Three Men in a Tub	23,712.08
Bear Facts	21,344.67
Canned Fishing	27,937.34 (direction and cast cost more than usual)
Mail and Female	19,914.54
Framing Youth	26,156.89
Pig Skin Palooka	37,224.82 (more on cast and sets)
Night 'n' Gales	30,000.56
Fishy Tales	29,398.75

Financial Performance of the MGM Features

Production No./Film Title	U.S./Canadian Gross Earnings	Foreign Gross Earnings	MGM/RCA Deductions from Studio's Percentage[a]	Negative Costs	Profit (or Loss)
F-1/Pardon Us	$536,401.20	$498,564.19	$192,187.09	$221,681.03	$198,312.44
F-2/Pack Up Your Troubles	417,029.41	595,668.53	124,102.66	146,811.65	274,289.08
F-3/The Devil's Brother	332,895.05	1,227,819.40	158,669.45	201,662.01	475,156.97
F-4/Sons of the Desert	357,909.24	756,158.50	128,455.47	165,705.06	299,711.26
F-5/Babes in Toyland	376,467.20	567,178.06	122,096.18	421,810.68	13,853.24
F-6/Vagabond Lady	278,357.49	196,107.95	96,843.39	542,263.87	(156,370.86)
F-7/Bonnie Scotland	408,395.76	959,204.03	143,990.46	447,031.55	186,575.18
F-8/The Bohemian Girl	370,923.17	722,742.09	96,314.21	348,850.91	172,433.28
F-9/Mr. Cinderella	207,541.53	66,798.94	40,840.11	301,333.29	—
F-10/Kelly the Second	341,361.82	125,032.04	57,162.41	263,502.04	—
F-11/Our Relations	366,245.95	532,400.84	98,686.72	430,823.59	2,165.53
F-12/General Spanky	240,091.35	39,099.06	45,161.84	275,777.47	—
F-14/Way Out West	257,696.28	2,472.89	38,648.07	361,541.18	—
F-15/Pick a Star	165,835.22	1,186.24	24,994.66	474,544.91	—
F-16/Nobody's Baby	213,255.89	1,121.98	32,000.53	323,593.86	(139,008.02)
F-17/Topper	12,233.51	495.00	2,221.30	720,625.30	—

Note: The U.S./Canadian and foreign numbers are gross earnings in U.S. dollars. This information came from a listing of earnings dated July 29, 1937. "Negative Costs" represents the total production costs of a film. Because F-9, F-10, and F-12 through F-17 were still in release in mid-1937, final profit or loss figures were not available when this list was compiled. The loss figure for F-16 came from a memo from Hugh Huber to Victor Ford Collins dated November 2, 1939. No feature received the production number F-13.

[a]Not counting the distributor's percentage of the gross.

Financial Performance of the United Artists Films

The primary source for the revenue figures below is a series of annual United Artists reports that cover the U.S. and Canadian box office for the years 1938–49. The figures are in U.S. dollars. The records for the years 1940 and 1947 were not available. Therefore,

1. For *There Goes My Heart*, box office totals for 1938 and 1939 are given. For *Zenobia*, *Topper Takes a Trip*, and *Captain Fury*, totals for 1939 are given. A number beside each film will indicate the number of weeks the film was in release at the time the total was calculated. For *The Housekeeper's Daughter*, *A Chump at Oxford*, *Of Mice and Men*, *One Million B.C.*, *Saps at Sea*, *Turnabout*, and *Captain Caution*, a less detailed summary sheet in the Hal Roach files that dates from January 31, 1942, has been used in place of the annual summary sheets to supply box office totals. For films released in 1941 and later, the UA annual report figures are used.

2. Although the UA features and wartime streamliners were still in release in 1947, the absence of box office information from that year has minimal impact on the accuracy of the profits stated, since most of the films were making their last theatrical rounds in subsequent-run venues that paid flat rental fees of between ten and twenty dollars per film. Thus most of the films were earning less than one thousand dollars per year by this point.

3. The absence of information for the year 1947 does affect the profit tally for *Comedy Carnival*, which was placed in release that year.

4. The absence of figures after 1949 somewhat affects the profit figures for both *Comedy Carnival* and *Lafftime*, since they continued pulling in meager amounts in subsequent-run venues through the early 1950s.

5. The absence of foreign figures for the feature films seriously affects the profit totals. The international market contributed a substantial portion of a film's total revenue.

6. The foreign figures for the streamliners are from a United Artists document entitled "World Wide Estimate of Gross on Roach Streamliners." The author has provided a figure for each film that is 65 percent of this gross, an average percentage of the producer's share for the various foreign markets. It must be remembered that these figures are based on UA's estimate.

7. Roach's production costs are included when known.

Thus, the table presented below provides only an idea, but not a definitive answer, about the financial performance of Roach's UA features and streamliners. The producer's share is the net earning on each picture paid to Roach from United Artists.

		Producer's Share		
	Negative Cost	U.S./Canadian	Foreign	Total
Features				
There Goes My Heart (63 wks)	N/A	410,699.94	N/A	N/A
Topper Takes a Trip (51 wks)	N/A	565,687.84	N/A	N/A
Zenobia (37 wks)	N/A	130,050.90	N/A	N/A
Captain Fury (33 wks)	N/A	537,858.05	N/A	N/A
The Housekeeper's Daughter	N/A	713,436.90	N/A	N/A
A Chump at Oxford	N/A	230,296.77	N/A	N/A
Of Mice and Men	336,524.21[a]	676,292.01	N/A	N/A
One Million B.C.	N/A	462,730.83	N/A	N/A
Saps at Sea	N/A	225,139.15	N/A	N/A
Turnabout	457,650[b]	515,152.49	N/A	N/A
Captain Caution	761,766.41	513,148.66	N/A	N/A
Road Show	N/A	284,393.68	N/A	N/A
Broadway Limited	N/A	257,304.74	N/A	N/A
Topper Returns	N/A	500,931.12	N/A	N/A
Streamliners				
Tanks a Million	98,049	182,956.61	100,750	283,706.61
Niagara Falls	105,770	157,215.02	61,750	218,965.02
All American Co-Ed	108,932	138,107.34	52,000	190.107.34
Miss Polly	118,854	144,781.97	58,500	203,281.97
Fiesta	178,044	134,186.84	61,750	195,936.84
Hayfoot	98,690	155,349.83	65,000	220,349.83
Brooklyn Orchid	115,682	152,822.52	52,000	204,822.52
Dudes Are Pretty People	114,982	108,177.63	29,250	137,427.63
About Face	105,057	153,375.51	55,250	208,625.51
Flying with Music	129,466	112,223.26	52,000	164,223.26
The Devil with Hitler	N/A	135,230.27	52,000	187,230.27
The McGuerins from Brooklyn	N/A	152,603.16	48,750	201,353.16
Calaboose	N/A	114,331.34	32,500	146,831.34
Fall In	N/A	154,253.75	42,250	196,503.75
Taxi, Mister?	N/A	156,051.59	42,250	198,301.59
Prairie Chickens	N/A	123,032.26	39,000	162,032.26
Yanks Ahoy	N/A	152,347.79	42,250	194,597.79
Nazty Nuisance	126,040.12	52,000	178,040.12	230,040.12
Streamliner pairs				
Hal Roach Comedy Carnival	N/A	321,948.98	N/A	N/A
Lafftime	455,631.28[c]	304,901.63	N/A	N/A

Note: N/A, not available.

[a]The negative cost for *Of Mice and Men* is incomplete, being based on a summary of costs after principal photography wrapped but before postproduction (editing, music scoring, etc.) commenced.
[b]The negative cost for *Turnabout* is based on the budgeted amount, not the final amount.
[c]This cost is for *Who Killed Doc Robbin?* only. The exact cost of the other half of *Lafftime, Here Comes Trouble,* was not available for review.

Notes

1. Introduction

1. It is also not intended as a biography of the many actors who worked for Roach or as a detailed chronicle of their films. Excellent books, many listed in the bibliography, have been written about the films and lives of Harold Lloyd, Laurel and Hardy, Our Gang, Charley Chase, and others.

2. "Studio That Fun Built Soon to Be a Memory," *Los Angeles Times,* June 28, 1963.

3. Henry Ginsburg to Mike Levee, Academy of Motion Picture Arts and Sciences, July 5, 1932, University of Southern California (hereafter, USC), Hal Roach Studios, Hollywood Museum Collection.

4. For a detailed examination of theatrical short subjects from the 1930s through the 1950s, see Leonard Maltin, *The Great Movie Shorts* (New York: Bonanza Books, 1972). For a look at the different short-subject production strategies of three studios during the 1930s, see Richard Ward, "Extra Added Attractions: The Short Subjects of MGM, Warner Bros. and Universal," *Media History* 9, no. 3 (2003): 221–44.

2. The Rolin Film Company, 1914

1. Janet Staiger, "Combination and Litigation: Structures of U.S. Film Distribution, 1896–1917," *Cinema Journal* 23 (Winter 1983): 41–72; David Bordwell, Kristin Thompson, Janet Staiger, *The Classical Hollywood Cinema: Film Style and Mode of Production to 1960* (New York: Columbia University Press, 1985), 398; Robert Sklar, *Movie-Made America* (New York: Random House, 1975), 33–47.

2. Bordwell, Staiger, Thompson, *Classical Hollywood Cinema,* 134–37.

3. Bordwell, Staiger, Thompson, *Classical Hollywood Cinema,* 157–59.

4. Buster Keaton and Charles Samuels, *My Wonderful World of Slapstick* (New York: Da Capo Press, 1960), 109–10.

5. Randy Skretvedt, *Laurel and Hardy: The Magic Behind the Movies* (Beverly Hills: Moonstone Press, 1987), 36; Bernard Rosenberg and Harry Silverstein, *The Real Tinsel* (London: Collier-Macmillan, 1970), 15–16; Mike Steen, *Hollywood Speaks!* (New York: G. P. Putnam's Sons, 1974), 363.

6. Rolin board of directors minutes, August 17, 1914, USC, Hal Roach Studios, Hollywood Museum Collection, business ledger 1914–21.

7. Rolin articles of incorporation, July 23, 1914, USC, Hal Roach Studios, Hollywood Museum Collection, business ledger 1914–21.

8. The amount of capital stock available in Rolin was ten thousand dollars, divided into one hundred shares at one hundred dollars per share. The amount of stock actually sold on the date of incorporation was only three hundred dollars, with Roach, Linthicum, and Nance each purchasing one share. Rolin articles of incorporation, USC, Hal Roach Studios, Hollywood Museum Collection, business ledger 1914–21.

9. Rolin board of directors minutes, August 17, 1914, USC, Hal Roach Studios, Hollywood Museum Collection, business ledger 1914–21.

10. Rosenberg and Silverstein, *Real Tinsel,* 16–17.

11. Rolin board of directors minutes, September 15, 1914, USC, Hal Roach Studios, Hollywood Museum Collection, business ledger 1914–21.

12. "Sawyer, Inc., Quarters Superb," *Moving Picture World,* July 11, 1914, 259.

13. Rolin board of directors minutes, July 30, 1915, USC, Hal Roach Studios, Hollywood Museum Collection, business ledger 1914–21.

14. Bordwell, Staiger, Thompson, *Classical Hollywood Cinema,* 401.

15. Pathé advertisement, *Moving Picture World,* February 28, 1914, 1058.

16. "Our Lawyers' Communication to the General Film Co.," Pathé advertisement, *Moving Picture World,* May 9, 1914, 835.

17. "Pathe Opens Exchanges," *Moving Picture World,* May 16, 1914, 975.

18. *Pathé Daily News* advertisement, *Moving Picture World,* June 20, 1914, 1630–31.

19. "Expediting Service," *Moving Picture World,* July 11, 1914, 284.

20. "Pathé in Mutual," *Variety,* October 31, 1914, 25.

21. George Blaisdell, "Charles Pathé, Film Publisher," *Moving Picture World,* November 14, 1914, 904–5.

22. Pathé advertisement, *Moving Picture World,* January 16, 1915, 314. "Pathé Freres' New Executive Offices," *Moving Picture World,* April 3, 1915, 79.

23. "Pathé Freres' New Executive Offices," *Moving Picture World,* April 3, 1915, 79.

24. Dwight Whiting, in New York City, telegrams to Rolin Film Company, March 25 and 26, 1915, USC, Hal Roach Studios, Hollywood Museum Collection, 1914–15 business correspondence file.

25. Hal Roach, in New York City, telegram to Rolin, October 14, 1915, USC, Hal Roach Studios, Hollywood Museum Collection, 1914–15 business correspondence file.

26. Rolin, telegram to Hal Roach in New York City, October 11, 1915, USC, Hal Roach Studios, Hollywood Museum Collection, 1914–15 business correspondence file.

27. Rolin, telegram to Hal Roach in New York City, October 11, 1915, USC, Hal Roach Studios, Hollywood Museum Collection,
1914–15 business correspondence file.

3. Lonesome Luke and the Glasses Character, 1915–19

1. Henry Jenkins, *What Made Pistachio Nuts?* (New York: Columbia University Press, 1992), 56–57.

2. Jenkins, *What Made Pistachio Nuts?,* 57.

3. David Bordwell, Janet Staiger, Kristin Thompson, *The Classical Hollywood Cinema* (New York: Columbia University Press, 1985), 99.

4. Whiting to Upson Company, April 19, 1916, USC, Hal Roach Studios, Hollywood Museum Collection.

5. Norbig to Rolin, August 28, 1915; Whiting to Norbig, August 28, 1915; Norbig to Rolin, July 15, 1915; and Whiting to Negative Reconstructing Company, March 21, 1916, USC, Hal Roach Studios, Hollywood Museum Collection, box 4, file 1915. Rolin to Pacific Laboratories, March 9, 1916, March 31, 1916, and March 4, 1916, USC, Hal Roach Studios, Hollywood Museum Collection, box 4, 1916 business correspondence. Rolin to H. V. Carter of San Francisco, undated, USC, Hal Roach Studios, Hollywood Museum Collection. Nick Harris detective report, USC, Hal Roach Studios, Hollywood Museum Collection, 1919 file.

6. Whiting to Twist, June 10, 1915, USC, Hal Roach Studios, Hollywood Museum Collection, box 4, 1915 file.

7. Whiting to Twist, August 4, 1915, USC, Hal Roach Studios, Hollywood Museum Collection, box 4, 1915 file.

8. Whiting to Twist, October 27, 1915, USC, Hal Roach Studios, Hollywood Museum Collection, box 4, 1915 file.

9. Whiting to Phillips Film Company, November 24, 1915, USC, Hal Roach Studios, Hollywood Museum Collection, 1915–20 file.

10. William Hodginson, Paramount, to Rolin, February 13, 1916, USC, Hal Roach Studios, Hollywood Museum Collection, 1915–20 file; Roach to Whiting, November 2, 1917, USC, Hollywood Museum Collection, business correspondence file.

11. Whiting to Roach, February 16, 1917, USC, Hal Roach Studios, Hollywood Museum Collection, business correspondence file.

12. Roach to Whiting, March 6, 1916; Whiting to Roach, April 10, 1916, USC, Hal Roach Studios, Hollywood Museum Collection, 1916 business correspondence.

13. Hal Roach Studios Collection; minutes of a special board of directors' meeting of December 19, 1916, USC, Hal Roach Studios, Hollywood Museum Collection; "News of the Film World," *Variety,* August 4, 1916, 26; "Rolin Comedian Dead," *Moving Picture World,* September 20, 1919, 1799.

14. Whiting to J. D. Stafford of the Lyric Theater, Chico, CA, October 14, 1916, USC, Hal Roach Studios, Hollywood Museum Collection, file 1916.

15. Whiting, telegram to Roach in New York City, August 11, 1916; Rolin to *Moving Picture World,* May 31, 1917, 1917 *Moving Picture World* file; Doane to Mae McGregor, March 16, 1918, 1918 file; Rolin to *Motion Picture News,* September 2, 1918, *Motion Picture News* 1915–20 file; all USC, Hal Roach Studios, Hollywood Museum Collection, box 4. Harold Lloyd, *An American Comedy* (New York: Dover Publications, 1971), 129.

16. Roach to Rolin, February 6, 1917, USC, Hal Roach Studios, Hollywood Museum Collection.

17. Whiting to Roach, February 7, 1917, USC, Hal Roach Studios, Hollywood Museum Collection.

18. Whiting to Roach, February 12, 1917, USC, Hal Roach Studios, Hollywood Museum Collection. File 1916, "Harold Lloyd Mentioned."

19. Roach to Whiting, October 27, 1917, USC, Hal Roach Studios, Hollywood Museum Collection, 1917 business correspondence file.

20. Whiting to Roach, October 28, 1917, USC, Hal Roach Studios, Hollywood Museum Collection, 1917 business correspondence file.

21. Roach to Whiting, October 28, 1917, USC, Hal Roach Studios, Hollywood Museum Collection, 1917 business correspondence file.

22. Roach to Whiting, October 29, 1917, USC, Hal Roach Studios, Hollywood Museum Collection, 1917 business correspondence file.

23. Whiting to Roach, October 31, 1917, USC, Hal Roach Studios, Hollywood Museum Collection, 1917 business correspondence file.

24. Randy Skretvedt, *Laurel and Hardy: The Magic Behind the Movies* (Beverly Hills: Moonstone Press, 1987), 41.

25. *Variety,* September 20, 1918, 41; "Pathe Program for March 2," *Moving Picture World,* March 1, 1919, 1235.

26. George Stevens quoted in John McCabe, *Laurel and Hardy* (New York: Ballantine Books, 1975), 10.

27. Roach to Whiting, February 8, 1917, USC, Hal Roach Studios, Hollywood Museum Collection, 1917 business correspondence file.

28. Roach to Whiting, February 16, 1917, USC, Hal Roach Studios, Hollywood Museum Collection, 1917 business correspondence file; Lloyd, *American Comedy,* 60–63.

29. Rolin to *Motion Picture News,* January 31, 1916, USC, Hal Roach Studios, Hollywood Museum Collection, box 4, *Motion Picture News* 1915–20 file.

30. Pathé advertisement, *Moving Picture World,* August 24, 1918, 1054.

31. "Harold Lloyd Is Making Distinctive Comedies," *Moving Picture World,* January 25, 1919, 514.

32. "Hal Roach in New York," *Moving Picture World,* June 8, 1918, 1409.

33. Whiting to Frank A. Garbutt of Famous Players–Lasky, May 4, 1917, USC, Hal Roach Studios, Hollywood Museum Collection, 1917 file; Roach to Brunet, May 19, 1919, USC, Hal Roach Studios, Hollywood Museum Collection, Pathé 1919 file.

34. "Iowa Exhibitor Holds a Harold Lloyd Comedy Week," *Moving Picture World,* June 14, 1919, 1676.

35. Doane to Walker, January 24, 1918, USC, Hal Roach Studios, Hollywood Museum Collection, 1917 file.

36. Whiting to Frederick Davidson of New York City, February 14, 1918, USC, Hal Roach Studios, Hollywood Museum Collection, 1918 file.

37. Minutes of a special meeting of the board of directors, April 4, 1918, USC, Hal Roach Studios, Hollywood Museum Collection.

38. Tom Dardis, *Harold Lloyd: The Man on the Clock* (New York: Viking Press, 1983), 89; Bernard Rosenberg and Harry Silverstein, *The Real Tinsel* (New York: Macmillan, 1970), 20.

39. Whatever the circumstances of Whiting's departure, there appears to have been little or no lasting acrimony between Roach and Whiting. The two were to have non-film-related business dealings throughout the 1920s and 1930s, most notably when Whiting served on the board of directors of Hal Roach's excursion into professional horse racing: the Santa Anita racetrack.

40. "Hal Roach Buys Whiting's Interest in Rolin," *Moving Picture World,* May 4, 1918, 681.

4. Pathécomedies, 1919–27

1. *Moving Picture World* (hereinafter *MPW*), September 6, 1919, 1449.

2. *MPW,* September 6, 1919, 1449.

3. "Lloyd Will Resume Work on New Series of Two Reel Comedies for Pathé Within a Month," *MPW,* October 4, 1919, 106.

4. Alf Goulding v. HRS, USC, Hal Roach Studios, Hollywood Museum Collection, box 5, Alf Goulding file 1921–23.

5. Tom Dardis, *Harold Lloyd: The Man on the Clock* (New York: Viking Press, 1983), 40.

6. Pathé ad on an unnumbered page quoting a review in *MPW,* February, 7, 1920.

7. Fred Quimby to Hal Roach, November 4, 1919, USC, Hal Roach Studios, Hollywood Museum Collection, 1919 Hal Roach–Fred Quimby file.

8. William McIntire to Rolin, January 3, 1920, and reply of Warren Doane to William McIntire, January 11, 1920, USC, Hal Roach Studios, Hollywood Museum Collection, Hal Roach Studios 1920–22 file.

9. Hal Roach to Fred Quimby, September 10, 1919, and reply of Fred Quimby to Hal Roach, September 13, 1919, USC, Hal Roach Studios, Hollywood Museum Collection, 1919 Hal Roach–Fred Quimby file.

10. Dardis, *Harold Lloyd,* 86.

11. Hal Roach to Fred Quimby, August 4 and 8, 1919, USC, Hal Roach Studios, Hollywood Museum Collection, 1919 Hal Roach–Fred Quimby file.

12. Hal Roach, in New York City, to Rolin, November 17, 1919, USC, Hal Roach Studios, Hollywood Museum Collection, "Hal Roach NY/C. H. Roach LA, November 1919" file.

13. Warren Doane to Railroad Commission, February 18, 1920, and September 20, 1920, USC, Hal Roach Studios, Hollywood Museum Collection, 1920–21 file.

14. Warren Doane to Southern California Edison of Santa Monica, August 5, 1920, USC, Hal Roach Studios, Hollywood Museum Collection, 1920 file.

15. Copy sent to *Culver City Courier* for Christmas edition, December 1920, USC, Hal Roach Studios, Hollywood Museum Collection, 1920 general file.

16. Board of directors minutes, 1921, USC, Hal Roach Studios, Hollywood Museum Collection.

17. Board of directors minutes, July 26, 1920, USC, Hal Roach Studios, Hollywood Museum Collection.

18. Pathé advertisement, *MPW*, July 14, 1920, n. pag.

19. Pathé advertisement, *MPW*, October 16, 1920, n. pag.

20. Hal E. Roach to Famous Players–Lasky, August 12, 1920, USC, Hal Roach Studios, Hollywood Museum Collection, 1920 file.

21. Warren Doane to Ben Shipman, September 24, 1925, USC, Hal Roach Studios, Hollywood Museum Collection, Ben Shipman file.

22. Hal Roach to Fred Quimby, September 29, 1920, USC, Hal Roach Studios, Hollywood Museum Collection, Hal Roach Studios 1920–22 file.

23. Hal Roach to Fred Quimby, August 6, 1920, USC, Hal Roach Studios, Hollywood Museum Collection, Harold Lloyd 1920 file.

24. "Lloyd Completes Last Comedy for Pathe; Starts Work for Associated Exhibitors," *MPW*, October 30, 1920, 1276.

25. "Three Reel Harold Lloyd Comedy to Be Featured by S. L. Rothafel," *MPW*, July 2, 1921, 107.

26. "Quality Led Rothafel to 'Star' Harold Lloyd, Says Arthur Kane," *MPW*, July 23, 1921, 426.

27. Pathé advertisement, *MPW*, April 8, 1922, 588.

28. Hal Roach to Jack Cohn, April 11, 1922, USC, Hal Roach Studios, Hollywood Museum Collection, Harold Lloyd 1922 file.

29. Harold Lloyd (actually ghostwritten by Joe Reddy), copy sent to *Health and Life* magazine, May 1, 1922, USC, Hal Roach Studios, Hollywood Museum Collection, Harold Lloyd 1922 file.

30. Lasky, in New York City, to Hal Roach, December 7, 1921, USC, Hal Roach Studios, Hollywood Museum Collection, Harold Lloyd 1921 file.

31. Dardis, *Harold Lloyd*, 88.

32. Hal Roach to A. S. Kane, February 21, 1922, USC, Hal Roach Studios, Hollywood Museum Collection, Harold Lloyd 1921 [*sic*] file.

33. Joe Reddy of Hal Roach Studios to publicity director of Associated Exhibitors, June 21, 1922; Hal Roach to Harold Lloyd, in New York City, November 6, 1922: both USC, Hal Roach Studios, Hollywood Museum Collection, Harold Lloyd 1922 file.

34. *MPW*, July 7, 1923, 52.

35. Harold Lloyd, *An American Comedy* (New York: Dover Publications, 1971), 89, 130.

36. *MPW*, July 7, 1923, 52.

37. USC, Hal Roach Studios, Hollywood Museum Collection, Harold Lloyd Corporation File.

38. Exhibitor review of *The Battling Orioles* under Pathé release section, *MPW*, January 24, 1925, 363.

39. W. B. Frank to Warren Doane, November 14, 1924, USC, Hal Roach Studios, Hollywood Museum Collection, box 5, 1924 file.

40. *MPW*, information from cast lists in reviews of several films in 1926.

41. Randy Skretvedt, *Laurel and Hardy: The Magic Behind the Movies* (Beverly Hills: Moonstone Press, 1987), 71–72.

42. "Hal Roach's Ninth Year with Pathe," *MPW*, September 8, 1923, 182.

43. A. H. Giebler, "News of the West Coast," *MPW*, February 4, 1922, 545.

44. "Four Hal Roach Comedy Companies Making Films to Be Released by Pathé," *MPW*, March 18, 1922, 267.

45. Leonard Maltin and Richard Bann, *Our Gang: The Life and Times of the Little Rascals* (New York: Crown Publishers, 1977), 18.

46. John McCabe, *The Comedy World of Stan Laurel* (Garden City, NY: Doubleday, 1974), 77.

47. During a trip to New York, Roach dictated in explicit terms a series of changes after a rough-cut screening of *General Spanky:*

1. Put back scene of Holmes going into house.
2. Put back walk with Spanky.
3. Take out closeup of Buckwheat's foot in whistle gag.
4. Take out idea of getting food.
5. Open sequence with Buckwheat going into watermelon patch. Go to inside of cave. Cut to Buckwheat leaving watermelon patch.
6. Cut out opening cave scene kids are swearing allegiance. Cut to Spanky.
7. Cut fort scene way down.

Hal Roach, on a business trip in New York City, to Hal Roach Studios, October 24, 1936, USC, Hal Roach Studios, Hollywood Museum Collection.

48. H. M. Walker to Hal Roach, November 8, 1922, USC, Hal Roach Studios, Hollywood Museum Collection, 1922 file.

49. Dwight Whiting to Kellogg Manufacturing Company, November 10, 1916, February 1, 1917, USC, Hal Roach Studios, Hollywood Museum Collection.

50. C. S. Sewell, "Hal Roach Calls Forces Together; Emphasizes Cleanliness in Films," *MPW*, June 17, 1922, 619.

51. "Pathe to Handle Ben Turpin and Mack Sennett Comedies," *MPW*, March 24, 1923, 407.

52. Maltin and Bann, *Our Gang,* 79.

53. W. B. Frank to Warren Doane, November 26, 1924, USC, Hal Roach Studios, Hollywood Museum Collection, Box 5, 1924 file.

54. W. B. Frank to Warren Doane, September 5, 1924, July Theatrical Totals, USC, Hal Roach Studios, Hollywood Museum Collection, box 5, 1924 file.

55. Gross sheet, November 28, 1925, USC, Hal Roach Studios, Hollywood Museum Collection, box 5, Warren Doane December 1925 file.

56. Warren Doane to W. B. Frank, October 21, 1924, USC, Hal Roach Studios, Hollywood Museum Collection, box 5, 1924 file. Ever-dissatisfied with Pathé, Roach in 1924 began production on a series of one-reel comedies starring Earl Mohan and intended for distribution by CBC (the forerunner of Columbia). A few of these films were produced before the CBC distribution deal fell through; the films were ultimately released as Hal Roach Comedies through Pathé.

57. W. B. Frank to Warren Doane, September 30, 1924, USC, Hal Roach Studios, Hollywood Museum Collection, box 5, 1924 file.

58. W. B. Frank to Warren Doane, September 30, 1924, USC, Hal Roach Studios, Hollywood Museum Collection, box 5, 1924 file.

59. Warren Doane to W. B. Frank, October 20, 1924, USC, Hal Roach Studios, Hollywood Museum Collection, box 5, 1924 file.

60. W. B. Frank to Warren Doane, November 14, 1924, USC, Hal Roach Studios, Hollywood Museum Collection, box 5, 1924 file.

61. Warren Doane to W. B. Frank, December 9, 1924, USC, Hal Roach Studios, Hollywood Museum Collection, box 5, 1924 file.

62. USC, Hal Roach Studios, Hollywood Museum Collection, box 5, 1925 Hal Roach Studios general folder, survey copy and responses.

63. Author interview with Hal Roach associate Richard Bann, August 1989, Los Angeles.

64. *MPW,* November 19, 1921, and later Pathé advertisements.

65. Pathé to Hal Roach Studios, April 8, 1927, USC, Hal Roach Studios, Hollywood Museum Collection, H. M. Walker New York April 1927 file.

66. Warren Doane to H. M. Walker, April 13, 1927, USC, Hal Roach Studios, Hollywood Museum Collection, H. M. Walker New York April 1927 file.

67. Fred Jackman, telegram to Hal Roach Studios, June 26, 1925, USC, Hal Roach Studios, Hollywood Museum Collection, Fred Jackman Co.—*Devil Horse*—June 1925 file.

68. Jack Roach, telegram to Hal Roach Studios, February 10, 1922, USC, Hal Roach Studios, Hollywood Museum Collection, 1922 Truckee Serial Co. correspondence file.

69. Jack Roach, telegram to Hal Roach Studios, February 10, 1922, USC, Hal Roach Studios, Hollywood Museum Collection, 1922 Truckee Serial Co. correspondence file.

70. Brandy (no first name given), telegram to L. A. French, June 19, 1925; Fred Jackman, telegram to Hal Roach Studios, June 26, 1925: both USC, Hal Roach Studios, Hollywood Museum Collection, Fred Jackman Co.—*Devil Horse*—June 1925 file.

71. Lloyd French, telegram to Warren Doane, June 25, 1926, USC, Hal Roach Studios, Hollywood Museum Collection, western co. on location Mopa, Nevada, June 1926 file.

72. "Roach Discontinues Westerns," *MPW,* September 25, 1926, 214.

73. "Short Subjects Merit More Recognition," *MPW,* June 6, 1925, 660.

74. "Hal Roach to Co-Feature Well-Known Fun Makers," *MPW,* May 16, 1925, 356.

75. Hal Roach, "A New Day—A New Policy," *Exhibitor's Trade Review,* January 2, 1926, 24–25; Hal Roach, "A New Trend in Short Comedies," *MPW,* April 3, 1926, 352.

76. "Hal Roach to Make Two Reel Dramas," *MPW,* December 11, 1926, 411.

77. Warren Doane, telegram to W. B. Frank, January 29, 1926, and W. B. Frank, telegram to Warren Doane, January 30, 1926: both USC, Hal Roach Studios, Hollywood Museum Collection, box 5, 1924 [*sic*] file.

78. W. B. Frank, telegram to Warren Doane, May 3, 1926, USC, Hal Roach Studios, Hollywood Museum Collection, box 5, 1924 [*sic*] file.

79. W. B. Frank to Warren Doane, April 2, 1926, and several items in a 1926 Hal Roach Studios file on Mabel Normand; Warren Doane, telegram to W. B. Frank, April 20, 1926: all USC, Hal Roach Studios, Hollywood Museum Collection, box 5, 1924 [*sic*] file.

80. W. B. Frank to Warren Doane, October 30, 1925, USC, Hal Roach Studios, Hollywood Museum Collection, box 5, 1924 [*sic*] file.

81. Warren Doane to W. B. Frank, December 7, 1925, USC, Hal Roach Studios, Hollywood Museum Collection, box 5, 1924 [*sic*] file.

82. Warren Doane, telegram to F. Richard Jones, January 27, 1926, USC, Hal Roach Studios, Hollywood Museum Collection, F. Richard Jones 1925–27 file.

83. Contract between Hal Roach Studios and Metro-Goldwyn-Mayer Distributing Corporation dated March 16, 1926, USC, Hal Roach Studios, Hollywood Museum Collection, box 42, MGM 1926–27 file.

84. Hal Roach Studios, telegram to Red Kann of the *Film Daily,* May 26, 1926, in answer to inquires from Kann, USC, Hal Roach Studios, Hollywood Museum Collection, box 6, 1926 file.

85. Hal Roach, in New York City, telegram to Warren Doane, April 26, 1926, USC, Hal Roach Studios, Hollywood Museum Collection, box 5, 1924 [*sic*] file.

86. Warren Doane to Fred Quimby, June 10, 1927, USC, Hal Roach Studios, Holly-
wood Museum Collection, box 6, Fred Quimby 1926–27 file; Warren Doane to H. M.
Walker, April 19, 1927, and H. M. Walker to Warren Doane, April 25, 1927, USC, Hal
Roach Studios, Hollywood Museum Collection, H. M. Walker New York April 1927 file.

5. Roach-MGM Short Features, 1927–33

1. *MPW*, November 13, 1926.
2. Hal Roach Studio–MGM contract, March 16, 1926, USC, Hal Roach Studios,
Hollywood Museum Collection, box 42, MGM file.
3. Quimby to Roach, December 20, 1926; Roach to Quimby, December 27, 1926;
Doane to Quimby, February 10, 1927; Quimby to Roach, February 11, 1927; Quimby to
Roach, February 12, 1927: all USC, Hal Roach Studios, Hollywood Museum Collection,
box 6, Fred Quimby 1926–27 file.
4. Doane to Gasner, April 19, 1927, USC, Hal Roach Studios, Hollywood Museum
Collection, box 10, 1927 general files.
5. Quimby to Roach, April 1, 1927; Roach to Quimby, April 2, 1927: both USC, Hal
Roach Studios, Hollywood Museum Collection, box 6, Fred Quimby 1926–27 files.
6. Roach to Quimby, June 16, 1927, USC, Hal Roach Studios, Hollywood Museum
Collection, box 6, Fred Quimby 1926–27 files.
7. Doane to Quimby, July 1, 1927, USC, Hal Roach Studios, Hollywood Museum
Collection, box 6, Fred Quimby 1926–27 files.
8. Quimby to Doane, undated, USC, Hal Roach Studios, Hollywood Museum Collection, box 6, Fred Quimby 1926–27 files; Luz to Doane, July 16, 1927, and Doane to
Luz, August 2, 1927: both USC, Hal Roach Studios, Hollywood Museum Collection,
box 10, 1927 general files.
9. Quimby to Roach, July 11, 1927; Doane to Quimby, August 1, 1927: both USC, Hal
Roach Studios, Hollywood Museum Collection, box 6, Fred Quimby 1926–27 files.
10. Quimby to Roach, August 5, 1927, USC, Hal Roach Studios Hollywood Museum
Collection, box 6, Fred Quimby 1926–27 file.
11. Doane to Roach, September 8, 1927, USC, Hal Roach Studios, Hollywood Museum Collection, box 7, Hal Roach New York August 1927 file.
12. Doane to Roach, September 14, 1927, USC, Hal Roach Studios, Hollywood Museum Collection, box 7, Hal Roach New York August 1927 file.
13. Quimby to Roach, October 10, 1927, USC, Hal Roach Studios, Hollywood Museum Collection, box 6, Fred Quimby 1926–27 file.
14. Roach to Quimby, December 17, 1927, USC, Hal Roach Studios, Hollywood
Museum Collection, box 6, Fred Quimby 1926–27 file.
15. Quimby, telegram to Roach, December 31, 1927, USC, Hal Roach Studios, Hollywood Museum Collection, box 6, Fred Quimby 1926–27 file.
16. Annual report of the directors to the stockholders of Hal Roach Studios, August 31, 1928, USC, Hal Roach Studios, Hollywood Museum Collection, general 1928
file.
17. United Artists–Victor contract, August 27, 1928, Wisconsin Center for Theatre
Research, United Artists Collection, Madison.
18. "35 of 40 Hal Roach Comedies to Have Synchronization," *MPN*, September 1,
1928, 725.
19. Doane to Roach, November 27, 1928, USC, Hal Roach Studios, Hollywood Museum Collection, stockholders reports box 1.
20. "Victor Engineers Start Work on Roach Stages," *MPN*, March 9, 1929, 754. The
trades preferred the term *talker* rather than *talkie* when discussing sound pictures.

21. Randy Skretvedt, *Laurel and Hardy: The Magic Behind the Movies* (Beverly Hills: Moonstone Press, 1987), 186.

22. Skretvedt, *Laurel and Hardy*, 59–66; board of directors minutes, December 23, 1929, USC, Hal Roach Studios, Hollywood Museum Collection, board of directors files.

23. Board of directors minutes, May 25, 1934, USC, Hal Roach Studios, Hollywood Museum Collection, board of directors file.

24. Brian Anthony and Andy Edmonds, *Smile When the Raindrops Fall: The Story of Charley Chase* (Lanham, MD: Scarecrow Press, 1998), 131.

25. Skretvedt, *Laurel and Hardy*, 52.

26. Skretvedt, *Laurel and Hardy*, 49–54.

27. Hal Roach to preferred stockholders, November 25, 1929, USC, Hal Roach Studios, Hollywood Museum Collection.

28. Incidentally, *Pardon Us* was the only Hal Roach feature to be shot in multiple languages, a practice being phased out in 1931, and, curiously enough, it featured Boris Karloff, who is not in the English version, as the heavy in the French edition.

29. John Douglas Eames, *The MGM Story* (New York: Crown Publishers, 1975), 5, 66–154.

6. The Demise of the Short Subject, 1933–38

1. *Motion Picture Herald* (hereafter *MPH*), June 1, 1935, 42. The $5,200 increase was due to the following: $650 to the Production Code Administration, $1,000 to Electrical Research Products, Inc., for the sound royalty, $550 for music copyrights and clearances, and $3,000 for costs associated with sound recording. In this estimate, Roach failed to mention the cost of the film and production time wasted due to flubbed dialogue.

2. Roach-MGM contract dated May 8, 1931, USC, Hal Roach Studios, Hollywood Museum Collection, box 42, MGM file.

3. Board of directors minutes, April 25, 1932, USC, Hal Roach Studios, Hollywood Museum Collection, board of directors file. Short subjects earnings-losses report, July 31, 1937, USC, Hal Roach Studios, Hollywood Museum Collection, miscellaneous reports file.

4. Doane to Roach in New York City, April 24, 1926, USC, Hal Roach Studios, Hollywood Museum Collection, April 1926 file; Roland Cummings, MD, to Doane, November 20, 1927, USC, Hal Roach Studios, Hollywood Museum Collection, box 7, 1927 general file.

5. Board of directors minutes, McGowan resignation, May 30, 1932, and verbal continuation agreement, June 21, 1932, USC, Hal Roach Studios, Hollywood Museum Collection, board of directors file.

6. Leonard Maltin and Richard Bann, *Our Gang: The Life and Times of the Little Rascals* (New York: Crown Publishers, 1977), 187.

7. Henry Ginsberg to Thomas Gerety, July 29, 1932, USC, Hal Roach Studios, Hollywood Museum Collection, Thomas Gerety MGM New York file.

8. Lew Maren to Gerety, July 29, 1932, USC, Hal Roach Studios, Hollywood Museum Collection, box 10, Thomas Gerety file.

9. Maren to Gerety, June 12, 1933, USC, Hal Roach Studios, Hollywood Museum Collection, box 10, Thomas W. Gerety MGM New York 1932 file.

10. Maren to Gerety, February 25, 1933, USC, Hal Roach Studios, Hollywood Museum Collection, box 10, Thomas Gerety MGM New York 1932 file.

11. Randy Skretvedt, *Laurel and Hardy: The Magic Behind the Movies* (Beverly Hills: Moonstone Press, 1987), 59–66.

12. Board of directors minutes, November 25, 1932, USC, Hal Roach Studios, Hollywood Museum Collection, board of directors file.

13. Felix Feist, telegram to Hal Roach, November 17, 1932, USC, Hal Roach Studios, Hollywood Museum Collection, box 18, Laurel and Hardy miscellaneous file.

14. Joe Rivkin to Sam W. B. Cohn, March 16, 1935, USC, Hal Roach Studios, Hollywood Museum Collection, box 10.

15. Board of directors minutes, May 25, 1935, USC, Hal Roach Studios, Hollywood Museum Collection, board of directors file.

16. Leonard Maltin, *The Great Movie Shorts* (New York: Bonanza Books, 1972), 85.

17. Tino Balio, *Grand Design: Hollywood as a Modern Business Enterprise, 1930–1939*, vol. 5, *History of the American Cinema* (New York: Charles Scribner's Sons, 1993), 28–30.

18. *MPH,* July 8, 1933, August 19, 1933, August 26, 1933, and many other issues through the summer and fall of 1933.

19. "Fate of Dual Bills May Rest in Hands of Supreme Court," *MPH,* February 1, 1936, 23; "Roach Parlays Feature Production into Six Features in His Stride," *MPH,* April 16, 1938, 23.

20. *MPH,* December 26, 1931, 10.

21. *MPH,* May 9, 1931, 12.

22. *MPH,* December 12, 1931, 17; *MPH,* October 22, 1932, 37.

23. *MPH,* May 6, 1933, 11.

24. *MPH,* December 9, 1933, 27.

25. *MPH,* January 26, 1935, 69. When Republic ceased active production in the 1950s, the facility was sold to the Columbia Broadcasting System and was renamed CBS Studio City. In this incarnation, it became home to many of CBS's filmed sitcoms (taped shows were produced at CBS Television City in Hollywood), including the MTM productions of the 1970s and 1980s. Thus Mary Richards and her WJM cronies gamboled on the very soundstages on which Andy Clyde, W. C. Fields, and Bing Crosby had done the same approximately four decades earlier.

26. *MPN,* May 24, 1930, 98; *MPH,* August 29, 1931, 31; Ephraim Katz, *The Film Encyclopedia* (New York: Harper and Row, 1979), 236–37.

27. *MPH,* April 22, 1933.

28. "Four Hal Roach Features Added to 32 Short Subjects," *MPH,* June 30, 1934, 16.

29. "Educational Seeks New Releasing Ally," *MPH,* January 22, 1938, 30.

30. "Hammons to Coast to Study Project," *MPH,* September 17, 1938, 56.

31. "Educational in Bankruptcy," *Hollywood Reporter,* February 1, 1940, 1.

32. "Hammons Returning," *MPH,* February 1, 1941, 8.

33. "Hammons on Third 'Hand,'" *MPH,* August 22, 1942, 50.

34. MGM to Roach, July 10, 1934, USC, Hal Roach Studios, Hollywood Museum Collection, box 42, Roach-MGM 1934–35 file.

35. Roach-MGM contract, February 20, 1936, USC, Hal Roach Studios, Hollywood Museum Collection, box 42, Roach-MGM 1936 file.

36. Victor Ford Collins to Emmett Thurmon of Affiliated Enterprises, June 4, 1936, USC, Hal Roach Studios, Hollywood Museum Collection, box 17, C. Chase file.

37. Breen to O'Brien, 1936, USC, Hal Roach Studios, Hollywood Museum Collection, box 17, Breen-PCA-MPPDA file.

38. "Chase, Roach Split After 17 Yrs. Ass'n," *Hollywood Reporter,* June 1, 1936, 1.

39. Full-page advertisement, *Hollywood Reporter,* June 1, 1936, n. pag.

40. Hal Roach Studios to Charley Chase, July 2, 1936, USC, Hal Roach Studios, Hollywood Museum Collection, box 17, miscellaneous C 1936 file.

41. W. F. Rodgers, MGM New York, to Hal Roach, August 28, 1936, USC, Hal Roach Studios, Hollywood Museum Collection, box 18, MGM file.

42. Roach-MGM contract, February 20, 1936, USC, Hal Roach Studios, Hollywood Museum Collection, box 42, MGM 1936 file.

43. S. S. Van Keuren to Hal Roach, November 2, 1936, USC, Hal Roach Studios, Hollywood Museum Collection.

44. "Mr. Roach Emerges," *MPH*, March 19, 1938, 7.

45. Roach-MGM contract, March 30, 1937, USC, Hal Roach Studios, Hollywood Museum Collection, box 42, MGM 1937 file.

46. "Roach Parlays Unit Production into Six Features in His Stride," *MPH*, April 16, 1938, 23.

47. "United Artists Plans 30 Features for '38–'39 and 12 Shorts in Color," *MPH*, June 18, 1938, 33. The twelve shorts were to be travelogues produced by World Windows, Inc.

7. From "A" Pictures to Streamliners, 1938–42

1. "Mussolini, Roach Sued," *Motion Picture Herald*, October 9, 1937, 9.

2. "Hal Roach Announces Big Deal as Mussolini Partner," *MPH*, October 2, 1937, 21–22.

3. "Mussolini, Roach Sued," *MPH*, October 9, 1937, 9.

4. Letter from MGM to Hal Roach Studios, December 29, 1938, USC, Hal Roach Studios, Hollywood Museum Collection, box 42, Roach-MGM 1938 file.

5. Contract between United Artists and Hal Roach Studios, May 16, 1938.

6. Contract between MGM and Hal Roach Studios, USC, Hal Roach Studios, Hollywood Museum Collection, box 42, Roach-MGM 1937 file.

7. MGM to Hal Roach Studios, May 12, 1938, USC, Hal Roach Studios, Hollywood Museum Collection, box 42, Roach-MGM 1938 file.

8. John McCabe, *Laurel and Hardy* (New York: Ballantine Books, 1975), 365. Interestingly, the hyphenated title of *Block-Heads* was the result of MGM's concern that audiences might confuse the simpler *Blockheads* on a theater marquee with *Blockade*, a concurrent United Artists release. MGM to Hal Roach, July 22, 1938, USC, Hal Roach Studios, Hollywood Museum Collection, box 15, Frank Ross file.

9. Loew's to Hal Roach, May 31, 1938, USC, Hal Roach Studios, Hollywood Museum Collection, box 42, Roach-MGM 1938 file.

10. Loew's to Hal Roach, May 31, 1938, USC, Hollywood Museum Collection, box 42, Roach-MGM 1937 file.

11. "Roach to U.A. for Eight Years," *Hollywood Reporter*, May 14, 1938, 1.

12. Tino Balio, *United Artists: The Company That Changed the Film Industry* (Madison: University of Wisconsin Press, 1987) 14.

13. Tino Balio, *United Artists: The Company Built by the Stars* (Madison: University of Wisconsin Press, 1976), 163.

14. "Fold-up of U.A. Dicker Admitted by Frank Capra," *Hollywood Reporter*, August 15, 1941, 1, 4.

15. United Artists Corporation annual stock report, June 1, 1946, 31.

16. Thomas Schatz, *Boom and Bust: Hollywood in the 1940s*, vol. 6, *History of the American Cinema* (New York: Charles Scribner's Sons, 1997), chap. 2, p. 21.

17. Arthur Kelly to Mary Pickford, September 16, 1941, Wisconsin Center for Film and Theatre Research, United Artists Collection, general correspondence, box 10-6, series 2A.

18. Schatz, *Boom and Bust*, 11–12.

19. Tom Walker to Hal Roach, December 17, 1938, USC, Hal Roach Studios, Hollywood Museum Collection, box 20, Hal Roach Studios New York 1938 file.

20. Hal Roach statement at United Artists sales convention, June 13 and 14, 1938, USC, Hal Roach Studios, Hollywood Museum Collection, box 20, Hal Roach Studios 1938 file.

21. Pan reviews criticizing story *and* direction include *Hollywood Reporter* of May 1, 1940, on *Turnabout* (3) and *Hollywood Reporter* of February 6, 1941, on *Road Show* (3).

22. Leonard Maltin and Richard Bann, *Our Gang: The Life and Times of the Little Rascals* (New York: Crown Publishers, 1977), 192–93; Ephraim Katz, *The Film Encyclopedia* (New York: Harper and Row, 1979), 354.

23. Leonard Maltin, *The Great Movie Shorts* (New York: Bonanza Books, 1972), 5.

24. Grace Rosenfield to Hal Roach, April 4, 1939; Ruth Burch to Grace Rosenfield, April 27, 1939, USC Hollywood Museum Collection, Hal Roach Studios.

25. Joseph Breen to Hal Roach Studios, August 11, 1939, USC, Hal Roach Studios, Hollywood Museum Collection, box 16, *Of Mice and Men* file. For an account of the censorship adventures of three other Roach productions of the era, *Topper, Turnabout,* and *Curley,* see Richard Ward, "Golden Age, Blue Pencils: the Hal Roach Studios and Three Case Studies of Censorship During Hollywood's Studio Era," *Media History* 8, no. 1 (2002): 103–19.

26. Frank Ross to Tom Walker, November 2, 1939, USC, Hal Roach Studios, Hollywood Museum Collection, box 20, Hal Roach Studios New York 1939 file.

27. Hugh Huber to Tom Walker, November 3, 1939, USC, Hal Roach Studios, Hollywood Museum Collection, box 20, Hal Roach Studios New York 1939 file.

28. Mary Pickford, telegram to Hal Roach, February 18, 1940. Burgess Meredith, who played the part of George, sent a telegram to Roach that read, "Saw the picture and to say the least was very proud to be in it," Buzz Meredith, telegram to Hal Roach, January 5, 1940. Marion Davies wrote, "Dear Hal, *Of Mice and Men* is one of the greatest pictures I have ever seen. . . . I was really quite overcome with its greatness," Marion Davies to Hal Roach, March 31, 1940. The lone dissenting voice was that of the author himself. John Steinbeck wrote director Lewis Milestone, "Dear Milly, I just saw the picture, 'Of Mice and Men.' I have a problem telling you what I think of it. The picture industry has wilted the language like the Surrealist Dali's watches. There are no good stiff adjectives left. Suppose I try to rebuild English from the bottom and say that it is a very good and very moving picture and that I am proud to be associated with it," John Steinbeck to Lewis Milestone, undated. USC, Hal Roach Studios, Hollywood Museum Collection, box 16.

29. Ross to Walker, December 26 and 27, 1939, USC, Hal Roach Studios, Hollywood Museum Collection, box 20, Hal Roach Studios New York 1939 file.

30. Ross to Walker, December 1, 1939, USC, Hal Roach Studios, Hollywood Museum Collection, box 20, Hal Roach Studios New York 1939 file.

31. *Exhibitors' News,* February 17, 1940, 3, Wisconsin Center for Film and Theatre Studies, United Artists Collection, Paul O'Brien files, series 2A, collection 2, box 10, file 4.

32. Edward Peskay to Ruth Burch, August 26, 1940, USC, Hal Roach Studios, Hollywood Museum Collection, box 28, United Artists file.

33. Mike Steen, *Hollywood Speaks! An Oral History of the Movies* (New York: G. P. Putnam's Sons, 1974), interview with Ruth Burch, 359.

34. Hal Roach to D. W. Griffith, May 13, 1939, USC, Hal Roach Studios, Hollywood Museum Collection, box 18, D. W. Griffith file.

35. Ibid.

36. D. W. Griffith, telegram to Hal Roach, May 22, 1939, Griffith file.

37. Florence McEnany, memorandum to Frank Ross, August 17, 1939, USC, Hal Roach Studios, Hollywood Museum Collection, box 16, *One Million B.C.* file.

38. Specific known dates on the Griffith tests are August 11, 1939, *Of Mice and Men;* August 11 and 25, October 10 and 28, 1939, *One Million B.C.* Additionally, Hal Roach directed tests for *One Million B.C.* from September through November 1. USC, Hal Roach Studios, Hollywood Museum Collection, box 4, *Of Mice and Men* and *One Million B.C.* files.

39. Frank Ross to Hugh Huber, December 19, 1939, USC, Hal Roach Studios, Hollywood Museum Collection, box 18, office memoranda file.

40. Mike Steen, *Hollywood Speaks,* interview with Ruth Burch, p. 359. "'Million B. C.' Spectacular," *Hollywood Reporter,* April 10, 1940, 3.

41. As for D. W. Griffith, he decided not to immediately return to Kentucky but rather to stay on the West Coast for a while, continuing to hope for a film assignment that never came. The final item in the Hal Roach Studios' D. W. Griffith file is the following March 1940 note from Roach's secretary to Griffith in Beverly Hills: "When your office was cleaned out, there were a number of things of a personal nature which I thought might be of interest to you and I am sending them to you. Hope you will stop in and see us again very soon," Ruth Burch to D. W. Griffith, March 9, 1940.

42. UA advertisement, *MPH,* June 18, 1938, 51.

43. "Roach Suspends Laurel," *MPH,* August 13, 1938, 56.

44. "Langdon Teams with Hardy as Laurel Is Dropped," *MPH,* August 20, 1938, 51.

45. "Sennett Resuming Production with Laurel as Star," *MPH,* September 17, 1938,

46. Jed Buell had also been the producer of a series of matinee musical westerns starring Fred Scott. In a generally unchronicled phase of his career, Stan Laurel had served as an executive producer on the last three films of this series: *Songs & Bullets, Knight of the Plains,* and *Rangers' Round Up* (all 1938).

46. Stan Laurel, telegram to Oliver Hardy, March 31, 1939, USC, Hal Roach Studios, Hollywood Museum Collection, box 18, Oliver Hardy file.

47. Tom Walker to Frank Ross, April 28 and June 1, 1939, and Arthur Kelly to Walker, May 16, 1939, USC, Hal Roach Studios, Hollywood Museum Collection, box 20, Hal Roach Studios New York 1939 file.

48. United Artists, cable from London to Tom Walker, May 23, 1939, USC, Hal Roach Studios, Hollywood Museum Collection, box 20, Hal Roach Studios New York 1939 file.

49. *MPH,* May 13, 1939, 45.

50. Murray Silverstone to Hal Roach Studios, April 11, 1939, USC, Hal Roach Studios, Hollywood Museum Collection, box 20, Hal Roach Studios New York 1939 file.

51. Telegrams: Walker to Ross, October 17, 1939; Ross to Walker, October 12, 1939; Ross to Walker, October 18, 1939; Ross to Walker, October 29, 1939: all USC, Hal Roach Studios, Hollywood Museum Collection, box 20, Hal Roach Studios New York 1939 file.

52. While there is no evidence to indicate that the four-reel version of *Chump* ever played in any theater at the time of its original release, there has been considerable confusion about the matter. UA apparently did release the four-reel version theatrically in the United States in 1943 as a "reissue." Blackhawk Films, a distributor of eight- and sixteen-millimeter film prints to collectors in the days before home video, released both the four- and six-reel versions of the film in the 1960s as part of a package licensed by Hal Roach Studios that included all of the surviving Laurel and Hardy films produced by Roach. Blackhawk's catalog description identified the four-reel version as the original domestic "streamliner" release and the six-reel version as the foreign release.

53. "Stan and Ollie as Gladiators in Next," *Hollywood Reporter,* December 21, 1939, 3.

54. "Laurel and Hardy to Roll Their Own," *Hollywood Reporter,* February 5, 1940, 4.

55. Ruth Burch to Tom Walker, April 29, 1940, USC, Hal Roach Studios, Hollywood Museum Collection, box 28.

56. Schatz, *Boom and Bust,* 45. Randy Skretvedt, *Laurel and Hardy: The Magic Be hind the Movies* (Beverly Hills: Moonstone Press, 1987), 373.

57. Edward Peskay to Ruth Burch, August 26, 1940, USC, Hal Roach Studios, Hollywood Museum Collection, box 28.

58. United Artists Salesman's Bulletin, November 4, 1940; Arthur Kelly to UA sales force, November 4, 1940, USC, Hal Roach Studios, Hollywood Museum Collection, box 28.

59. "Indie Production Money Tough," *Hollywood Reporter,* December 20, 1940, 1, 2.

60. "Roach Sets $6,000,000 Budget for Six Pictures in 1940–41," *Hollywood Reporter,* May 6, 1940.

61. Hal Roach to Will Hays, August 8, 1940, USC, Hal Roach Studios, Hollywood Museum Collection, box 28, Reconstruction Finance Corporation (RFC) file.

62. Jessie Jones, RFC, to Will Hays, September 23, 1940, USC, Hal Roach Studios, Hollywood Museum Collection, box 28, RFC file.

63. J. E. Brulator and Company to Hal Roach, October 1, 1940, USC, Hal Roach Studios, Hollywood Museum Collection, box 28, RFC file.

64. Arthur Kelly to UA sales force, February 12, 1941, USC, Hal Roach Studios, Hollywood Museum Collection, box 28.

65. "Roach Parlays Unit Production into Six Features in His Stride," *Motion Picture Herald,* April 16, 1938, 23, 24.

66. Peskay to Burch, December 11, 1940, USC, Hal Roach Studios, Hollywood Museum Collection, box 28.

67. Executives at RKO (November 27, 1940) and Twentieth Century–Fox (October 30, 1940) to Hal Roach, USC, Hal Roach Studios, Hollywood Museum Collection, box 22, MPPA file.

68. Harry Brandt, telegram to Hal Roach, April 24, 1941, USC, Hal Roach Studios, Hollywood Museum Collection, box 29.

69. Peskay to Burch, March 14, 1941, USC, Hal Roach Studios, Hollywood Museum Collection, box 28.

70. An interesting footnote to United Artists' acceptance of streamliners from Roach was the dilemma of trying to book them in theaters that customarily played only a single film. In these cases UA was forced into the position of trying to convince the managers to book a *first* feature to play with the Roach second feature, an embarrassing situation considering that UA, as a distributor of "prestige" pictures, had always been in the forefront of the battle against the "double feature evil." Hal Roach to Peskay, October 10, 1941, USC, Hal Roach Studios, Hollywood Museum Collection, box 28.

71. "U.A. Keeps Old Policy; 25–30 Pix," *Hollywood Reporter,* April 11, 1941, 1, 4.

72. Peskay to Arthur Kelly, February 27, 1941, USC, Hal Roach Studios, Hollywood Museum Collection, box 29.

73. Hugh Huber, telegram to Hal Roach in New York City, March 5, 1941, USC, Hal Roach Studios, Hollywood Museum Collection, box 29.

74. Paul O'Brien, letter to Edward Raftery, June 24, 1941, Wisconsin Center for Film and Theater Research, United Artists Collection, Paul O'Brien files, 190-4, series 2A.

75. Peskay to Hal Roach, July 3, 1941, USC, Hal Roach Studios, Hollywood Museum Collection, box 28.

76. "Cash receipts and distribution expenses—streamliners" file, October 2, 1942, USC, Hal Roach Studios, Hollywood Museum Collection, box 29.

77. "Roach's Streamliner Panic," *Hollywood Reporter,* August 5, 1941, 3.

78. Exhibitor reviews of *Fiesta, About Face,* and *Hay Foot* under United Artists head-
ㄱg, *MPH,* November 7, 1942, 45; exhibitor reviews of *Fiesta, Hay Foot,* and *Brooklyn
rchid* under United Artists heading, *MPH,* August 1, 1942, 60.

79. Roach-UA contract, February 6, 1942.

80. Report of the Film Conservation Committee as forwarded to Roach by Mitchell,
Silberberg, and Knupp, July 9, 1942, USC, Hal Roach Studios, Hollywood Museum
Collection, box 28.

8. Fort Roach, 1943–48

1. Bob Thomas, *Walt Disney: An American Original* (New York: Pocket Books, 1976),
178–219.

2. Affidavits by H. M. Walker, Warren Doane, Earl Wisdom, Dwight Whiting, August 1917; Hal Roach, telegram to Dwight Whiting, November 2, 1917; Dwight Whiting, telegram to Hal Roach, November 2, 1917: USC, Hal Roach Studios, Hollywood
Museum Collection, 1917 business correspondence file.

3. Dwight Whiting to Pvt. G. L. Hanes, December 15, 1917, USC, Hal Roach Studios, Hollywood Museum Collection, 1917 correspondence file.

4. Major General Charles McK. Saltzman to Hal Roach, July 6, 1925, USC, Hal
Roach Studios, Hollywood Museum Collection, U.S. Reserve Corps file, 1925–27.

5. Hal Roach, telegram to Saltzman, July 21, 1925, USC, Hal Roach Studios, Hollywood Museum Collection, U.S. Reserve Corps file, 1925–27.

6. Hal Roach to Lt. Col. J. E. Hemphill, Washington, June 27, 1927; Roach, telegram
to Hemphill, October 10, 1927; Roach, essay and letter to Saltzman, November 1, 1927:
USC, Hal Roach Studios, Hollywood Museum Collection, U.S. Reserve Corps file.

7. C. W. Thornton to Hugh Fulton, March 17, 1943, USC, Hal Roach Studios, Hollywood Museum Collection, 1942–43 file.

8. Ulio, Adjt. Gen., Washington, telegram to Hal Roach, June 26, 1942, USC, Hal
Roach Studios, Hollywood Museum Collection, box 29.

9. Roach, telegram to Ulio, July 6, 1942, USC, Hal Roach Studios, Hollywood Museum Collection, box 29.

10. Ulio, telegram to Roach, July 9, 1942, USC, Hal Roach Studios, Hollywood Museum Collection, box 29.

11. *Los Angeles Examiner,* July 30, 1942; power of attorney document signed by Roach,
October 9, 1942, recorded June 21, 1943.

12. "Rumor Govt. Deal on Educ. Lot," *Hollywood Reporter,* October 17, 1940, 1, 4;
"ERPI Clamps Down on Educ. Lot," *Hollywood Reporter,* November 8, 1940, 1, 3.

13. C. W. Thornton to Special Separate Committee Investigating the War Program,
October 12, 1942, USC, Hal Roach Studios, Hollywood Museum Collection, 1942–43
file.

14. Thornton to Roach, September 18, 1942, and Thornton to Hugh Fulton, March
17, 1943, USC, Hal Roach Studios, Hollywood Museum Collection, 1942–43 file.

15. Edward C. Raftery, UA, to Paul O'Brien, October 23, 1944, Wisconsin Center for
Film and Theatre Research, United Artists Collection, 190-4, series 2A.

16. Roach to Hal Roach Studios, June 8 and 22, 1943, USC, Hal Roach Studios,
Hollywood Museum Collection, 1942–43 file.

17. "Vic Mature Issues Roach Ultimatum," *Hollywood Reporter,* October 14, 1941, 2;
"Roach, Mature Pull Up to Peace Table," *Hollywood Reporter,* October 22, 1941, 7.

18. Minutes of the Hal Roach Studios board of directors meeting of October 26, 1942,
USC, Hal Roach Studios, records of the board of directors; Hal Roach Studios "Receipts

and Disbursements," September 15–October 15, 1945; Ruth Burch to Edward Peskay, December 28, 1940, USC, Hal Roach Studios, Hollywood Museum Collection, box 28

19. Thomas Schatz, *Boom and Bust: Hollywood in the 1940s,* vol. 6, *History of th American Cinema* (New York: Charles Scribner's Sons, 1997), chap. 11, p. 13.

20. Court record, Hal Roach Studios v. Film Classics, Inc., July 25, 1946. By the tim it ceased theatrical production and after ownership of some of its productions was transferred to other entities (i.e., Harold Lloyd and MGM), the Hal Roach Studios film library would ultimately contain approximately 758 silent shorts, 271 talking shorts, 9 silent features, 39 talking features, and 22 streamliners.

21. Hal Roach to J. A. Berst, October 15, 1926, USC, Hal Roach Studios, Hollywood Museum Collection.

22. Kodascope catalog, undated, USC, Hal Roach Studios, Hollywood Museum Collection, Misc. C 1936 file.

23. Contract between Hal Roach Studios and Frederick Gerke, October 30, 1935, USC, Hal Roach Studios, Hollywood Museum Collection, Misc. C 1936 file.

24. "'Gypsy' Shows Invade Hinterland with 16mm," *Motion Picture Herald,* May 25, 1940, 13, 14.

25. Contract between Hal Roach Studios and Post Pictures, November 5, 1942, ratified by Hal Roach Studios board of directors March 18, 1942, USC, Hal Roach Studios.

26. H. W. Schroder, UA, to Paul O'Brien, March 9, 1949, Wisconsin Center for Film and Theatre Research, United Artists Collection.

27. H. J. Muller, UA, to Hal Roach Studios, March 14, 1950, Wisconsin Center for Film and Theatre Research, United Artists Collection.

28. Hal Roach to Milton Bren, April 5, 1946, USC, Hal Roach Studios, Hollywood Museum Collection, 1946 "B" misc. file.

29. Tino Balio, *Hollywood in the Age of Television* (Boston: Unwin Hyman, 1990), 3–4.

30. Hugh Huber to J. H. Rosenberg, Bank of America, August 27, 1945, and S. S. Van Keuren to Walter M. Johnson, October 29, 1945, USC, Hal Roach Studios, Hollywood Museum Collection.

31. Mike Steen, *Hollywood Speaks! An Oral History* (New York: G. P. Putnam's Sons, 1974), Hal Roach interview, 371; Hal Roach to Robert Lynch, Loew's, Inc., September 10, 1946, USC, Hal Roach Studios, Hollywood Museum Collection, "L" miscellaneous 1946–55 file; Douglas Gomery, *The Hollywood Studio System* (New York: St. Martin's Press, 1986), 180.

32. Hal Roach to Gradwell Sears, UA, May 7, 1947, Wisconsin Center for Film and Theatre Research, United Artists Collection.

33. Mitchell, Silberberg, and Knupp, Attorneys, to Robert Rubin, Loew's, Inc., September 12, 1945. Grace Rosenfield to Hal Roach, October 27, 1945, USC, Hal Roach Studios, Hollywood Museum Collection, "Our Gang" Correspondence file.

34. Hugh Huber to J. H. Rosenberg, Bank of America, August 27, 1945, USC, Hal Roach Studios, Hollywood Museum Collection, Bank of America National Trust and Savings file.

35. Hal Roach Studios board of directors minutes, June 29, 1946, April 17, 1947, May 22, 1947, USC, Hal Roach Studios.

36. Board of directors minutes, July 22, 1946, USC, Hal Roach Studios, Hollywood Museum Collection.

37. Hal Roach Jr. to Hal Roach Sr., July 25, 1947, USC, Hal Roach Studios, Hollywood Museum Collection, "production schedules file, revised July 19, 1946."

38. Bernard Rosenberg and Harry Silverstein, *The Real Tinsel* (London: Collier-

Iacmillan, 1970), Hal Roach interview, 23. The production file for *Who Killed Doc obbin?* reveals that the final production cost was a whopping $455,631.28, due, in part, ɩ a forty-six-day production schedule. The streamliners Roach produced in the early 40s characteristically had been shot on a twelve- to eighteen-day schedule.

39. Hal Roach to Robert Lynch, Loew's, Inc., September 10, 1946, USC, Hal Roach Studios, Hollywood Museum Collection, "L" miscellaneous 1946–55 file.

40. Contract between Hal Roach Studios and United Artists, May 2, 1947, Wisconsin Center for Film and Theatre Research, United Artists Collection.

41. *New York Times,* June 8, 1947.

42. Lloyd T. Binford to United Artists, September 9, 1947, Wisconsin Center for Film and Theatre Research, United Artists Collection.

43. Herb Gelbspan to Eric Johnson, January 12, 1955, USC, Hal Roach Studios, Hollywood Museum Collection.

44. Hal Roach Studios–United Artists contract termination, February 9, 1948, Wisconsin Center for Film and Theatre Research, United Artists Collection.

45. Hal Roach Studios MGM 1948–53 file, and Hal Roach to Margot Grahame, May 7, 1948, both at USC, Hal Roach Studios, Hollywood Museum Collection, MGM 1948–53 file.

46. Hal Roach to Dore Schary, December 16, 1948, USC, Hal Roach Studios, Hollywood Museum Collection, MGM 1948–53 file.

47. *Fortune,* April 1949, 142, 144, quoted in Thomas Schatz, *Boom and Bust: Hollywood in the 1940s,* vol. 6, *History of the American Cinema* (New York: Charles Scribner's Sons, 1997), 347.

48. Law offices of O'Brien et al. to Charles E. Millikan, November 9, 1948, Wisconsin Center for Film and Theatre Research, United Artists Collection.

49. Hal Roach to General Muir Fairchild, May 26, 1948, and Fairchild to Roach, June 21, 1948, USC, Hal Roach Studios, Hollywood Museum Collection.

9. The Man Who Bet on Television, 1949–60

1. "The Man Who Bet on Television," *TV Guide,* June 11, 1955, 5.

2. Ibid., 6.

3. "Film v. Live Shows," *Time,* March 29, 1954, 78.

4. Hal Roach Sr. to Hal Roach Jr., September 7, 1949, USC, Hal Roach Studios, Hollywood Museum Collection, Hal Roach Jr. TV file.

5. "The Man Who Bet on Television," *TV Guide,* June 11, 1955, 6.

6. "Film v. Live Shows," *Time,* March 29, 1954, 78.

7. William Arnold to Hal Roach Sr., July 1, 1948, USC, Hal Roach Studios, Hollywood Museum Collection, 1948 "A" misc. file.

8. Hal Roach Sr. to Hal Roach Jr., September 26, 1949, USC, Hal Roach Studios, Hollywood Museum Collection, Hal Roach Jr. TV file.

9. Hal Roach Sr. to Grace Rosenfield, October 16, 1948, USC, Hal Roach Studios, Hollywood Museum Collection, Grace Rosenfield–New York office 1948 file.

10. Hal Roach Sr. to Hal Roach Jr., September 12, 1949, USC, Hal Roach Studios, Hollywood Museum Collection, Hal Roach Jr. TV file.

11. Hal Roach Sr. to Hal Roach Jr., November 30, 1949, USC, Hal Roach Studios, Hollywood Museum Collection, Hal Roach Jr. TV file.

12. Hal Roach Sr. to Hal Roach Jr., second letter of November 30, 1949, USC, Hal Roach Studios, Hollywood Museum Collection, Hal Roach Jr. TV file.

13. S.. Van Keuren to Hal Roach Sr., December 1, 1948, USC, Hal Roach Studios, Hollywood Museum Collection, Apex file. In light of the motion picture industry's

attitude toward telefilm production, it is interesting that a member of Apex Productions' board of directors was Harry Cohn, the president of Columbia Pictures.

14. Hal Roach to Sidney Harris, June 10, 1949, USC, Hal Roach Studios, Hollywoo Museum Collection, "H" miscellaneous file.

15. Hal Roach Studios board of directors minutes for June 28, 1950.

16. Hal Roach Studios board of directors minutes for July 20, 1950.

17. Executive committee of the board of directors minutes for July 12, 1950.

18. Executive committee of the board of directors minutes for August 22, 1950.

19. Hal Roach Studios board of directors minutes for November 24, 1950.

20. USC, Hal Roach Studios, Hollywood Museum Collection, *Three Musketeers* file, *Hurricane at Pilgrim Hill* file, Television–Magnavox Company file.

21. *New York Times*, January 10, 1952, 34.

22. Memo from S. S. Van Keuren to Hal Roach, June 11, 1951. When Lucille Ball and Desi Arnaz formed Desilu and announced their intention to produce a situation comedy on film on the West Coast, Roach studio management made a bid to lease production space for what was tentatively being called *The Lucille Ball Show: My Favorite Husband,* a variation on the title of Ball's popular radio series. Ball and Arnaz ultimately chose other facilities, so *I Love Lucy* was filmed elsewhere.

23. Tim Brooks and Earle Marsh, *The Complete Directory to Prime Time Network TV Shows* (New York: Ballantine Books, 1985), 805.

24. Hal Roach Studios board of directors minutes for June 7, 1951.

25. Hal Roach Studios board of directors minutes for August 2, 1951.

26. Hal Roach Studios to creditors, August 3 and August 28, 1951, board of directors minutes ledger.

27. Hal Roach Studios board of directors minutes for September 12, 1951.

28. "Freeman, Roach See Upped Quality, No 'B' Pix in Industry Future; TV Forecast as New Cradle of Talent," *Variety,* December 12, 1951, 18.

29. Ibid., 5.

30. Brooks and Marsh, *Complete Directory,* 582. In an interesting turn of events, *My Little Margie* actually made a transition from television to radio. The radio version premiered on CBS in December 1952 and ran for the life of the television series with the same cast but different scripts from its television sibling.

31. *New York Times*, March 23, 1953, 28.

32. *New York Times*, January 22, 1953, 20.

33. Herb Gelbspan to Hal Roach Jr., May 5, 1955, USC, Hal Roach Studios, Hollywood Museum Collection, Herb Gelbspan–New York office file.

34. "No Laughing Matter: Laurel and Hardy Find Themselves on TV . . . for Free," *TV Guide,* April 23, 1955, 15.

35. *New York Times*, March 1, 1955, 21.

36. Ibid.

37. Hal Roach Sr., memorandum to staff, February 28, 1955, USC, Hal Roach Studios, Hollywood Museum Collection, Hal Roach Studios, transfer or sale file.

38. Hal Roach, Sr. to stockholders and claimants, March 1, 1955, USC, Hal Roach Studios, Hollywood Museum Collection, Hal Roach Studios, transfer or sale file.

39. USC, Hal Roach Studios, Hollywood Museum Collection, Hal Roach Studios records of transfer or sale, 1955.

40. "The Man Who Bet on Television," *TV Guide,* June 11, 1955, 6.

41. "Hollywood Is Humming," *Time,* October 29, 1951, 48.

42. Ibid.

43. "Film v. Live Shows," *Time,* March 29, 1954, 78.

44. Tino Balio, *Hollywood in the Age of Television* (Boston: Unwin Hyman, 1990), 32.

45. *New York Times,* October 6, 1955, 59.

46. *New York Times,* October 20, 1955, 71.

47. *New York Times,* December 8, 1955, 75.

48. Larry James Gianakos, *Television Drama Series Programming: A Comprehensive Chronicle, 1947–1959* (Metuchen, NJ: Scarecrow Press, 1980).

49. "Studio Cites Rise in TV Script Cost," *New York Times,* August 29, 1956, 59.

50. USC, Hal Roach Studios, Hollywood Museum Collection, Hal Roach Studios, transfer or sale file.

51. Hal Roach Jr. to George Shupert, June 19, 1956, USC, Hal Roach Studios, Hollywood Museum Collection, American Broadcasters 1953–57 file.

52. Report of the trustees to the U.S. District Court for the Middle District of Pennsylvania in the matter of Hal Roach Studios and Rabco TV Productions, Debtors, May 26, 1961 (hereafter referred to as "Trustees report"), 17–18, USC, Hal Roach Studios, Hollywood Museum Collection.

53. *Broadcasting,* June 2, 1958, 44.

54. "Hal Roach Units Get New Owner," *New York Times,* May 28, 1958, 51.

55. *Broadcasting,* June 2, 1958.

56. "New MBS Owner Guterma: Optimist Moving into 'Depression-Proof' Trade," *Broadcasting,* September 22, 1958, 46.

57. "Guild, Roach Sign VTR Pact," *Broadcasting,* September 22, 1958, 10.

58. Trustees report, 26; Hal Roach Studios to Distributors Corporation of America, February 3, 1959, USC, Hal Roach Studios, Hollywood Museum Collection, DCA file.

59. Trustees report, 19.

60. "Guterma's Tangles Thicken: Mutual, Guild, Roach Add to Involvements," *Broadcasting,* February 23, 1959, 56.

61. Trustees report, 21, 35, 40.

62. *Broadcasting,* February 23, 1959, 56.

63. Trustees report, 18.

64. *Broadcasting,* February 23, 1959, 56.

65. Trustees report, 4, 33, 40, 41, 46.

66. "Guterma Guilty: Awaits Sentencing in Detention House," *Broadcasting,* February 1, 1960, 78.

67. "Roach Fined $500 in Propaganda Case," *Broadcasting,* June 27, 1960, 9.

68. *Broadcasting,* June 27, 1960, 9.

69. "Film-Maker to Resume," *New York Times,* March 23, 1960, 33.

70. Trustees report, 53.

71. *New York Times,* December 21, 1962, 5.

72. *New York Times,* January 24, 1963, 5.

73. *New York Times,* May 22, 1963, 35.

74. *New York Times,* March 30, 1962, 18.

75. Richard Bann, interview by author, Beverly Hills, CA, August 28, 1989.

76. *Broadcasting and Cable,* June 27, 1994, 7.

77. Richard Bann, interview by author; *Broadcasting and Cable,* June 27, 1994, 72.

10. Conclusion

1. For insight into Stan Laurel's behavior during this period, read Randy Skretvedt's *Laurel and Hardy: The Magic Behind the Movies* (Beverly Hills: Moonstone Press, 1987). A brutally frank discussion of Laurel may be found in *Stan* by Fred Lawrence Guiles (New York: Stein and Day, 1980).

ˈbliography

rchives

al Roach Studios Collection, Department of Special Collections, Doheny Library, University of Southern California, Los Angeles.

Production Code Administration Files, Margaret Herrick Library, Academy of Motion Picture Arts and Sciences, Beverly Hills, CA.

United Artists Collection, Wisconsin Center for Film and Theatre Research, State Historical Society, Madison.

Journals and Newspapers

Broadcasting (later, *Broadcasting and Cable*)
Exhibitors' News
Exhibitor's Trade Review
Hollywood Reporter
Los Angeles Examiner
Motion Picture Herald
Motion Picture News
Moving Picture World
New York Times
Time
TV Guide
Variety

Books and Articles

Anderson, Christopher. *Hollywood TV: The Studio System in the Fifties.* Austin: University of Texas Press, 1994.

Anthony, Brian, and Andy Edmonds. *Smile When the Raindrops Fall: the Story of Charley Chase.* Lanham, MD: Scarecrow Press, 1998.

Balio, Tino. *Grand Design: Hollywood as a Modern Business Enterprise, 1930–1939.* History of the American Cinema, 5. New York: Charles Scribner's Sons, 1993.

————, ed. *Hollywood in the Age of Television.* Boston: Unwin Hyman, 1990.

————. *United Artists: The Company Built by the Stars.* Madison: University of Wisconsin Press, 1976.

————. *United Artists: The Company That Changed the Film Industry.* Madison: University of Wisconsin Press, 1987.

Bann, Richard. Author interview. Beverly Hills, CA, August 28, 1989.

Bergan, Ronald. *The United Artists Story.* New York: Crown Publishers, 1986.

Bordwell, David, Kristin Thompson, and Janet Staiger. *The Classical Hollywood Cinema: Film Style and Mode of Production to 1960.* New York: Columbia University Press, 1985.

Brooks, Tim, and Earle Marsh. *The Complete Directory to Prime Time Network TV Shows.* New York: Ballantine Books, 1985.

Capra, Frank. *The Name above the Title.* New York: MacMillan, 1971.

Crafton, Donald. *The Talkies: American Cinema's Transition to Sound, 1926–1931.* New York: Charles Scribner's Sons, 1997.

Dardis, Tom. *Harold Lloyd: The Man on the Clock.* New York: Viking Press, 1983.

Doherty, Thomas. *Pre-Code Hollywood.* New York: Columbia University Press, 1999.

Eames, John Douglas. *The MGM Story.* New York: Crown Publishers, 1975.

Everson, William K. *The Films of Hal Roach.* New York: Museum of Modern Art, 197

———. *The Films of Laurel and Hardy.* New York: Citadel Press, 1967.

Gehring, Wes. *Parody as Film Genre.* Westport, CT: Greenwood Press, 1999.

Gianakos, Larry James. *Television Drama Series Programming: A Comprehensive Chron icle, 1947–1959.* Metuchen, NJ: Scarecrow Press, 1980.

Gomery, Douglas. *The Hollywood Studio System.* New York: St. Martin's Press, 1986.

Guiles, Fred Lawrence. *Stan.* New York: Stein and Day, 1980.

Jewell, Richard B., with Vernon Harbin. *The RKO Story.* London: Octopus Books, 1982.

Katz, Ephraim. *The Film Encyclopedia.* New York: Harper and Row, 1979.

Keaton, Buster, and Charles Samuels. *My Wonderful World of Slapstick.* New York: Da Capo Press, 1960.

Lastra, James. *Sound Technology and the American Cinema.* New York, Columbia University Press, 2000.

Lloyd, Harold. *An American Comedy.* 1928. New York: Dover Publications, 1971.

MacGillivray, Scott. *Laurel & Hardy: From the Forties Forward.* Lanham, MD: Vestal Press, 1998.

Maltin, Leonard. *The Great Movie Comedians.* New York: Crown Publishers, 1978.

———. *The Great Movie Shorts.* New York: Bonanza Books, 1972.

Maltin, Leonard, and Richard Bann. *Our Gang: The Life and Times of the Little Rascals.* New York: Crown Publishers, 1977.

McCabe, John. *The Comedy World of Stan Laurel.* New York: Doubleday and Company, 1974.

———. *Laurel and Hardy.* New York: Ballantine Books, 1975.

———. *Mr. Laurel and Mr. Hardy.* New York: Grosset and Dunlap, 1966.

Reilly, Adam. *Harold Lloyd: The King of Daredevil Comedy.* New York: Collier Books, 1977.

Rosenberg, Bernard, and Harry Silverstein. *The Real Tinsel.* London: Collier-Macmillan, 1970.

Schatz, Thomas. *Boom and Bust: Hollywood in the 1940s.* Vol. 6, *History of the American Cinema.* New York: Charles Scribner's Sons, 1997.

———. *The Genius of the System.* New York: Pantheon Books, 1988.

Schickel, Richard. *Harold Lloyd: The Shape of Laughter.* New York: New York Graphic Society, 1974.

Sklar, Robert. *Movie-Made America.* New York, Random House, 1975.

Skretvedt, Randy. *Laurel and Hardy: The Magic Behind the Movies.* Beverly Hills: Moonstone Press, 1987.

Sova, Dawn. *Forbidden Films.* New York: Facts on File, 2001.

Staiger, Janet. "Combination and Litigation: Structures of U.S. Film Distribution, 1896–1917." *Cinema Journal* 23, no. 2 (Winter 1983): 41–72.

Steen, Mike. *Hollywood Speaks! An Oral History.* New York: G. P. Putnam's Sons, 1974.

Stokes, Melvyn, and Richard Maltby. *American Movie Audiences: From the Turn of the Century to the Early Sound Era.* London: BFI Publishing, 1999.

Terrace, Vincent. *Encyclopedia of Television: Series, Pilots and Specials.* New York: Baseline Books, 1986.

Thomas, Bob. *Walt Disney: An American Original.* New York: Pocket Books, 1976.

Vazzana, Eugene. *Silent Film Necrology.* Jefferson, NC: McFarland and Company, 2001.

Ward, Richard. "Golden Age, Blue Pencils." *Media History* 8, no. 1 (2002): 104–19.

Richard Lewis Ward is an associate professor at the University of South Alabama. He is a lifelong fan of the Hal Roach Studios, having been introduced at an early age to its films on television in the 1950s. He strives to introduce the uninitiated to the joys of silent comedy, and to that end he regularly organizes film screening series. He also writes and directs an occasional short comedy film. His homage to French writer, director, and actor Jacques Tati, entitled *Doppelgangster* (2001), won a Golden Lion at the George Lindsey–UNA Film Festival in 2003.